Why Your Pastor Left

by

Christopher D. Schmitz

I think it vitally important that churches understand pastors are not gods and, as such, can be stressed, stretched, broken, and burned—while many studies exist reflecting data on pastoral stressors, most of that data was collected 1-2 decades ago!

Updating those statistics is something of a passion of mine. If YOU or a SPOUSE *are*, or *have ever been*, a vocational or volunteer minister (official ministerial staff) would you help me update those old stats?

I want to collect data that more accurately reflects the current culture of ministry. (Because there were many surveys in the original data, I use the same verbiage as the original queries, which I understand is less than perfect wording at times,) Early information collected from nearly 200 respondents and wives indicate the overwhelming majority of stats (see the collected and sorted information in the appendices,) remains current; by updating those older numbers we can see which ones remain relevant, have reached "critical mass," or have improved with time and culture shift.

If you would like to lend your voice, please take a 5-10 minute survey by typing the following link into your browser or scanning the QR code below.

https://goo.gl/xq7mDG

Christopher Schmitz – Why Your Pastor Left

Christopher Schmitz – Why Your Pastor Left

James Dobson's newsletter (August 1998):

> Our surveys indicated that 80 percent of pastors and 84 percent of their spouses are discouraged or are dealing with depression. More than 40 percent of pastors and 47 percent of their spouses report that they are suffering from burnout, frantic schedules and unrealistic expectations. We estimate that approximately 1,500 pastors leave their assignments each month, due to moral failure, spiritual burnout or contention within their local congregations.

> Why are pastors struggling? There are many causes. The Fuller Institute of Church Growth found in 1991 that 80 percent of the clergy feel their families have been negatively impacted by the church, and 33 percent consider the ministry to be an outright hazard to their families. Financial burdens are common as well. The majority of pastors are heavily in debt, due to college and seminary expenses. These and other problems lead often to serious marital conflict and family dysfunction. Unfortunately, the embarrassment or gossip within the church leads some couples to avoid needed counseling services.

"An unwritten expectation of our profession is that successful pastors should not have unhappy parishioners. There are incompetent pastors, of course, but there are clergy killers also."
  --G. Lloyd Rediger, PhD. The Clergy Journal (August 1993)

A new study by the Barna Group indicates that one of the least favorite biblical principles might well be "Obey your spiritual leaders, and do what they say. Their work is to watch over your souls, and they are accountable to God. Give them reason to do this with joy and not with sorrow" (Hebrews 13:17, NLT). (Barna Group, Nov. 2010)

One of America's most famous ministers, Jonathan Edwards (*Sinners in the Hands of an Angry God,*) was fired by his Northampton Church in 1750 after 23 years in that pulpit. A major part of his dismissal was his insistence that his parishioners live lives reflecting their claimed beliefs. In other words, they should practice what they heard preached. After refusing to administer communion to those without such evidence, Edwards was fired on June 22, 1750, by a vote of 230 to 23.

"In one year, 27 ministers in my district were forced to resign their pastorates, without charges of wrongdoing, unethical behavior, or immorality. Many because they were causing growth. Most cases it was the power bloc that ran the church that had them removed. Many have lost their pastorates, many their reputations and many have lost their enthusiasm about staying in the ministry."
  --Kent Crockett in *Pastor Abusers: When Sheep Attack Their Shepherd*

Table of Contents:

Introduction

I remember when I was a child in elementary school; I had a teacher who would always tell my class that we acted like a bunch of "chickens with their heads' cut off." Of course, kids get curious about such things, so I took to a library to learn about how nerves and the body react with the sudden severing of its head. Even as a child I wondered how a headless chicken could run. Did it maintain a sense of balance or just flop on the ground and shake? I'd never seen a chicken butchered; my imagination was enough for me, as a child. But I *have* seen many organizations sever their own headship and I have seen their bodies flail wildly in the after effects. Some run, and some fall; *all* bleed.

The church is the "body of Christ." I know people who've lost limbs and organs and have been able to continue living life, often with only minimal impairment. But there are certain parts of our bodies that are vital—we die without them. Pastors, Godly leaders, are of high importance and few parishioners ever understand the sacrifices that many ministers make on behalf of their flock. We must take care to not assassinate our body. We are mandated to the high calling of evangelizing the world! Churches must stop playing the butcher and be the healer.

If you ask the typical "Joe on the street" to name a famous pastor other than Billy Graham, chances are you will get a name like Jim Baker, Jimmy Swaggart, or Ted Haggard. Because of the headlines generated by those above (as a sample of fallen ministers,) the first thing that comes to mind for parishioners who hear that a minister is stepping down, has been removed, or is

Christopher Schmitz – Why Your Pastor Left

transitioning out of a current ministry is this question: "What sin did they fall into?"

Our culture has led us to assume that any pastor moving on—especially when he or she does so at the request of their congregation—has committed some moral failure. The last few decades have been dominated by headlines involving moral and ethical failures, including Ted Haggard's drug and prostitution scandal, divorce and financial misconduct from public figures like Benny Hinn and Todd Bentley, and institutional bankruptcy at iconic campuses such as Schuller's Crystal Cathedral or Oral Roberts University. The memory of these headlines loom above us, causing the general public to conclude that ministers are prone to corruption and secret sins available especially to those placed in areas of privilege.

However, in the last few years, I've discovered that pastors removed for moral failure and/or gross sin are in the vast minority. Far more ministers are forced out, terminated, or simply burnout under pressure and fade away, than those who exploit or abuse congregations or misuse their authority. And yet, we rarely see the villain pastor as the exception, not the rule. This is a cultural irony in the west when we so readily admire the "tainted hero." Typically, America no longer reveres spiritual leaders as heroes, neither are they allowed to be human.

As a minister, let me say that a Godly pastor's heart beats and bleeds for even those people. Please understand that this book is not meant to cause hurt or division in any group, nor is it meant as a rant about negative experiences.

Christopher Schmitz – Why Your Pastor Left

I hope that this book will be read by not only pastors, clergymen, and church staff, but by frequent and infrequent churchgoers across America. I want you to understand a pastor's heart; I want to expose the tribulations which many pastors tolerate in order to fulfill their calling. I also want to help you cope with the loss of your pastor, if applicable.

In the west, the number of qualified pastors consistently declines; the American church is in crisis. While endeavoring to help the wounded heal and cope through a difficult time, my primary goal in this book is to point out several specific "ministry killers."

Above all else, we must remember the great commission and the two greatest commandments. We (the Church) should be focused on winning souls to the Kingdom and let love rule above all else. God must be our utmost head and the object of our worship, faith, and life; love must prevail in every circumstance—not legalism or religiosity. Jesus did not spare his contempt for subscribers of religiosity as they sought to use their man-made piety to regulate and manipulate an eternal, omnipotent God. I often paraphrase Jesus' words about the second greatest commandment this way: "If you can just do Love correctly—genuinely and as God demonstrates and calls, then everything else in life will work out."

See, God is Love. "Christian" in the original language can translate as a paraphrase of "little Christ," essentially, a copycat (or at least, this is supposed by many and at the least it means "Belonging to the household/family of Christ.") If we are faithful imitators of Him, then our own lives will be

Christopher Schmitz – Why Your Pastor Left

characterized by divine love: love that should be visible from the outside-in and felt from the inside-out.

We must get better at love if we are to be better Christians. Here is a quick refresher from 1 Corinthians 13:4-7 "Love is patient, love is kind. It does not envy, it does not boast, it is not proud. It is not rude, it is not self-seeking, it is not easily angered, it keeps no record of wrongs. Love does not delight in evil but rejoices with the truth. It always protects, always trusts, always hopes, always perseveres." NIV

Here are some sobering statistics.

A survey[1] of pastoral subscribers to Leadership, Christianity Today, and Your Church found the following results regarding "forced exits":

- Nine out of ten pastors (91%) know three to four others who have been forced out of pastoral positions.
- One-third of all pastors (34%) serve congregations who either fired the previous minister or actively forced his or her resignation.
- Nearly one-fourth (23%) of all current pastors have been forced out at some point in their ministry.
- 10 % of dismissed/replaced pastors left pastoral ministry altogether.
- 46% cite conflicting visions as the precipitating cause of their termination.
- 38% cite personality conflict with board member(s) as the cause.

    Of those ministers forced to exit:

---

[1] John C. LaRue, Jr. "Forced Exits: a Too-Common Ministry Hazard." Your Church, 1996.

Christopher Schmitz – Why Your Pastor Left

- 13 percent were directly fired,

- 58 percent were forced to resign,

- 29 percent resigned because of perceived pressure.

- A similar survey[2] by the Southern Baptist Convention found that 66% of respondents had "conflicts with powerful members," a finding thirty points higher than the Christianity Today poll.
- The Southern Baptists also found that, of those churches that fired pastors, 78% had also terminated *previous* pastors or staff members.

The fact of the matter is that many pastors are burned up, burned out, or have been just plain burned by the church, and the modern church has made it a habit of doing so. The stress of ministry weighs heavily on a pastor and on his or her family (and most of these stressors are not part of the calling as a pastor, but are extra, human burdens we put on him or her). Many jobs are stressful, but most other jobs, at least in America's highly-regulated culture, include some form of compensation or control that keeps that worker efficient and safe. For example, airline pilots are required to take a certain amount of rest/personal time between each flight so that they don't become fatigued. Likewise, we ought to make every effort to safeguard our ministers. Ministry is one of the few vocational areas not policed and regulated by some government group; Pastors often get no severance package and cannot receive unemployment benefits in

---

[2] Krejcir, Dr. Richard J. "Statistics on Pastors." Into Thy Word. n.d. http://www.intothyword.org/apps/articles/default.a (accessed August 2014).

Christopher Schmitz – Why Your Pastor Left

the wake of a dismissal. Because of the nature of the Church, we should never require someone to tell us to support our leaders: God already told us that (just for starters, read 1 Tim. 5:17,18; Matt. 10:10; Lk. 10:7; 1 Cor. 9:14,) and yet a dismissed minister immediately becomes an island, more lonely and abandoned than ever. Adherents to Scripture shouldn't need admonishment, and yet, too often clergy fall under the heavy load of disillusionment, dishonor, or financial pressure bestowed upon them.

In a group conversation, hotly discussed was peoples' tendency to jump to conclusions and make wrong decisions. Most of those assumptions were based on faulty, preconceived expectations that had hardened like concrete years before. My wife pointed out the need for proper training and education in churches for even the simplest things. In a college course she'd taken in preparation for a teaching degree, she'd been taught that, "We cannot expect students [people] to know anything that we have not specifically/purposefully taught them."

That is an area the church must improve in: teaching people. Do you remember not knowing how to talk, or looking at a book and not being able to identify letters and words? It is the obligation of those with wisdom and knowledge to share that with any who seek it. There exist many preconceived notions within the church, imaginary trip wires leading to bombs within the pews. Whether they be social mores, old grudges, or staunch traditions, a detonation is never the responsibility of the one who steps on the landmine, but rather the fault of the bomber who planted it. Let's take a fortune-cookie nugget of wisdom from Star Wars' Yoda; sometimes we must "unlearn what we have learned."

This is a book about love. Love rejoices in truth. Sometimes we don't like to hear about the painful, fallout side of ministry, yet it exists and should be addressed. To prevent causing hurt to more people, we must honestly look hard at the things the church has done to cause pain in others so that we can prevent repeating these mistakes. Without understanding these things, we cannot be kind, we find it difficult to trust, and we *will not* persevere.

Statistics are not in our favor. But still, love perseveres.

Chapter 1

(Rebel sheep and dying flocks)

The western church is dying. This is a fact, though some might attempt to dispute that statement; on paper things don't look good. The 2007 Yearbook of American and Canadian Churches reports a membership increase of 0.82% in the top 25 denominations, however twelve of those twenty-five did not offer a report at all, and many of those denominations that reported increases count membership for life (even if that "member" joins and never again attends, or even joins a new church elsewhere.)[3]

It's true; many churches are doing quite well. Some churches are experiencing growth and revival, but as a whole, we are in decline. A cancer survivor might say that they feel fine; all the while their body is shutting down and dying of new, undiagnosed tumors. "I feel fine." A hospital analysis shouldn't be ignored based on feelings. We cannot live in denial that the Church is in decline.

The United States Census Bureau Records, denominational reports, and the Assemblies of God U.S. Missions department offer these statistics:

- Every *year* between 4,000 and 7,000 churches close.[4]

- Half of all churches in the US did not add any new members to their ranks in the last two years.[5]

---

[3] Lindner, Eileen, ed. The 2007 Yearbook of American and Canadian Churches. Nashville: Abingdon Press, 2007.

[4] (Rainer n.d.)

[5] Krejcir, Dr. Richard J. "Statistics and Reasons for Church Decline." Church Leadership. n.d.

Christopher Schmitz – Why Your Pastor Left

- There were about 4,500 new churches started between 1990 and 2000 and a 20 year average of about 1,000 per year.[6]

- Every year, 2.7 million church members fall into inactivity.[7]

- From 1990 to 2000, the combined membership of all Protestant denominations in the USA declined by almost 5 million members (9.5 percent), while the US population increased by 24 million (11 percent).[8]

- At the turn of the last century (1900), there was a ratio of *27 churches per 10,000 people*; as compared to the close of this century (2000) we have *just 11 churches per 10,000* people in America![9]

- In keeping with the above ratios, there should have been over 38,000 new churches commissioned to keep up with the population growth.

- The United States now ranks third following China and India with populations of residents who are not professing Christians; in other words, the U.S. is the third largest "un-reached people group" in the world.[10]

A 2009 Barna report[11] finds:

---

http://www.churchleadership.org/apps/articles/default.asp?articleid=42346 (accessed 2014 August).

[6] Ibid.

[7] Ibid.

[8] Ibid.

[9] Ibid.

[10] Ibid.

[11] Barna, George. "Gracefully Passing the Baton." The Last Christian Generation? December 7, 2009. http://fourpercent.blogspot.com/2009/12/gracefully-passing-baton-by-george.html (accessed August 2014).

Christopher Schmitz – Why Your Pastor Left

- Volunteerism in churches is down by an alarming 21% since 1998

- Adult Sunday school involvement has declined by 17% since 1998.

Here is a trend tracked by Francis A. Schaeffer Institute of Church Leadership Development (FASICLD). According to this poll data,[12] "frequently" is defined as attendance at least two times per month:

- 22% of Americans "frequently" attended church in 1992, including Orthodox, Evangelical, or Protestant.

- 20.5% of Americans "frequently" attended church in 1995

- 19% of Americans "frequently" attended church in 1999

- 18.0% of Americans "frequently" attended in church in 2002

The western church is rapidly becoming a collection of loose, wandering flocks. Sheep refuse to follow the guidance of any shepherd in our day; they are content to meander along their own path of self-enlightenment. Moreover, they demand that they be allowed to do this and even encourage others to do likewise. Disenfranchised shepherds have become a sight all too common: lonely pastors on a hillside, often covered with sheep bites and the stink and manure of the uncommonly vicious animals he tried to tend.

David Fisher's book, *21st Century Pastor,*[13] quotes one of my favorite writers, George Hunter, who addresses the problem of Christian decline in our culture. "The result of culture quakes and shakes is an increasingly unchristian

---

[12] (Krejcir, Statistics and Reasons for Church Decline n.d.)
[13] Fischer, David. The 21st Century Pastor. Nashville: Zondervan, 1996. 2

Christopher Schmitz – Why Your Pastor Left

America. George Hunter claims that 120 million Americans are virtually secular. They have no Christian influence, no Christian memory or vocabulary, and no Christian assumptions or worldview. Hunter believes America is actually the largest mission field in the Western world, noting that the percentage of practicing evangelical Christians in Uganda, once a Western mission field, is higher than in America."

Western culture is independent-minded. We so value personal freedom that, very often, we refuse to follow the leadership of any other. Personally, I grew up as a part of what I call the "Walt Disney Generation." We WDGs were told that anything they wanted to do was possible; all you needed was positive thinking. You want to be the next president, princess, or rags-to-riches hero? Perfect, just believe in yourself. WDGs also got the soft end of the stick when it came to self-esteem. School programs were designed to boost a child's ego, even in the face of abject reality. Programs, counselors, books, teachers, and parents all informed us we were great at everything, even when we weren't made for those things. That's why we see a row of petite little girls in ballerina uniforms plié during a Swan Lake recital, and there's a fat kid in the back trying to keep up. (Please don't think I'm attacking anyone—I was a fat kid as a child, I've been there and suffered through that before I got comfortable with who I was in my own skin.) The thing is, God built us all to excel at different things, be they physical or mental, we all have niches of skill, and we all have limitations. The Ugly Duckling story doesn't tell us we all can be the best at the same thing, but that we are beautiful in our different ways *when we accept ourselves for who we are.*

17

WDGs are raised to disbelieve in the limitations; this was a contributing factor to the eventual destruction of absolute truth and the rise of post-modern thinking that has occurred in recent decades. WDG thinking gave us a generation that believes each person deserves to sit in the Oval Office or in some lofty executive chair. Those spaces, however, are limited, and ignoring the reality of that only encourages rebellion against authority and discontent within any assembly, be they secular or religious. The WDG mindset is still encouraged today through a variety of media.

One of the problems within western churches is that they are full of people who believe *they* would make a better leader than he or she whom God called to the helm already. Watchers of the NFL call them arm-chair quarterbacks and the analogy works across the board. Arm-chair quarterbacks can't pay attention in church because they are distracted by comparing every aspect of the church to either their own hypothetical scenario, or the preacher down the road. They don't see their leader as good enough of an administrator as the last guy; he or she isn't a better worship leader than Sister Ethel. Arm-chair quarterbacking plants doubt and makes people question whether God really called this pastor: it erodes a ministry's foundation.

It's a hard time for us WDGs when we realize that the world doesn't revolve around us. The funny thing is, many churchgoers are old enough to remember days long before Steam Boat Willy, and they, too, often have this very same attitude. Developing the belief that another is more gifted or talented than your pastor is one thing, (I won't even deny that it could be true,) but it is another matter entirely when someone begins to act out on this assumption.

Christopher Schmitz – Why Your Pastor Left

Pastoring is not a matter of gifts or ability; it is a matter of calling. Too often, people squeeze their pastor, trying to fit him or her into the mold that they envision as their ideal leader. That manipulation is simply wrong. The pressure he or she feels exerted upon them often feeds directly into burnout, which is a chief factor sending pastors out of the ministry.

Plain and simple, many people want their pastor to become someone else; when sheep try to change their pastor or his ministry, the fuse is lit. Even when this "squeezing" takes place in private meetings between the leadership of the church, it harms a pastor's ability to lead. Like all people, pastors need to be challenged and held to high standards, encouraged to learn and advance themselves, but not manipulatively so.

Typically, the pressure to conform happens like a bully shaking down kids for milk money. "Give me what I want or me and my friends will beat you up." If pastors don't meet the playground bully, they often deal with the whiner, "If we don't play the game *my way* I'm taking my ball and going home!" Most of us have acted like one or the other at some point in our lives. It's simple human nature, but it certainly exerts a great deal of negative influence on pastors, who we are directed to love and support.

Negativity and stress drain people. That drain acts like a crack in a car's oil-pan: the engine runs hotter and hotter without the correct amount of oil, and eventually, the entire engine seizes up and quits—causing permanent damage in the process—literally burning out.

Here are some findings from various surveys and studies that reflect the stressors relating to this burnout epidemic.

Christopher Schmitz – Why Your Pastor Left

- 80% of pastors believe the pastoral ministry has negatively affected their families[14] (Life Enrichment Ministries - 1998)

- 25% of all pastors don't know where to go for help if they have a personal or family conflict or concern. 33 percent have no established means for resolving conflict.[15] (George Barna - 2002)

- 40% have no opportunity for outside renewal like a family vacation or continuing education. There is a very clear relationship between the amount of time a pastor takes for personal renewal and his satisfaction in his job.[16] (George Barna - 2002)

- At any given time, 75% of pastors in America want to quit.[17] (Church Resource Ministries - 1998)

- More than 2000 pastors are leaving the ministry each month[18] (Marble Retreat Center 2001)

- A 2005 survey of clergy by the Board of Pensions of the Presbyterian Church also took special note of a quadrupling in the number of people leaving the profession during the first five years of ministry, compared with the 1970s.[19]

- In May, 2010 the Clergy Health Initiative, a seven-year study from Duke University, published the first results of a continuing survey. Compared with neighbors in their census tracts, ministers reported

---

[14] Wheeler, Dr. Raiford S. A View from the Parsonage. Maitland: Xulon, 2012. 34
[15] Ibid.
[16] Ibid. 35
[17] Ibid.
[18] Ibid.
[19] (Vitello 2010)

Christopher Schmitz – Why Your Pastor Left

significantly higher rates of arthritis, diabetes, high blood pressure and asthma. Obesity was 10 percent more prevalent in the clergy group.[20]

- Sunscape Ministries of Colorado reported that in all denominations nationwide, 1,600 ministers per month are terminated or forced to resign their pulpit.[21]

The negative influence of pastoral burnout reverberates throughout traditional church bodies. Many of our children and grandchildren have become casualties of a system that has ramped up exterior judgment and regulation. Christ's primary directive for our horizontal relationships (how we interact with follow man) is to reflect *His* love.

Relationship based ministry has been called a passing fad by some, viewed as just a buzzword or a trend popular in the Emergent Church culture. The church needs to understand that this ministry philosophy has been around at least as long as Christ. The basic concept is derived directly from scripture.

I grew up in church, but most of my friends were from outside its walls. Even as a kid I recognized that the people inside didn't have true relationships with each other—they were just familiar faces sitting in the same, usual pew. I simply followed suit.

---

[20] Ibid.
[21] Kent Crockett and Mike Johnston. Pastor Abusers: When Sheep Attack Their Shepherd. Whole Armor Press, 2012. 5

21

Christ established the church, but He *died* so that He could restore the *relationship* of love between mankind and the triune Godhead. He died so we could know Him.

"Isn't this just an Emergent Church fad?" In seventeenth century, the monk known as Brother Lawrence wrote many letters (later compiled into the book The Practice of the Presence of God,) in which he stated, "We must know before we can love. In order to know God, we must think of Him; and when we come to love Him, we shall also think of Him often, for our heart will be with our treasure." You can't *know* someone without a relationship; we cannot love those whom we do not know.

Perhaps one of the reasons the Church is upside down is that we've forgotten what the church really is. We are all familiar with sayings such as, "The church is not this building, but the people within," but the cumulative cliché has stolen the meaning behind the statement. We pay the notion lip service, but never scratch below the surface.

In his blog, author and pastor David Foster said, "The gap between following Christ and being committed to a church is growing."[22] That statement hit me like a ton of bricks. Foster's statement indicates that believers, especially the rising generation, will cling to their personal faith and relationship with Christ. However, they are actively leaving behind the overly-sanitized traditions and man-made institutions that make up a standard Sunday Morning Liturgy.

Foster also notes that, in the context of the emergent church movement, the question has been raised: Do we try to reach people, or build a church? He

---

[22] Barna, George. Revolution. Tyndale: Carol Stream, 2006.

Christopher Schmitz – Why Your Pastor Left

points out that this is not supposed to be an either/or ultimatum. It should be both/and. This question reflects just how far we've gone in forgetting what the church really is and what it was meant to be. Preacher's often say, "Christ loved the church so much that he laid down His life for it." I have often argued against that very sentiment, because I know that I was a sinner and He laid it down for *me*, church background regardless. The preacher's statement is a paraphrase taken from Ephesians 5:25; the Greek word for church is ekklēsia, which means a gathering/community of believers/saints either on Earth or in Heaven (or both). It's a broad term.

Actually, both statements are true! The problem is one of the English language: we use the same term for the people as we do the building and lose the nuances of context that surround the word.

So just what is the church? What's it for? How did we ever confuse the two? Why do we even need to bother with the argument? "Forget this nonsense; let's just do church!" as some of my older colleagues might say.

In *Revolution*, George Barna estimates that the local church is presently the primary form of faith experience and expression for about two-thirds of the nation's adults. He projects that by 2025 the local church will lose roughly half of its current "market share" and that alternative forms of faith experience and expression will pick up the slack. Churches have already been rocked by the noncommitment of "church hoppers" and the absence of "Lone Ranger Christians," those people who say, "I'm a believer but I refuse to attend any church for (insert various reason.) I can worship God just as well at home, on my own." I can't imagine that any new, alternative form (which abandons the

23

Assembly/Gathering of Believers–see Hebrews 10:25,) can be healthy or scriptural.

Barna's research indicates that in just a few years' time, we will have lost HALF our current influence. Our cultural influence, even *now*, is not enough to keep pornography and obscenities off television networks or encourage the stability of the American family. If we are outraged over the flood of rampant ungodliness which stalks our children and the general decay of social morals through Hollywood, the music industry, education outlets, and the Internet, understand that it stems primarily from the decline of our influence on culture.

Half our influence means society can behave twice as badly before anyone will cry out against them or weep on their behalf. When the church, sometimes referred to as societies' conscience, bleeds to death, Immorality becomes the new morality. Do we care about fixing the church once the numbers show our methods cause our own deterioration? Currently, "*the primary form of faith experience and expression*" is causing people to abandon our God in droves. It is time to reevaluate that machine.

What is church now? Is it different than how it was in biblical times? If it is different, then shouldn't Bible-believing Christians attempt to do something to get us back to the scriptural model? The most telling question is this: are we even familiar enough with Scripture to know what that model looks like?

24

Chapter 2

(Forgotten Church)

The median number of adults who attend a mainline church on any given weekend is just 99 adults (George Barna - 2009).[23]

"And Joshua the son of Nun, the servant of the LORD, died, being an hundred and ten years old. And they buried him in the border of his inheritance in Timnathheres, in the mount of Ephraim, on the north side of the hill Gaash. And also all that generation were gathered unto their fathers: **and there arose another generation after them, which knew not the LORD, nor yet the works which he had done for Israel**. –Judges 2:10 KJV."

This passage from Judges depicts exactly what happens to a nation—even a nation with hardcoded religious beliefs—when it's culture-influencers exit the scene. Once Joshua and the last of those who marched around Jericho died, the next generation lives in ignorance (possibly of their own design, or "dumb on purpose.") *"The primary form of faith experience and expression"* in our culture has always been routed through the church. Western culture and the church are reciprocal influencers, but the Church has begun to fade, largely because many people don't understand exactly what it is?

---

[23] The Barna Group, Ltd. "Report Examines the State of Mainline Protestant Churches." Barna Group. December 7, 2009. https://www.barna.org/barna-update/leadership/323-report-examines-the-state-of-mainline-protestant-churches.

Christopher Schmitz – Why Your Pastor Left

So what is the church? How would *scripture* define it? If we want to be accurate in our search for truth, we should examine the source of truth, God's Word. What was the church in the times of Christ, versus what it is now?

To get started in that search, we must first look at "sanctification." Western Christians rarely understand the idea of sanctification, or the process of continually trying to become more like Christ, literally conforming to His image and putting on Christlikeness so that the inner-self changes to align with *His* character. The western/American idea of what a Christian should look like has really become list of dos and don'ts. This is the same trap that Pharisees fell into: religiosity, which makes their faith more about *them*, than about God.

Many problems stem from that thinking. First and foremost is that it exempts personal freedoms. The list follows traditions rather than scripture, keeping believers inside a box, secluded within a comfort zone that renders them ineffective in the world. Second, it encourages people to compare their level of commitment/holiness versus each other, even if subconsciously. It is pharisaical religion: relegating faith to a checklist of chores and prohibitions. It forgets the relationship aspect between us and Christ. Sanctification, walking alongside Jesus in our daily lives, is "becoming more like him," not "meeting prerequisites."

So how does that relate to this issue of church? We typically look at church as a weekly assembly to attend as a matter of religious duty. Jesus lives in a box and we come to visit Him every once and a while; the elite do it at least once a week, some of us just on Easter and Christmas. People live like heaven on Sunday and play like hell the rest of the week.

Christopher Schmitz – Why Your Pastor Left

Church is so much more than just the weekly gathering for singing songs, giving money, and listening to a preacher. Church has become synonymous with the idea that your duty to God is met by attending meetings in some building which, statistics show, is the average Americans least favorite place to go.

See, a Christian life, truly lived, already contains all the aspects that we see reflected in "standard" church services. Those attributes should include prayer, reflection/reading of scripture, worship (which is not described as mere singing), sacrificial generosity, an attitude of learning. A true Christian life makes the Sunday Service practically redundant except for that it's a corporate and visible display—it is the community/relationship aspect of our faith.

A Christian life, one of sanctification, is a journey. The believer walks alongside Christ, becoming more like Him. That being the case, he or she will exhibit all of the traits listed above. These are publicly displayed in traditional Sunday services; they are done corporately to edify and encourage each other. Our understanding of church should be that we come together in a community setting, having all things in common (see Acts 4:32). Perhaps we need not, because of our culture, actually share all worldly possessions, but it would behoove us to at least attempt having a common *mind* and *goal*, that is, to elevate Christ above us.

If a person's Christianity (which could literally be translated as the amount to which they imitate Christ,) is lived in their daily lives, then we gather on Sundays to meet specific purposes. We honor the Sabbath, a day of remembrance and dedication to the Lord. This serves as a gateway for many to

27

come and visit a church and become acquainted with it. The primary reason that we gather together is to share *ourselves* with each other in unity of our bonds to Christ.

The community aspect of a weekly gathering is so that we can build lasting, solid friendships. With solid relationships forged, we have the ability to minister to each other, hold each other accountable, help each other, exercise spiritual gifts, teach each other, and practice love—all in the name of our Savior. When a visitor previews a service where they see those things occurring, they want in.

In regards to the question of the Sabbath/commandment from the Old Testament in regards to the New Covenant, I take a logical approach. It's often taught that those Old Testament laws reinforced by the New Testament must still be obeyed (or obeyed with clarified meaning under the light of Christ's or the Apostles' teaching.) Hebrews 10:25 teaches us not to give up on gathering together, something which the early believers continued. Simply put, we are to remain carrying on the spirit of the Sabbath: corporate, regular joining as a community of faith.

I personally think that we've made too much of our liturgies. Most churches I'm familiar with (even the "non-liturgical" ones,) have developed some sense of standing liturgy: a typical method or service order for function and flow. The service order becomes nearly as holy as Scripture itself! I've often heard pastors quip that their church might split if they abandoned pre-service coffee and doughnuts.

Christopher Schmitz – Why Your Pastor Left

Must we have our standard coffee and doughnuts to see people saved? Whenever people get so hung up on the details of the service order, I get irked. Why do we even need to have a regimented service? We don't need four songs, announcements, offering, and a three-point sermon to assemble together and discover God in our midst. We can still have an orderly gathering in the name of God without it looking *anything* like the traditional, western church service. Matthew 18:20 tells us we only need to be *together*.

See, we get so focused on the body of the building that we forget about building the body. While preparing to write this I traveled through Tennessee. I saw multiple signs advertising places where a new church was soon to be built. While so many individual churches lock their doors forever, languishing and bleeding their flock, the western church still spends billions every year in real estate: new buildings, fixtures and decorations… all creature comforts. Church was never meant to be about our comfort levels!

CHURCH IS NOT THE SUNDAY MORNING RITUAL! In fact, if the primary focus of your local church is your Sunday service, I think you have lost focus. Sadly, this is the case in the *majority* of our American services. In fact, in Galatians Paul literally damns those who try to distort the message of the church by making it more legalistic; he speaks harshly about pleasing people rather than seeking souls. Church cannot be about pleasing the founders—the desire to please people is usually the root of displeasing God. Simply doing a "nice service" is a placebo: nothing really happens, there is no growth, but everyone is happy—nobody rocked the boat. Pleasant church services perpetuate a nursing home mentality: make your patrons comfortable and keep the environment

Christopher Schmitz – Why Your Pastor Left

pleasurable for whatever years remain. Childbirth, on the other hand, is messy and painful and bloody—yet life is birthed in the struggle of the moment.

Church *is the people*... the service, then, is a regular gathering meant to refresh those relationships. Just driving down the highway with fellow believers, sharing our hearts and how God has been active in our lives can be "church." Scripture does not mandate a service order, or even the necessity of a traditional sermon, songs/hymns, possible call for a response, etc. Why would it? It only tells us to continue meeting together for our common purpose in Him.

Our *lives* should be sermons. The mandate to proclaim the Gospel is not an obligation of just the pastor. Romans 10:14b (KJV) says "How shall they believe in him of whom they have not heard? And how shall they hear without a preacher?" The word preacher is not a pastoral title here. The Greek word is kērussō and it simply means "a herald, as in a town crier." Verbally, publicly proclaiming the truths of God should already be a part of a Christian's life

A lifestyle of Christ-likeness should be the *daily walk* of a believer, not a weekly checklist. The gathering within the upper room in the book of Acts is undeniably an example of believers gathering and "having church," as some might call it. They met in neither synagogue nor "church building" nor temple. It is not recorded that they played organ, hymns, or choruses. There was no recorded sermon or offering, no special number or announcements. The only qualifier was that they "were all together in one place" (Acts 2:1) and we see that they were all with one mind (Acts 1:14).

The most effective "church service," then, might include a football game rather than a sermon. (Note, I'm not in favor of eliminating public

Christopher Schmitz – Why Your Pastor Left

proclamation of the Gospel, but am in favor of varying the Church's traditional approach to outreach. A church that does only "fellowship" services becomes a social club. But there is a social element that we must incorporate—that "community" of faith aspect is a major part of a believer's baptism, one of the two sacraments ordered by Jesus.)

I recall one disagreement with an interim Pastor who was fifty years my senior. He decided to cancel the church's annual Superbowl "fellowship" night in order to substitute it with a Sunday evening service. His opinion was that we fellowship was trivial compared to "doing church;" we would not skip a regular evening "church service". His argument was "what if God wants to do something in someone's life that night? I won't deny God any opportunity to move in His body." I don't disagree with his premise, but I think the data reflected God had been utilizing a different method to call in new people.

God can move wherever we allow Him. The evening service was already sparsely attended, but attendance numbers had little to do with my argument. The event had been an annual "non-threatening" event where people could invite their friends to come inside our building and have some fun while meeting members of our congregation and possibly get connected. I could name three specific individuals in our church that gave their hearts to the Lord during an altar call, but first visited at a friend's invitation to the "Superbowl Sunday" event. The event built bridges to members of the community and bolstered relationships within the congregants.

Comfort compelled this pastor to do it the way he had always done it before—even in the face of data and at the possible expense of forfeiting souls

31

from the harvest. He operated on the premise that *God cannot work anywhere except within MY liturgy.* This is rigid, inflexible faith that denies God the opportunity to work.

My argument wasn't considered; we "had church." Attendance barely registered in church records. No divine healings occurred within the service; no persons responded to an altar call for salvation. No visitors attended. To my knowledge, nobody who attended looks back to that evening's service as the turning point in their life, or the hook that drew them into a relationship with God.

Some things in life are lifestyles, not just simple decisions. Worship is an example, an attitude of honoring God with all that you are, surrendering yourself to Him; it is not the songs that we sing, but the impetus behind them. This is the definition of more than eighty percent of the ancient words penned in all scripture used to express "worship," it is not mere song-singing. Worship is something that we should do ALL THE TIME in our private lives as Christians—worshipping is not just a corporate, Sunday morning block of music. Likewise, church reflects so much more than our modern understanding of it (or lack thereof.)

The Sunday service is meant for the corporate observance of our faith—the details of which should already be happening *every day* for the believer. Jewish history gives us insight into how we ought to structure this. I hear the complaints already; I know that we are not Jews. There are New Testament examples of the early church meeting in the Synagogue, so the Synagogue is relevant.

32

In the synagogue, any man who felt himself qualified could seek permission to teach on the Sabbath. That's right, there was no pastor/rabbi/priest running the Synagogue, nobody regulating the pre-planned order of service/schedule. They did, however, have a "Head of Synagogue," he was voted in from the local body to act as the authority of the local synagogue, sometimes also occupying the role of the hazzan, (the person who leads any vocal prayers or worship. The position, often modernly called a cantor, was not a "paid" position such as a Levite or priest.) In Jesus' time, any respected teacher or Rabbi who passed through an area was often sought out to teach in the local synagogue. (Nowadays, I travel through and try to drop in and connect with local pastors in towns I visit; I can't seem to get in to meet the leader of a group between 50-300 congregants, let alone address a congregation.)

The Jewish idea of synagogue treats it as more of a community hub than a dedicated religious center; it served as the local school, civic center, etc. They didn't always have a set liturgy. They read and taught from the Torah, but their typical "sermon" or teaching on Sabbath was more reflective on how God fits into their daily walk or how He recently impacted this week's speaker... the message had real life application. It more resembled the "small group" model.

Ray Vander Laan writes at FollowTheRabbi.com[24]:

"...it is likely the main focus of the early gatherings of Jewish people was simply the need to maintain their identity as a people living

---

[24] Vander Laan, Ray. "He Went to the Synagogue." Follow The Rabbi. n.d. http://followtherabbi.com/guide/detail/he-went-to-synagogue (accessed August 2014).
Vitello, Paul. "Taking a Break From the Lord's Work." New York Times, Augus 2, 2010: A1.

Christopher Schmitz – Why Your Pastor Left

in a foreign and pagan country. That the synagogue began as the center of the Jewish social life is confirmed by the fact that it was the community center in the first century as well. The synagogue was school, meeting place, courtroom, and place of prayer. In some towns, the synagogue may even have provided lodging for travelers. It was the place where small groups of Jewish students assembled for Scripture reading and discussion of the Torah and oral tradition. This meant that worship and study, friendship and community celebration, and even the governing of the community were all done by the same people in the same place.

Although the *hazzan* was in charge of worship services, the prayer leader, readers, and even the one who delivered the short sermon could be any adult member of the community. All were recognized as being able to share the meaning of God's Word as God had taught them in their daily walk with him. In this way, the community encouraged even its youngest members to be active participants in its religious life. Jesus's encounter with the wise teachers in the Temple courts was unusual not so much because of his age, but because of the wise questions he asked…"

The church is supposed to be all about Christ, God's grand plan to redeem fallen man; at some point the culture shifted and the focus become the sheep, rather than the Shepherd. Author David Foster points out that many people have come to embrace Christ, but cannot stand his Bride. People enjoy Jesus, but can't stand the Church. Foster says:

34

"It really is sad to see that Christians have gotten the reputation of being mad, angry, negative, and condemning.

Since when did Christianity become anti anything? My interpretation of the message of Christ is that God is for us. Yes we are broken and our brokenness causes the pain we see in the world. But didn't Christ come to reconcile, to redeem, and to restore?"[25]

It is unfortunate that *we, the Bride of Christ*, have let ourselves get to this point. It's like a person whose long-time friend gets married; they cannot tolerate the company of their old friend's new spouse. This always leads to a relational drift. As the bride, we ought to try to please our betrothed and become better than we currently are. I believe it is one of the aspects and duties to which we are called in this process of "making ourselves ready," (Revelation 19:7) that is to say that we are not yet ready for the marriage of the Lamb.

So let's address that problem. (Aside from the *not making herself ready*,) the Church has become only about *what they are against*. If the unbelieving world knows only a few things about churches, they know this:

They are against homosexuality.

They are against abortion.

They believe they are always right (and by contrast, I am wrong).

They want my money.

---

[25] Foster, David. "Anne Rice Announces She's Leaving Christianity. I Knew That Would Happen. Did You? ." DavidFoster.TV. august 2, 2010. http://www.davidfoster.tv/anne-rice-announces-she's-leaving-christianity-i-knew-that-would-happen-did-you/ (accessed August 2014).

Christopher Schmitz – Why Your Pastor Left

They hate the details of my life; (they want me to change and be like them,) thus, they don't like *me*.

What is conspicuously absent from this list? Jesus! More people today know about the judgmental attitudes in the church and the likelihood that they'll see an offering plate than they do about our dedication to the risen Messiah! How can this be? It's like our "Christian" holidays: Christmas is about holiday shopping and presents (commercialism) and Easter is that time of the year children get to drink wine in church.

Outsiders can easily see that the church is composed of people. And yet we, inside the church, so often overlook how outsiders cannot see the one person that should be glaringly visible: Jesus Christ.

God wants unbelievers to see the appealing aspects of His character in His body. The church should reflect the abundant love of Christ—a love that has no walls or boundaries and that loves regardless. Thus, the love of our God, who literally defines himself as love, should be visible. Our body should be unified; untarnished holiness and righteousness must be clear. Forgiveness and nonjudgmental attitudes should cover those differences that exist between any congregant and his fellow man. The people, the Church, should mirror these things.

Christian music group Casting Crowns alluded to it in a song: *We are the body*. We are the materials that make up what we call Church. It is not a dwelling, or an office, a hallway, or room. It is not tied to a geographic location. "Church lived out" might be as simple as two Christian guys in a boat, trying to

Christopher Schmitz – Why Your Pastor Left

catch some fish. And I mean that literally, not just as a Christianese term for evangelism.

Sometimes plain speech can hurt; here's the first stubbed toe. Very few pastors leave their Church because of the condition of the building. Rather, a pastor leaves under good conditions (the calling of God who moves resources according to His divine purpose,) or he/she leaves under poor conditions (and under the direction and will of *human* purpose.)

When a pastor leaves for human reasons, and under a negative context, understand that he or she may have left because of *some of us*. Perhaps one from the flock somehow damaged him or her, or changed situations beyond a pastor's ability to perform his or her duty. Maybe the pastor was fired, or maybe they were just worn out. One thing I am certain of: the primary reason people leave ministry is not because of God, God is perfect. The reason is people, or human circumstances beyond their control.

Many people never know what circumstances under which a pastor departs. Just as we blur terminology by calling both the people and the structure, "church," we often say that our pastor was simply "called elsewhere," when in fact, they were directed by human guidance (be it their own, or another's.)

I don't know your situation, or your churches' circumstances. I don't want to put a label on anything or make blanket statements because no two situations are the same. A local church body's values, vision, and structure often have an impact on the longevity of his or her stay, and upon the state of a pastor's exit. Understanding your home church is the first step towards coping with the loss of a pastor and guarding against future man-made factors; these

Christopher Schmitz – Why Your Pastor Left

often influence a pastor to depart before their call has been fulfilled, before their tasks have been fully accomplished.

Knowledge of yourself, who you are in Christ, is necessary to maintain a healthy body. Whether through an act of choice, physical death, sickness, or God's calling, every church will eventually find itself without a pastor at some point, and local leaders will need to rise into roles of leadership to see it through until a new shepherd is installed.

Chapter 3

(The Destructive Power of Autonomy)

Why in the world would a book about pastoral longevity need a chapter about free will, a highly theological issue that many of our most highly-educated, religious leaders can't agree on? *Churches are people*, and free will is a critical component woven into the fabric of our humanity. Much of who we are is made up out of those choices we make. We are, at least in part, defined by the actions we choose. A person who chooses to lie is a liar; someone who kills with premeditation is a murderer.

I know that I can't wrap up an argument that's been raging between Armenians and Calvinists for nearly half a millennium, but free will issues invade many aspects of this book. It's not my intent to solve that argument; there are points I can agree with on both sides of the argument. While I wouldn't claim to be a "Calminian," which is a term colloquially given to a firm middle-ground belief, nor do I claim any title to label my specific point of view, I think the truth is somewhere in between the two extremes of the debate.

It's critical we understand what freedom and power we have as human beings in regards to free will. Free will factors into both of these warring theologies. The differences only become divisive when either side's beliefs are taken to an extreme.

Taken to the far edge, Calvinism becomes staunchly predestination and stifles free will—humans have no capacity to make their own decisions (fatalism). This comes about chiefly from the second point of TULIP (an acronym for the five points of Calvinism.) The U stands for Unconditional Election, a doctrine that attempts to explain which persons can achieve salvation, how they do it (or actually, how it is done *to them,*) and why. This potentially throws out free will in that, taken to the extreme, God forces his will upon ours—we don't have any say in the matter. Throughout my ministry, I've known many parents who want to dictate where their kids attend college, the jobs they work, the people they date or marry. Their children are usually resentful; nobody wants to be another's puppet, higher power or not. The extreme of this concept removes hope and purpose from the lives of those other than the minority "elect."

On the other hand, taken to extremes, Arminianism infringes on the sovereignty and power of God. The modern concept of Arminianism, taken to the edge, elevates human authority above the rule and dominion of God. Extreme Arminianism places God as beholden to us: *we* choose to respond to the grace He chose to bestow on us. In this idea, the child tells the parent about his or her college, jobs, marriage prospects, etc. The child is entitled, having a wealthy father; the children wind up spoiled. Here, Christ died for the sins of all to bring us all to redemption, but *only we* choose to accept or reject it—we have all the cards, God can do nothing without our permission. He wanders the planet begging people to sign up for his "retirement plan."

People look at the wrong issue here. Generally, both doctrines believe in the importance of human free will as it relates to salvation. The only theological sparring is over the issue of where the power lies. God opens a door to eternity that no other can open. When a person, through faith in Christ,

Christopher Schmitz – Why Your Pastor Left

accepts the gift of salvation they are walking through that door. The question is who is the one doing the work and flexing their muscle in the soteriological (doctrine of salvation) debate? My point of view: it doesn't matter. Can humanity even understand the process of divine election? Did Christ come for everyone or for only the elect of God; could we all be chosen? Ultimately, since we cannot answer those things, the Calvinist and the Armenian must present the Gospel to all people. The crux of the matter is this: only Jesus Christ had the power to do what was accomplished at the cross; each one that accepts Him must walk through that door opened by grace—they consciously, willfully, move themselves through that door. Regardless of the theological bent, free will is still exercised in all but extreme viewpoints, views which can only be held if a person directly ignores scripture that speaks contrarily.

See, we tend to pick and choose our own beliefs about God's operative ability based upon how we feel at the moment of need. When something we perceive as bad happens to us or our loved ones, we tell ourselves that it will all be better... that this is a product of divine operation. When our neighbor's dog gets hit by a car we remind them of Romans 8:28 which says, "All things work together for good," and often neglect to mention that this is a *conditional* promise: you must love the Lord.

Ultimately, because we don't want to accept the fact that *we* can do bad things, which *cause negative consequences*, we like to pass the buck on to God and blame His sovereignty. I've encountered situations such as this. For example, Bob is a member of a church; he is a decent, moral person, but not a very good worker. Bob spends too much time at the water cooler and tends to be late for work; he tends to arrive unprepared for meetings. Stacked against his coworkers, he draws the same money and benefits but does less work and isn't as qualified as the rest. One day, Bob's boss realizes that he can replace Bob with a motivated intern for a fraction of the price and increase output. Jobless, Bob goes home saddened until his neighbor reminds him that, "all things work together for those who love the Lord." Bob feels happy. His neighbor insists that there must be some new, better job, or other blessing that God has ordained him to receive, just around the corner. Maybe Jesus wants Bob to play the lottery?

Is Bob's story familiar? We have all known a Bob. We forget that Bob could lose a great deal financially, which hurts him, but we look forward to God's next blessing on Bob. We've all seen a Bob wait for that next big thing, and watched it never come. See, we essentially blame God in this model. When *our* expectations don't come to pass, we villainize God's character because of the expectations we give *Him*. Most likely, God initially blessed Bob with that job he wasn't quite qualified for, but Bob failed to follow up on his end and work to maintain or improve his skills. God *already* blessed Bob, but Bob failed to grab a hold of it firmly. It's like Bob was handed a box of fine crystal goblets, Bob didn't firmly grab the box and let it slip to the floor, where the contents shattered... logically, he's not entitled to a *larger* box with *more expensive* crystal to replace what he just dropped.

Using that mentality, we can blame anything on God. He becomes our punching bag and ATM machine. I have seen this attitude applied to a disturbing number of church and governmental politics. It's the WDG mentality in action; it's also an influence in the church of comfort.

Christopher Schmitz – Why Your Pastor Left

One pastor I served under prayed and fasted for many days prior to a vote of re-election. He had served that church for the last five years and the body had consistently grown, both numerically and with maturity. A number of "human factors" played into the vote that followed that Sunday morning service. Days before the vote, a letter had been "accidentally" sent out by the board indicating that the minister's job *did not* hang in the balance—this was not clearly retracted prior to the vote. There had been a coup brewing in the days surrounding the all-church business meeting. Following the meeting, the members of the board publicly stated which way they voted: all but one voted against their pastor remaining in his calling.

Just prior to casting the ballots, the chairman of the board called for a few seconds of prayer, asking God to instruct His people in the way they should vote. The outcome was not a unanimous decision. So was God confused, then, or did people let their personal desires and human motivation influence the way they voted? Somewhere, human will intervened. Either the minority of voters (who were able to influence the vote and eject the pastor) were wrong and let their emotion guide the decision (and some later admitted such) or the Pastor and majority of voters were wrong and the divine call of God for the pulpit; the minister's call was a figment of his imagination. Which person more likely hears the voice of God, a pastor who is educated, retains years of committed ministry experience, prays and fasts in his or her search for answers, or are untrained laity more likely to accurately discern His will? There is much to be said for spiritual maturity.

Christopher Schmitz – Why Your Pastor Left

The previous scenario is all too common. Where does free will enter this situation?

I have no doubt in my mind that both sides of the ballot were composed of voters who love the Lord and are called according to His purpose. But was this outcome, the forced exit of the pastor, really God's will for the church?

Did God reveal His will to the voters who prayed, at most for several minutes, rather than the pastor who prayed and fasted for three days and knew in his spirit that his call to that church was not released? Why did God allow people to be hurt in this process? Why did some people discern God's will as being opposite of the outcome? Was the pre-vote dissention also part of God's plan?

In similar situations, I've seen people turned away permanently from God, frustrated to such a degree that they abandon all belief and hope in God. *That is not* His *will*.

Was this God's will? My thoughts, being directly involved, were no. And yet, things have gone well in that church since their pastoral headship was transferred. The ministries are running at least as strong as ever. But this is God's will anyway: that His church gains ground for the Kingdom. He is still capable of working evil deeds into something new and good, so we can't necessarily judge the decision by that fruit because God endures with His people, even when they habitually do wrong.

Most churches that fire their pastor have already done so previously (78% of them according to the study by the Southern Baptist Convention[26]); the

---

[26] Whitehead, William. "Praise the Lord, Fire the Pastor!" Spiked Online.

Christopher Schmitz – Why Your Pastor Left

replacement always receives a honeymoon before a congregation's fickleness is revealed. It's like remarriages, many people know someone who's in their third, or fourth marriage. Ask anyone who has been married for at least a decade and they will tell you how their marriage dynamics changed after the first few years; expectations shift and passion waxes and wanes.

Ultimately, we *shouldn't* judge if this was His will because *we are not called* to judge it, nor are we capable of such an act. There are, however, many byproducts of the process and the aftermath of such a decision that are clearly outside God's will. If these things are not God's will, then they must be products of another's decision. There are only three influencing parties: God's will, human free will, or possible satanic influences.

How damaging is it when a church suddenly finds itself directionless, or at least pastorless? There is a proverb, taken almost verbatim from Zechariah 13:7 (Jesus also quotes it in Matthew 26), "Strike the shepherd and the sheep will scatter." This is exactly what happens when a shepherd is struck down; being "struck down" implies the forcible actions of another party—it is different than a call to depart a flock or pasture.

The end result of our pushing the Romans 8:28 mentality is that people have often become fatalists, at least when it suits them. How many times have you heard people try to console you with the idea that "Everything happens for a reason?" I disagree with the notion that all tribulations arise from God's testing. Everything happens *because* of a reason. Sin causes death; God doesn't desire

---

November 13, 2007. http://www.spiked-online.com/newsite/article/4073 (accessed 2014 August).

Christopher Schmitz – Why Your Pastor Left

death, rather life. Sometimes people sin, bad things happen in this world, but they are a direct result of *our* actions, not a wrathful deity trying to move his pawns about the galactic chessboard or get a point across. Human beings mess up, plain and simple, and those actions may cause negative consequences to ripple through the lives of others.

However, God can turn our shoddy, human decisions and failings into something glorious. Just because He often does that, does not mean that he intended for us to fail in the first place. That brings us back to the Arminian/Calvinist debate.

The *debate*, we must remember, only has a bearing on the power of human choice when it comes to the decision of accepting Christ's salvation. Centuries of debate have pressed the issue into other realms, broadening the reach of the argument. As far as our everyday lives go, we all constantly make decisions, neither doctrinal position argues against that.

God gave us the option to choose to live in obedience to His voice, or to our own desires. Sometimes those things align, but never do they *always* align, and we ALL choose to go our own way at times.

God is in the business of fixing flawed, sinful people (and even those of us who're only just a *little* imperfect). We all possess the ability to make mistakes and commit sins, but God is awesome enough to take our red-checked, failed tests from the trash bin of life and make paper-mâché out of it, forming something unexpected and perfectly wonderful.

Human tendency is to believe that we're as good as we feel we are. In my experience, church people believe that God wants only the best for them and is continuing to take them from one level of blessing to another. They fail to realize, though, that God's view of blessing is quite different than ours. *Our view of blessing is defined by terms of our own comfort and pleasure rather than personal growth; God will often bless us with a thorn in our side to keep us humble, dependent on Him, etc.*

We think that the Christian life is a continual, uphill walk of blessings and each tier brings more bliss than the last; that overlooks the passages regarding the valley of death and the promises of suffering. Christianity is a life of challenge and difficulty, yet it promises ultimate satisfaction and personal development at the very end. See, God cares more about WHO YOU ARE than about how comfortable you are.

It's true that God is generous and the very definition of "a good father," one who gives us good things that we need (Matt 7:9, 10). God also enjoys giving us the creature comforts that we like, but never at the expense of our character. Those things might be ours as we continue striving becoming more like Christ; obedience is the currency of heaven—but we might not be able to spend it till we're there.

People acting contrary to God's will while proclaiming they are His tool reminds me of the movie *Kingdom of Heaven* (20th Century Fox,) Ridley Scott's historical epic revolving around the Christian and Muslim battle over Jerusalem during the 12th century crusades. In the film, bloodthirsty warmongers desiring the death of Muslims announce, "An army of Jesus Christ, which bears his holy cross, cannot be beaten." Then, they proclaim, "There must be war. God wills it!" In rebuttal to the comment, "I would rather live with men than kill

Christopher Schmitz – Why Your Pastor Left

them." The scene illustrates the problem that I've identified: based on *human* feelings and presuppositions, we label *ungodly* actions as *His* will because those actions were perpetrated by "Christians"—it must be so since we march to war under the banner of "His Holy cross," (I hope you catch the sarcasm.)

Humans of influence and position tend to believe that, because they are in place of privilege or position, they must be a reflection of God's will. *Their* desires must be *God's* desires. That is why we vote our own desires and interests in church board meetings and claim that God endorses the democratic process. Is God's will reflected through the legal and political systems? To answer yes would endorse the outcome of Roe v Wade and legitimize abortion; it makes God schizophrenic regarding homosexual marriage and various immoralities legalized in *some* regions and prohibited in *others*.

There *is* a human free will component. Our flesh wars with the plan of God. This is normal; it's when we cease to struggle that we find ourselves running downhill in our own purposes, seeking the low road rather than uphill path.

God never promised earthly bliss. God's goodness is not contingent upon our personal happiness. God *does* promise, though, to take those horrible, messed up things that we do (and even blame God for) and turn them into good things. He turns even our failures into redemption, which is wonderful, yet it's a far better testimony if we stopped telling the world that our hurtful decisions were done because "God wills it!"

We have the ability to go our own way, to do our own thing—this is the part of the free will He gave us. The best way, however, is to choose to go

God's way. And how do we know what His will is, except when we strive for spiritual maturity and listen for the gentle voice He so often speaks in.

Learn His voice and learn His language. Understand that the language of man and the language of God are different. As a pastor friend once said, "God speaks God and man speaks man. We must become mature, and rely on His Spirit for the interpretation."

Chapter 4

(Disillusionment in Ministry)

The most prevalent of all Ministry Killers is Disillusionment in Ministry. The reason it especially dangerous is that it's nearly always overlooked. It's so easy to fall into that it can happen by accident; Pastors' Wives' or close friends (or even a pastor's self-talk) can push him or her into disillusionment.

What do I mean by disillusionment? It could easily be defined as thinking of one thing as if it was something else: believing an apple is an orange, or that the sky is purple. Disillusionment is usually the case when communication has broken down or reality hasn't been addressed. For instance, if a person has been taught all their life that a hand grenade is a tennis ball and handed a bag of grenades and a racquet, it won't be long until he's trying to serve or return grenades. Not the safest situation, but it's one that is frighteningly similar to many modern pastorates. We often play games with explosives while we think the score is love-love... and then, boom! Many pastors, especially those still fresh from pastoral training, Bible College, Seminary, or other ministry positions often walk into a minefield while honestly believing that they're tiptoeing through tulips.

Several years after I graduated from Trinity Bible College, I had an opportunity to visit the campus with some prospective ministry students. I enjoyed my visit and had the opportunity to stay with a friend who was formerly a student in a ministry I worked in who now attended my alma mater.

While touring the campus, I walked the halls with another college student I'd played ball with years prior. He'd been a freshman when I was a graduating senior, and he'd become a mutual friend of my impromptu roommate. Being more connected on the campus, he knew where many of my graduating classmates were and the condition of their ministries. Remember, this is before the social networking scene hit the Internet.

Of my classmates, I viewed myself as the least. I didn't have much going for me. Most all of them were better connected than I, who'd been a transfer student and didn't have the opportunity to build some of those critical relationships in the dorms or share quirky learning experiences with professors as an awkward freshman. I viewed these classmates as potential major contributors to powerful, effective ministries.

In the main administrative corridor hung framed displays with photos of previous graduating classes. One by one, this student ticked off my former classmates who'd burned out, dropped out, or been kicked out of ministry. What really shocked me further was news of divorce and even abandonment of faith altogether.

It really hammered my psyche. Professors often quoted the statistical data that an associate pastor only lasts about nine months, on average, at his or her church. That was a stat that I had determined to defy. Many of those whom I'd graduated with were still going strong, but far too many had given up in so little time. Too many had bombed out and burned bridges, never to be welcomed back into ministry; some might never return to a church, save weddings or funerals.

51

We began to speculate. Why? Why had so many fallen away in so short of a time. Did they not believe that God would see them through trials; did they give in to temptation? This was the moment when I began to realize that there existed a certain lack of preparation for young ministers. My education was more than adequate in preparing me to study, to preach, and to fulfill the duties of a pastor. I left starry eyed and ready to battle against the powers and principalities of the world. Those starry eyes were the things that still needed education; most wounds that truly harm a pastor come from friendly fire.

Much fuss has been made about that nine-month statistic. I personally vowed to never back down, not to contribute to the seeming fickleness of staff pastors. After all, doesn't the same calling of God that directs a Senior Pastor also direct a youth pastor or a music pastor? Shortly after this visit began a deeper realization: it isn't always the choice of a pastor that they leave their ministry. In fact, leaving a church is the most heart-wrenching thing a minister can do to oneself.

This realization started when I and every single pastor friend in my personal circle of contacts (across three states) found themselves suddenly excused from their ministry for various reasons, and not one of them being for moral failure or sin issues. Many of these were seasoned veterans. At least one of them had been on staff for nearly a decade. All of them had children to feed. It happened within a period of a few weeks; each found themselves told that they needed to resign for various reasons.

Personally, I'd just missed nine-month mark in my ministry; that alone threatened to destroy me with guilt and shame. One neighboring pastor I'd met

Christopher Schmitz – Why Your Pastor Left

as I was forced out asked me, "But aren't you *called* to minister here? How can you just accept this as their will and move on?" I'd realized that a called shepherd can still be rejected by his or her sheep, or be cast out by another, higher ranking shepherd. (This is why I discussed freedom of choice earlier.) God calls pastors to their office; He opens those doors, but human beings have the option to slam shut those doors, often pinching our fingers in the threshold. It happens far too often.

Nobody talked about this in college. One might overhear stories or have some personal knowledge of situations where a pastor was dismissed for whatever reason, but there wasn't any specific address concerning the difficulties a pastor faces in ministry.

In college, ministry is a pipedream. Your parishioners will be loving and shower you with love and respect; they will walk with you as you reveal the things of God to them from His Word.

Sometimes we pastors allow ourselves to buy into the dream of disillusionment; it's more pleasant than the alternative. We can easily get so hung up pining for the "best-case" scenario that we have trouble finding the joys of ministry from within the trenches. It is easy, even for a pastor, to forget that following Christ means we will have trouble in our life (1 John 3:10-13.) It seems some aspects of the prosperity gospel have worked their way even into pastoral expectations, despite a broad rejection of the "theology."

Even ministers find it easy to confuse personal comfort with feelings of effectiveness; when you feel good and life's outlook looks promising, you feel you must be in the will of God. When things become hard, and scriptures

53

promise that they will, a pastor tends to become disillusioned. YOU as a church member can help us! Showing affection to your pastor, regardless of your viewpoint or feelings on his or her ministry, will help stave off disillusionment.

Ministry is about people. That carries its own set of problems: people, being inherently evil (Romans 3:23) are not always very nice, or even pleasant to be around. Many pastors often joke that they would love the ministry if it weren't for the people. The truth of the matter is ministry takes thick skin. While this may be mentioned in passing during a minister's training, our desire to focus on the positive aspects of ministry tends to preclude any possibility of hardship in how we envision our future congregations. Accentuate the positive, eliminate the negative, and ignore the middle ground is poor advice for the pastorate, or any sort of management.

Younger pastors tend to drop out early in their careers if they haven't developed thick skin. I was watching the Harry Potter book and movie series, reviewing it from a Christian perspective for some others, when I noticed something that Harry's school did and Bible College's should pick up on. To prepare the students for fierce opposition from their enemies, all students attended a mandatory class called "Defense Against the Dark Arts." While it's not quite correct to view our parishioners as enemies, we should better prepare our next generation of leaders for the conflict and survival that is inevitable when dealing with people.

In *Why Men Hate Going to Church*, author David Murrow makes the keen insight that we have watered down the strength of the church by de-masculinizing it. For the most part, men don't act like men, and if they show up

54

at all they are uninvolved or detached. Murrow says, "If men are to return to church, we must let them be men. Ferocious, aggressive, risk-taking men. We can no longer expect men to act like proper Victorian ladies."[27] In Order of the Phoenix, Harry Potter must sit under the tutelage of one Professor Umbridge. She is an obvious rip on the feminine ideals and control exerted by religious women (under which so many churches languish under a death-grip). One of the aspects of this femininity is the avoidance of conflict. But conflict is there, just brewing below the surface! Men tend to meet conflict head on, resolve it, and advance. Most men are not afraid of conflict; they enjoy watching men slug it out in the ring or on the court because they know that victory is bred in it. Conflict must be addressed and resolved in order for sincerity and Truth to prosper.

Because the church *is* people, there tends to be drama. Drama is a part of life, a natural result of personality and emotional clashes. Personal battles and gossiping, backstabbing attacks within a pastor's flock inevitably fatigue him or her. They don't always kill a pastor's ministry, but they take an unnecessary psychological toll. Disillusionment and drama is the HIV of ministry killers— while they don't always kill, they lower protection against other diseases and eventually another ministry-killer finds weakened resistances and overwhelms a pastor. Under disillusionment, the Call of God becomes less real and seems more a product of imagination or some emotionally triggered response in years previous.

---

[27] Murrow, David. *Why Men Hate Going to Church.* Nashville: Thomas Nelson, 2005. 144

Christopher Schmitz – Why Your Pastor Left

You can help your pastor by asking him or her about the specifics of their call to ministry. Validate their call. Partner with them by believing and holding them to that call; ask them to preach about it and share it. Forgetting the circumstances of their call is the first symptom of disillusionment. The loss of call warps a pastor's sense of self-value, identity in Christ, and sense of effectiveness; it indicates disillusionment is on the horizon.

Immature believers populate every church. Oftentimes, these people believe themselves to be mature. When I think of the term "immature" I am reminded of when my son was a toddler and could barely walk or even stand under his own power. He needed help to stand and would grab my two hands to stabilize himself as he'd run around the house. As great as this short period of time was, he soon learned to do these things on his own. I was not only proud of his achievement, but soon taught him to do more advanced things. When I mean "Immature Believer," I am talking about someone who needs a pastor's constant hand-holding to do basic, simple tasks. You can probably think of someone in your own church that has their minister on speed dial and calls over the slightest disruption of life. An immature believer tends to focus more on getting their pastor's help to guide them through a situation rather than seeking help from God's Word and relying on His presence first and foremost.

God is the ultimate source—we should run to Him first. When a believer who supposes himself or herself to be mature, but chiefly relies on either their own answers or the solutions of another person (be they a minister, deacon, or talk show host, etc.) they are actually immature. Their actions tend to nickel and dime a pastor's time and resolve, wearing it away over time,

56

Christopher Schmitz – Why Your Pastor Left

remolding the pastor's vision of his or her ideal church into something less than God's intent.

A pastor's vision for his or her church is closely tied to their self-worth, just as keenly as it is to his or her calling. It is a picture of their hopes and dreams as guided by God: a thing to be carefully planned for and strived to attain. Immaturity whittles down the ability to achieve that vision. Basically, it restrains the ability to accomplish God's purpose, and thus the Pastor's purpose; it's like dangling a treat in front of a dog's nose and yanking that treat away every time the dog reaches for it. Disillusionment. If you've ever seen this done, a dog eventually stops reaching for it. It gives up, desperately desiring the treat, but no longer willing to continue reaching.

Despite all the buzz that popular ministries and books have generated, there still exists a significant lack of discipleship in the American Church. Mainly, this is because of human refusal to grow. We have the tendency to merely attain status quo. We are happy to perform the minimum required amount of work and barely get by. Most church attendees are happy to just make it into Heaven by the skin of their teeth. Many of our sheep are satisfied to never move, never develop Christian character. Many are content to let a pastor come and feed them, and refuse to move on to forage on their own—worse yet, many even demand this of their pastor. They get upset when prodded to mature, yet this encouragement is the definition of discipleship: encouraging/teaching another to be more Christlike.

Personally, I expect any person in places of influence or authority to be mature (1 Tim. 3:6). This means not only progressing in personal sanctification, but encouraging others along that same path. Immature believers who think themselves mature don't like this expectation; it chafes their pride, as 1 Tim 3:6 points out. It's more work than they intended to do, and causes disconnection between lay leaders and the Pastor, causing that drama that works against God's plan for the body.

Mature believers should "buy-in" to the Pastor's leadership. You may disagree, even offer counsel and suggestions that are different or contrary to the Pastor's direction or vision for the church, but ultimately understand that it is the Pastor who is accountable to God for achieving His will. The pastor is divinely called. Everything flows downhill; there is a chain of command to the Kingdom of God. If a pastor genuinely seeks after God's heart, God will communicate His direction and desires to the *Pastor*. We must be careful not to sever the head of our leadership and replace it with another, especially our own.

Support your minister, even when you disagree with him or her. Disillusionment. Nothing is more disheartening than when influential sheep live in open mutiny.

The topic of congregational rebellion doesn't get talked about much, mostly because we *feel* discussing past failures might be detrimental to the body. Life cannot be led by mere feelings. I prefer to talk about the past; addressing problems does not make me an enemy of Jesus. He knows just as well as I do that His bride is *not yet* ready for the wedding feast. (Revelation 19:7; 21:2,9.) We are not perfect. This is not a divisive or bitter thing to say; it is simply a truth from the Word of God. Just as those in the church are not fully sanctified,

Christopher Schmitz – Why Your Pastor Left

the church as a whole is not yet ready; it can't be ready until it achieves perfect holiness in the presence of the groom at the designated time.

I understand the one who loves His bride, and I know that there are many out there who believe talking about problems within the church undercuts our own strength as a body. From the point of view of the unsaved, the fact that we are not willing to address the problem is already undercutting our credibility and robbing our ability to effectively witness. Discussing our own weaknesses with the intent of building ourselves up, does not tear down the Bride.

Jesus knows us; He knows the Bride. The Bride has *not yet* made herself ready and the only way to make ourselves ready is to first discover what is lacking. Failure or reluctance to address the situation only creates a chink in our armor, making it easier to suffer critical wounds from the enemy or from friendly fire (whether intentional or accidental).

Understand that we are not perfected yet. This step of sanctification will never be achieved until we are united with our savior on the other side of life.

I said that *I was not prepared* after college. By that, I mean that I couldn't see through my starry-glassed eyes that the world, even the church, was composed of fallen, sinful people. Suddenly discovering that a church isn't perfect and is even set against you hastens disillusionment.

One night I was praying and I clearly felt God speak to me. During my prayer, I cried out to God, frustrated with religious people in my church who'd been turning out new converts, driving away those who'd suffered hurts and turned to the church for help, only to be further hurt. "Don't these people care

Christopher Schmitz – Why Your Pastor Left

that I want to show your love to the sinners?" I'd vented. God gently responded, "Remember that these are just a different type of sinner."

My favorite kinds of people are those who don't try to hide who they are. It amuses me when people suddenly find out that I am a pastor. They often backpedal in their speech and try to start changing how they talk and apologize for any profanity. Personally, I love hearing the occasional profanity in church. Not profanity for the sake of offending others, but the genuine speech and conduct of a new believer that hasn't yet been trained how to act on the outside but is only chiefly concerned about how his inward man has been regenerated. As discipleship/sanctification progress, those things fade away until BOTH the outside man and the inward one resembles Christ. I am not offended by profanity—public sins do not lessen my desire to show you Christ's love!

We cannot expect spiritual empowerment for the kingdom of God until we surrender our right to be offended by those in the world, (or by other Christians, and by those that think they are). Divisions of offense and stumbling blocks reveal the Churches' disunity. We don't value the things of God as we should and so our passions become disjointed. We only pay lip service, it seems, to a passion for our Creator and for reaching out to His creation. This is why we don't personally share our faith, but leave it up to "the professionals." A survey by Lifeway Research shows that 78% of Christians have not shared their faith in the last six months.[28] Other research suggests that most never will.

---

[28] Lifeway Research. "Study: Churchgoers Believe in Sharing Faith, Most Never Do." Lifeway Research. January 2, 2014.
http://www.lifewayresearch.com/2014/01/02/study-churchgoers-believe-in-sharing-faith-most-never-do/ (accessed August 2014).

Christopher Schmitz – Why Your Pastor Left

Being genuine is one of the two primary things I've always stressed in my ministries. Unfortunately, we've been trained that we must look and act a certain way on the outside. The outward and inner-man don't match up. We try to look like Christ on the outside, but more resemble Judas in the inside; while this is done with the best of intent, it's why hypocrisy reigns in our western churches. Be genuine. I'd rather know who is struggling with certain problems so that I can work with them, encourage them, help them approach their problems without having to first delve through layers of obfuscation.

Proverbs 27:5 says, "Better is open rebuke than love that is concealed." I would rather openly know who hates me than be loved in secret by people who never share that feeling publicly. Traveling from the Midwest Bible Belt, I got off a train in downtown Seattle. Within one hour I'd seen more open homosexuals than in all my years previous. I fell in love with an aspect of them… not with homosexuality, but with the idea of people who don't hide who they are, whether sinner or saint. At least you know whom you are dealing with, for better or for worse, and can plan accordingly. Being real and genuine makes everything so much easier and doesn't substitute tennis balls for hand grenades.

Christopher Schmitz – Why Your Pastor Left

Chapter 5

(Abusive Boards & Power Struggles)

During King Ahab's reign, and the subsequent reign of his offspring (at the ultimate direction of Queen Jezebel,) Israel was in complete disorder as people with human and/or ungodly intentions directed the kingdom. Anytime people try to usurp God's purpose and plan for His people, the result is friction. From the start, God's plan for Israel was for God to be their head. Man has always begged to differ.

As humanity crept in and brought with it a system that continually failed its people and grew in corruption Israel forgot and even forsook God. We are so fortunate that He sends us divine appointments. In the Old Testament, He sent many prophets to try and recall His people to His purpose.

Throughout Ahab's reign, the wicked king and his evil wife combat these prophets. I find it interesting how God did not destroy the gruesome twosome long before He did. In His mercy, God allows leaders countless opportunities to turn their hearts back to Him. Part of this is related to our free will, in my opinion. He gives us continued grace so that we might choose to turn to Him; were that not the case, He wouldn't bother giving us those continued opportunities to change our hearts and mend our ways—there would be no point. Also, God (who ultimately requires perfection,) sometimes seems less fickle than man. Just as David refused to assassinate King Saul, his predecessor, because Saul was the anointed king, God strived with a series of ungodly kings, allowing them the possibility of turning their hearts back.

Christopher Schmitz – Why Your Pastor Left

Eventually, God has enough. God directs Elisha to send a nameless (though recognizable) prophet in 2 Kings 9 to anoint Jehu as the new king. Jehu slaughters the old line and starts over, tearing down the rampant Baal worship in the country, and with a few simple words, had the harlot-queen Jezebel flung from her safe tower. The chaos plunged the countries of Israel and Judah into turmoil. Temples were burned, people died, there were wars and feasts. This was conflict, and it's what happens within our own walls. Our battles are more of the cold-war/subversive variety, but the fallout is the same.

Conflict is present. As long as the church is full of people, there will be a constant source of drama and variance of opinions. It is our obligation to handle ourselves in a Godly manner and follow the God-given manual for Christian conduct (yes, I mean the Bible.) There are a number of good books on the market that approach this topic from a scriptural basis, so it's not my attempt to provide a guide for that here. My endeavor is to point out that there are really two sides to church conflict: God's side and the other one.

God's Side: God wants for His plans to succeed, but loves us so much that he doesn't force them upon us without our consent. In fact, His plans (and by extension, the salvation of mankind) are so important that Jesus came and lived a perfect life and was brutally tortured and killed on our behalf just so that a minority of people would choose to serve Him. His plans are so grand and you are so loved that God literally came and died in order to make the option of success possible for you. He didn't send a Jehu and destroy what existed, just scrap it all and start over. He made a way in His love and grace. God is amazing.

63

While His plans are of the utmost importance (and are perfect in every way,) we tend to think of our own life in terms of personal comfort. Because of the post-modern mindset in the western culture we view matters of right and wrong based on how we feel and in the moment. This is moral relativity at its heart. If we like it: it's labeled good and Godly. This is idolatry at the core; it becomes lower-case G godly to us. When we judge the results of supposed divine activity as either God's will or not, based upon our own pleasures, we judge God Himself, and thus elevate ourselves into His place.

Ultimately, and with divine calling, God appoints leaders and sets them over his flocks. For all our wooly bleating and cleverly crafted vision statements, only the head shepherd, God, is able to truly appoint a shepherd to guide His flock. As the owner of the flock, it is the Head Shepherd's job, not the job of the sheep, to pick the best person for this job (and ultimately be responsible to that calling with his or her life! In the context of modern Christianity, there is no such awful, heavy, or potentially rewarding a call as that of the pastor.)

It is a Christian's duty to uphold and support our leader, to encourage him or her, and to guard against their assassination. It is true that sometimes the leadership may become distracted (by people, circumstances, or even sin,) but that does not lessen the severity and burden of the divine call upon their life. Assassination or rebellion is not the answer. I point out that the assassination at Jehu's hands came after decades of suffering, prayer, and conflict and the eventual word directly spoken by God to the prophet Elisha. Unless you can verify that you are walking in very footsteps of a great Old Testament prophet

64

such as him, then I question a person's ability or directives that trump a pastor's divine appointment (which is almost always prayerfully verified and previously agreed upon by godly counsel. I'm also skeptical of any dissenting member of the laity who claims to have heard from the Lord and initiates the removal of a pastor if that person voted to install the pastor under the same premise of believing it to be God's will—except in the case of gross sin.)

Though a pastor is called, he or she is still human. Our humanity does not remove divine appointment. The calling of God remains the same until He removes or redirects it. His Spirit strives with his chosen ones just as it always has.

The Other Side: Sometimes, as is in the story of Jezebel and Ahab, the motivators can go beyond ambition and human selfishness. I don't want to preclude the possibility of demonic influence on the part of each and every case. I am not a "demon under every bush" sort of preacher. I think that we often give the devil to much due, but understand how serious it was spoken in Ephesians 6:12. We battle not against flesh and blood, but against powers and principalities, things of a spiritual dimension. While I believe that this is sometimes the case, it is something to be discerned in the moment rather than assumed as the first response.

Very often we assume things to be the work of Satan when they are merely ungodly things or actions perpetrated by humans exercising their fallen nature. We are fully capable of sinning against God without the motivation of the Devil. It is in our nature, a product of original sin. Demonic forces are content to let us destroy ourselves with limited involvement; they've witnessed

Christopher Schmitz – Why Your Pastor Left

the chronicle of human history which is full of self-destruction. As I once quipped to one disgruntled pastor, I believe that, typically, in many church conflicts, we can read Ephesians 6:12 to read, "We battle not against flesh and blood, but against powers and church secretaries."

Humans are very good at scheming and seeking influence. Look at the media; the most interesting thing to our culture is discovering dirt on someone else, especially someone of influence or authority; because that fallen sin-nature, the image of original sin, our nature hates authority and craves rebellion, so we innately desire seeing those in positions of influence fail. One of the greatest self-satisfying feelings in the world is to be told that you are better than someone else when that individual is very good at their job or is respected in their field.

This is what church splits are made of, when the faction opposed to the senior pastor courts the sympathy of a staff or associate pastor by whispering hollow praises into his or her ear. It need not be a staff pastor; it could be the church janitor, or even you. We are all susceptible to the arrogance that these situations breed and we find it easy to justify actions that result in a coup when we pull in the opinions and supposed good-intentions of others.

Gossip is one of the most damaging, hurtful, and prevalent sins within the traditional, western church today. Our congregations are filled with "catharsis addicts" who just need to "get something of my chest." It's an excuse to fool you into entertaining gossip. Don't give an ear to them; they will lasso you into a group of people in that camp opposed to God's side of the conflict.

If you are not standing with the pastor, who can admittedly be wrong at times, then you are in danger of crossing the battle lines into the other faction (or have already fallen into it.) Pray for your pastor. Encourage him and challenge him in private and give him your advice—but don't mandate that he or she follow it because God is the chief counsel, and all the field experience and expertise that a layperson may possess is insanity in the face of God's omniscience.

If you saw the movie Moneyball, you might understand what I mean. It's based on a true story of the Oakland Athletics baseball team. Needing to start from square one in rebuilding the team, and given almost no money to do it, Coach Bill Beane built a team that would operate as a true team, this included players with strengths that would cover each other's weaknesses. It was labeled as madness and the coaches refused to operate the lineup as Beane intended until he took extreme action. Staffers quit and his job was in jeopardy; he was a laughingstock—until the team broke the league record for consecutive wins.

Human judgment too often clouds what God wants to do in our midst; we aren't big-minded enough to be able to see God's vision for us. We anthropomorphize God, ascribe human characteristics to Him, and thereby limit Him and His capacity to work. I mean this: if Sunday morning attendance figures are down, if Sunday School is declining, or if church income is falling, our tendency is to blame the pastor for these things. We are limited in our thinking and can't believe that God would use those things to direct or motivate us. We are conditioned to believe that those declines are evil or the product of ungodliness when it is just as likely that it is a product of human choices or of

God doing something new and unconventional. Here specifically, scripture says as much; there *will* be a falling away (Matt. 24:10, in addition to many other passages).

One youth pastor I knew grew his youth group to well over a hundred students in a relatively rural area. It was the epitome of ministerial success. Then God began to turn his heart. He looked at his ministry and realized he'd become an entertainer; students arrived and had fun with activities but they did not grow in the Lord; students were entertained by good music, but they did not worship; students closed their eyes, but they did not pray. This pastor confessed to his students that God was not pleased with mere numbers, but wanted to take them deeper and into a true relationship with Him. As he began discipling students, he quickly grew that large ministry down to less than ten attendees. "Big church" is not much different. When the chips are down, many adults back off rather than rise to the challenge of sincerity.

It is God's desire to take us deeper, rather than broader. We cannot influence on a broad, horizontal field until we have gone deeper in our vertical relationship with him. This is why the pastoral call is so critical and is such a heavy burden! The length and breadth of our horizontal influence is directly proportional to the depth and substance of our relationship with the Almighty God of Heaven; our authority will never long supersede the median level of that relationship!

Because of the multiple dimensions of our relationship, we cannot judge a pastor's effectiveness, or his obedience to God's voice, by annual reports, data collections, or surveys. This is an area where we CANNOT judge a work by its fruit. We are simply not qualified to judge. I offer only one piece of evidence to support this theory: you are not God.

God, in His infinite love for us, appointed pastors and leaders to disciple and develop us. Many of Jesus' analogies accurately compare us to smelly, farmyard animals. We fall down and get dirty easily, we follow things we should not and demand our own way, and we easily die in our own self-destructive tendencies. We need caring leaders. We must let God be the good shepherd and let the pastor be accountable to Him, ultimately, not to sheep.

Only God is God; shepherds are shepherds; and sheep are sheep. Sheep make sheep. Shepherds lead sheep and train other shepherds. And this is how God designed it.

Many of us imitate King Ahab/Jezebel and do our own thing; others walk in the footsteps of King Josiah who partnered with the father of the prophet Jeremiah and brought spiritual renewal and revitalized the kingdom. Parallels of a broken system abound within church history, as do examples of the pendulum being reversed.

Jeremiah was an unfortunate case. The book blows me away every time I read it. There are so many parallels between Jeremiah and America/the Western Church. We see a country that is supposed to be God's chosen people; our country claims to be "one nation under God." Israel was very successful both financially and militarily; the USA has long held that prestige, even when she is in decline. Religion was fervent; our religiosity and spirituality reaches pinnacles.

Christopher Schmitz – Why Your Pastor Left

In Jeremiah's time, corrupt forces overthrew the leadership. We find false prophets rising up and making bold proclamations from the temple floor so that the people followed their "feel-good" advice rather than swallowing the "bitter pill" of correction that the true prophet preached. (Hananiah proclaims in Jer.28 that everything will be fine—that God will destroy Babylon within two years and bring back the temple vessels—this and other "prophetic utterances" came from demonic spirits, see Jer.23. In short time, Babylon attacked and subjugated the entire country.) I don't want to alienate anyone by mentioning names, but some high-profile evangelists who hold sway in our country have issued time-stamped prophecies that have failed to come to pass. What spirit have they listened to? We sometimes allow false doctrines into our theology: things such as "name it-claim it" theology, God = a cosmic gumball machine theology, and prosperity gospel teachings in addition to other age-old heresies warned against in scripture.

We live in times with such similarities; you'd think we'd heed these parallels and guard our minds. If you're reading this, I hope you're doing just that. The sad and final parallel is that nobody (or very few) listened to Jeremiah after the earliest days of ministry under King Josiah had passed. Jeremiah wandered and preached God's Word faithfully and was often abused and mistreated, but Scripture does not reveal to us any persons changing their ways and turning to God. Rather, they assassinated the character of the prophet and followed a popular opinion that validated the opinions and comforts of the general populace. Note: comfort and success *do not* confirm you are living within God's will.

70

Christopher Schmitz – Why Your Pastor Left

I lift weights and exercise to keep in shape. My wife dislikes pain. One night I confessed to her that I kind of like being in a little pain. The muscle aches remind me that I'm useful, that I've been working out and am achieving progress. I don't like pain for the sake of some sadomasochistic urge, but because I acknowledge that perfect comfort is generally the fruit of lethargy and uselessness. Are you comfortable in your church? Where do you volunteer? Have you done *anything*? The active ones in the church who strive the hardest to achieve the will of God sometimes share Jeremiah's trials and suffer ridicule, outcast, turmoil, character assassination, physical pain, and emotional stress. If you shy away from pain even in the face of some greater prize, then neither weight lifting nor vocational ministry is a fit for you.

Prophets brought the Word of God in the Old Testament. Whether it was good or bad, it was adamant truth. After the new covenant and in the days of the New Testament early church, more authority was given to man. In light of the charge to every believer to go and make disciples of all people, Jesus empowered everyday lay-people to do the active work of the church. This was, in essence, the very first "viral-marketing" campaign. Everyone who is a believer has been called to spread this good news and walk in the authority and power of Christ. But, as Peter Parker/Spiderman's wise Uncle Ben counseled, "With great power comes great responsibility." Will we use that authority and power we've been given to support God's mouthpiece, as when Josiah propped up Jeremiah? Or will we be like Ahab or Jezebel and seek to silence Elisha? Each of us has power and influence, even the lowliest of us.

Christopher Schmitz – Why Your Pastor Left

After painting her face, Jezebel went to the tower window and mocked God's chosen one, the newly anointed King Jehu. Jehu called for support, seeing the cowering servants behind the evil queen. Those servants rose up and gave God's enemy a shove out the window where she fell to an ignominious death and was devoured by dogs, fulfilling prophecy and allowing God's plans to move forward.

So very often, internal church conflicts arise and people form party platforms within our churches. This isn't right, but more tragic is when people refuse to run in church-political races (for the appointment to a deacon or board member seat) because they think it might be divisive to the body should they suffer as an alternative vote between candidates. Individuals and groups may lobby the pastor or become seated on a board or gain influence and begin to bind up any progress that may be in God's will. This is not always the case when someone seeks position in church—but it sometimes happens and parishioners should remain vigilant. Every time I've seen this happen has been because pastor's plans exceed the comfort zone of influential individuals or parties. Hindering a Godly pastor's vision is the same as refusing the will of God.

Conflict can be good. It is valuable for taking counsel and seeing new viewpoints and finding middle ground that might not have been conceived of. It can reveal new growth never thought possible. A muscle cannot be strengthened without the stress of small tears that natural healing resolves. However, power struggles and conflicts not handled in a healthy way destroy individuals and churches. Continued resistance is like a wound that refuses to heal and causes permanent damage.

The heaviest fallout always happens to those caught in the crossfire of warring factions. Many churches endure situations that absolutely should not exist under the delusion that conflict will lead to greater harm. Sometimes those who think themselves the lowliest, the untested, the unappointed, must rise up and take a side, standing for God's anointed Jehu. It was the eunuch servants that kicked Jezebel from the window and restored peace.

Sometimes you just need to throw that Jezebel out. Everything about the story of Jehu's installment reflects the authority and ability available to nameless individuals who support God's will. It was a nameless servant who anointed Jehu and it was unnamed slaves that booted the evil queen through the sill.

Our churches need more Godly people willing to step up, act in authority they have never before wanted, and run for church positions. They might breathe fresh life into the body of the church. Has your church had the same people on its board or leadership/advisory teams for decades, rotating one or two around because of a mandatory bylaw? Change that if you want to see something new happen. It's been said that, "the definition of insanity is to keep on doing the same thing and expecting a different result." We can't expect something new or mighty to happen in our churches if the leadership has stagnated in creature comfort. As I mentioned before, the church is declining, dying. Something needs to change so that God can freely move.

The Church desperately needs a new revitalization. If we desire to see God move as he did in the days of the early church, then logically we should apply principles we can glean from scripture regarding the early church.

Christopher Schmitz – Why Your Pastor Left

Specifically, we need to revamp our church leadership infrastructures. I'm not necessarily saying that churches reform/reincorporate or start from scratch as matter of principle: that would create chaos. Rather, we must look at what they did in the early church and figure out how to apply the principles of their church leadership/appointment and polity.

I mentioned in a previous chapter that the early synagogue had a much different system of rule. While our "church structure" is an extension of that earlier body, we have some similarities and differences. In the formative periods of the church, the similarities were much greater than they are today; one of the similarities is found in the principle of Eldership. I won't rehash that here, but I will recommend a book if you are interested in learning more about the subject: see Biblical Eldership by Alexander Strauch (Lewis and Roth).

The modern concepts of church boards (business) and deacon boards and elder boards are not scripturally mandated. I am not, as some might, recommending that we throw out the baby with the bathwater. I am not in favor of dismantling the entire hierarchy and structure of the modern church; some of what we have in terms of modern church polity has been born out of cultural factors and logical necessity. Many groups have, however, lost sight of the principles behind the church model.

The apostles, in Acts chapter six, found that they weren't able to spend the time they needed in prayer and study because of the demands of the ministry. They asked the people to select deacons in order to take some of the burden of ministry off of the apostles. Deacons are meant for actual, hands-on

Christopher Schmitz – Why Your Pastor Left

ministry. Deacons are doers; they are the oars to a ship—not the guidance system.

Currently, our most common concept of church polity (in terms of protestant denominations) is some form of one or multiple boards that either "advise" or are set over the pastor. For example, the pastor is a person who has experience, a skill set, and the education required to preach from the Word properly, oversee the ministries of the church, and visit shut-ins and widows. The Church board will often be sat upon by Deacons who handle the "business aspect" of the church. These deacons might be Elders, or there might be a separate "Elder Board." The Elder Board often functions in an advisory capacity.

In our human reasoning, this seems like a logical approach to govern a church full of self-willed, autonomous individuals. There are many checks and balances inherent in this system, but there are some fundamental flaws to it as well. I want to repeat that I am not advising any parties to hack their structure apart and restart—a process that just might eventually bring them full circle. I want to pull out, however, that there are *human* flaws in this system, which is full of the democratic process. It is susceptible to the same influence, compromising, and corruption that modern politics are replete with.

The problem is one of value. When the pastor, the elected/hired/called spiritual head of the congregation lays a hold of a vision for God's Kingdom advancing, the business minded board tends to ask itself how they can compromise between personal comfort, their respectability within the community, finances, and appeasing the pastor. Comfort be damned! We

Christopher Schmitz – Why Your Pastor Left

humans forget that the word Passion translates as "suffering." Jesus died a horrific death for us so we can be saved, not so we can be respected in our community! Jesus says in Matt 5:13 that if we are unwilling to be the salt of the word then we are good for nothing except throwing in the trash! Strong words, and they belong to Jesus, not me, also they were directed to His *followers*, not the lost.

So what happens when people don't share the same value as the pastor in this model? Church strife inevitably creeps in. It's a fundamental issue. The board sees itself as the caretakers and gatekeepers of the church's finances/business. When their value system varies from the pastor's, they won't be able to agree on due courses of action. Worse yet, they may begin to see each other as enemies.

On the flip side, the board may see critical need to hire a new church janitor and the pastor might have a different idea. If the pastor is trying to encourage the people in stewardship principles, he or she might be suggesting individuals in the body rotate this duty to meet this need as an act of service. When we start seeing certain areas of church control as beyond the boundaries of the leader's influence, we run into problems. It's the same in our spiritual life; we cannot compartmentalize our life. Cut off even the excretory system from the influence of the brain and we will have *major* problems. This all comes back to the issue of submission—something we naturally rebel against!

The Bible never endorses blind submission, mind you. We are not called to blindly follow any leader. Even the advice of angels is subject to discernment and testing.

Christopher Schmitz – Why Your Pastor Left

Strauch's book states, "Scripture also expressly commands the congregation to obey and submit to its spiritual leaders (Heb 13:17, James 5:5)... The requirement to submit, however, is not meant to suggest blind, mindless submission. Nor does it suggest that elders are above questioning or immune from public discipline (1Tim 5:19). The elders are most assuredly answerable to the congregation, and the congregation is responsible to hold its spiritual leaders accountable to faithful adherence to the truth of the Word."[29]

I don't want to suggest that there's never been a pastor that didn't belong in a pulpit. We know that some "pastors" have no business with God! There are checks and balances already, though. We need not setup a system that subjugates the chief leader of the assembly by forcing him to process God's vision and directives through a series of boards, committees, and forms that would make a Volgon grin.

We so desperately need unity at this point in church history. If the church body had a united vision, passion, and sense of value, there would be no conflict. Disagreement would be pointless because the body would have all things in common. Because commonality is such a rare thing when it comes to values and opinions, humans tend to utilize the democratic process—a government model never endorsed in Scripture. Logically, the democratic process leads to anarchy and chaos within the church body. When popular opinion prevails over the will of God—with true Believers as the minority of any culture, even Christianized culture—the moral absolutes of God's Word will

---

[29] Strauch, Alexander. Biblical Eldership: An Urgent Call to Restore Biblical Church Leadership. Colorado Springs: Lewis and Roth, 2003.

Christopher Schmitz – Why Your Pastor Left

always take a backseat to the majority will of immoral man. Still, it is commonly used in many systems of church polity and in every "congregational style" system of church government.

In a congregational style of church government, Deacons/Board Members take an overseer role in the direction and guidance of the church. The only thing needed for a person's will to triumph within this style of church government is to persuade key individuals within their assembly so that they have the number of votes necessary to wrest total control over to the course demanded.

As a friend of mine once stated, "The mind boggles when considering how it is that a young man would sense the call of God upon his life, complete a pastoral degree from a reputable Bible college, serve as an assistant pastor to gain experience, and then find himself in a situation where untrained deacons force him to take a back seat while they 'run' the church." I agree; but had I been told this in college, I might have had a harder time pursuing a ministerial career.

The Greek word for "deacon" is diakonos. It translates as servant, slave, or employee. Never do we see any deacons in the New Testament in a governing role. They serve; deacons are always the servants helping their pastor do their job well. They are never placed over the pastor as his or her governor. They are in a supportive role, partners to the pastor, but placed under them, not over them.

Scriptures teach that the deacons (servants) are to take care of the business of the church under the pastor's direction. There is a distinction listed between Elders and Deacons; Elders are listed in a greater capacity and held in higher honor than any other. In other words, the spiritual leader's authority (a pastor, first and foremost,) supersedes the authority of those who are the servant leaders. Simply put, coups led by anyone bearing the title of Deacon (or no title at all) which pursue authority, be it for a pastor's removal or whatever, and is outside of a scriptural mandate for obedience to the body's spiritual headship: i.e. this is sin!

Because this sin is so common, it has become widely accepted as "just another human problem" in our churches, another of the "challenges to effective ministry." IT IS SIN! Cast it out from your midst! Strife between church leadership is a common experience. Pastors are routinely challenged, denigrated, and cast out. The resultant disillusionment and discouragement is a ministry killer.

That said, I understand the flip side of the coin. There are people attempting to play the role of pastor yet whom are the furthest thing from qualified or worthy of such a high calling. It is critically important that we guard against such an egregious error as installing one who is not divinely called to service. However, it is not the role of a deacon to be this watchman. It is the specific duty of an Elder (who by way of the qualifications of such must also be capable of working in the same capacity as the one pastor to whom they are trying to install—Elders must be capable of fulfilling the duties of a deacon but also trained and capable of teaching and fulfilling the duties of the pastor if called upon.) The duties of a pastor are not to just deliver sermons! Were that

Christopher Schmitz – Why Your Pastor Left

the case, they would be nothing more than religious motivational speakers. What are the duties then, the difficult standard to which a pastor must stand upon?

Dr. John MacArthur included an anonymous layman's advice regarding pastors in the last of his FAQ's in his book Rediscovering Expository Preaching:[30]

> Fling him into his office. Tear the "Office" sign from the door and nail on the sign, "Study." Take him off the mailing list. Lock him up with his books and his typewriter and his Bible. Slam him down on his knees before texts and broken hearts and the flock of lives of a superficial flock and a holy God.

> Force him to be the one man in our surfeited communities who knows about God. Throw him into the ring to box with God until he learns how short his arms are. Engage him to wrestle with God all the night through. And let him come out only when he's bruised and beaten into being a blessing.

> Shut his mouth forever spouting remarks, and stop his tongue forever tripping lightly over every nonessential. Require him to have something to say before he dares break the silence. Bend his knees in the lonesome valley.

---

[30] MacArthur, Dr. John. Rediscovering Expository Preaching. Nashville: Thomas Nelson, 1992. 348-49

Christopher Schmitz – Why Your Pastor Left

Burn his eyes with weary study. Wreck his emotional poise with worry for God. And make him exchange his pious stance for a humble walk with God and man. Make him spend and be spent for the glory of God. Rip out his telephone. Burn up his ecclesiastical success sheets.

Put water in his gas tank. Give him a Bible and tie him to the pulpit. And make him preach the Word of the living God!

Test him. Quiz him. Examine him. Humiliate him for his ignorance of things divine. Shame him for his good comprehension of finances, batting averages, and political in-fighting. Laugh at his frustrated effort to play psychiatrist. Form a choir and raise a chant and haunt him with it night and day—"Sir, we would see Jesus."

When at long last he dares assay the pulpit, ask him if he has a word from God. If he does not, then dismiss him. Tell him you can read the morning paper and digest the television commentaries, and think through the day's superficial problems, and manage the community's weary drives, and bless the sordid baked potatoes and green beans, ad infinitum, better than he can.

Christopher Schmitz – Why Your Pastor Left

Command him not to come back until he's read and reread, written and rewritten, until he can stand up, worn and forlorn, and say, "Thus saith the Lord."

Break him across the board of his ill-gotten popularity. Smack him hard with his own prestige. Corner him with questions about God. Cover him with demands for celestial wisdom. And give him no escape until he's back against the wall of the Word.

And sit down before him and listen to the only word he has left—God's Word. Let him be totally ignorant of the down-street gossip, but give him a chapter and order him to walk around it, camp on it, sup with it, and come at last to speak it backward and forward, until all he says about it rings with the truth of eternity.

And when he's burned out by the flaming Word, when he's consumed at last by the fiery grace blazing through him, and when he's privileged to translate the truth of God to man, finally transferred from earth to heaven, then bear him away gently and blow a muted trumpet and lay him down softly. Place a two-edged sword in his coffin, and raise the tomb triumphant. For he was a brave soldier of the Word. And ere

he died, he had become a man of God.

In this light, the duties of a pastor, and by extension also an Elder, becomes unnervingly difficult. It is enough to dissuade one from reaching for such a title and should be enough to intimidate any truly God-fearing deacon from reaching beyond his or her station.

I see that there is an attempt to compromise between deacon/board members grabbing for some of the authority of an Elder, but not the responsibility. They take the power and influence that it brings, but not the obligation. It is a well-intentioned, yet misguided, effort to guard against a "dictator pastor."

In lieu of the common misconceptions regarding pastors, deacons, board members, and elders, many churches have solved the problem of pastor-dictators by simply placing a board over the pastor. Whether specifically outlined or unspoken, it is understood that this board will either keep the pastor in line or fire him. This unbiblical methodology, combined with discorded vision, will that strip the pastor of his or her authority to lead how God directs. That is a recipe for rebellion. We must return, at least in heart, to the scriptural model.

How does your church's reality line up with the appointment of your pastor and how does it differ from the early church? Pastor and evangelism expert David Wheeler tells a story about candidating for a senior pastor position at a Texas Baptist church. He was passed over by the selection committee for a

83

very particular reason. They were bluntly honest in their reasoning: "We want our pastor to be much more concerned with the affairs of the church and the present membership… to be in the office every day from 9:00 a.m. until 5:00 p.m. in case we call or drop by… frankly, you are way too evangelistic for us."[31] I imagine it was very uncomfortable for this church to admit the reality of their situation: that they did not want God's will to move within their midst. They sought *Personal Comfort* rather than obedience to God's Word. I think I might be sadly wrong, though, they might have been perfectly fine with denying God the ability to move, work, and redirect as needed. Wheeler comments on the situation, "Two thousand years ago [a group] of Christ followers had misplaced priorities… Unfortunately many Christians today have the same perspective."[32]

So what were the priorities of the early church? If the exact structure and formation are less important than the priorities and value system, what about it made it so successful?

The emphasis of the church was Jesus! It's just that simple. The focus was on Jesus, not on the building or an after service meal, it was all Jesus: knowledge that He changed lives, heals, and makes us slaves to righteousness and victory! Because He poured out the Holy Spirit and empowered them to each have the single most important role in the lives of others, even unto changing the course of human history: the opportunity to lead others to the foot of the cross.

---

[31] Earley, David and Wheeler, David. Evangelism Is: How to Share Jesus With Passion and Confidence. Nashville: B&H Academic, 2010. 129
[32] Ibid.

Christopher Schmitz – Why Your Pastor Left

This concept of "backyard" missions impacted every step of their life. This lifestyle permeated every part of their being. They understood that the neighbors across the backyard fence were the next generation of converts, that their place of employment was a mission field, that nothing in life was as valuable as the free gift of Christ's love. That is why the church grew! This must be our value as well if we seek anything beyond eventual atrophy and the death of our congregations.

We must allow a pastor to lead and understand the power and conviction of a pastor's divine calling over the flock—this is something that is in God's hands not our own. In our western, independent culture we have asserted ourselves so much that we are no longer capable of submitting to Godly authority; we've become like the church in Jeremiahs time. We do whatever WE want within HIS temple, ignoring Him completely, claiming our sins are within His will because they occur within His temple or are committed by His people (and it's usually a *self-appointed* group laying claim to that).

1 Timothy 3 contains a list of requirements for a pastor. Verse 5 requires the pastor of a church to be ruling his own house well, otherwise "how shall he take care of the church of God?" Paul, the author, draws a direct parallel between the pastor over the church and the same as the man over his house. The word is proistemi which means to set over, to superintend, preside over, be over. I do not know many men who take a vote with their six year olds over what to eat for supper: we'd have candy sandwiches for every meal. Neither do we give an equal vote to teenagers; we would have anarchy in the home. Paul instructed us to have strong pastors that can govern their "Christian family" with the strong

Christopher Schmitz – Why Your Pastor Left

hand that it sometimes needs. If there is rebellion in the home, correction must be made. It used to be that if our children rebelled, they'd have to learn some of the harsh realities of life via the school of hard-knocks. The modern church has, unfortunately, shifted this balance of power.

This shift happened decades ago. I remember about the time it began happening in the home. While in high school, I remember the headlines of the newspapers: "Mom, I want a divorce." Children sought emancipation and were given free reign by the government to do as they pleased; some of these cases might have been justified, but our culture seized upon this new ideal and it wasn't long before an inflated Social Services department began entertaining every claim of so-called abuse in the home. A person could no longer spank their child in public without a visit from the police or spank a naughty child in the home for fear of eventual reprisal.

Pastor-dictators should not be welcome in leadership. We do need to protect our congregations from the Stalins and Mussolinis that grasp for pulpits, but we have swung the pendulum too far in the other direction. In the interest of protecting the innocent, we overthrew the system. Fact of the matter is, and any parent of a child ages three to seventeen knows firsthand, nobody is innocent. To rule your own house well, discipline and a clear chain of command *must* be part of the equation.

The thinking, as directed by our culture, is that anybody who takes responsibility or control is evil. The truth of the matter is that ungodly men in any leadership positions can ruin a church. They need not be an ungodly "pastor" to do so; much more damage has been done in recent times by lay-

86

leaders (usually elected through political means rather than confirmed or installed by elders or fellow pastors,) rather than by clergy.

If a pastor is ever deterred from bringing a word of correction, then something is awry. If he is *afraid* to do so, then he is not ruling God's house well—the balance of authority is so far out of line that your pastor is not able to fulfill his Scriptural and/or Spiritual directives. Either way, it is disobedience, either on the part of the pastor for living in such fear of mortal men and their human influence, or it's those who have hoarded power and authority that is not their due. Unfairly, this situation almost never negatively impacts a deacon or board member whom has seized that power. In every case I've encountered, it is the pastor who pays the price. He or she is excused from their ministry in either scenario, once the communion elements hit the fan, or he or she must clean up the fallout of the divisiveness.

The concerns I have raised are not popular for discussion. Clergy have generally weathered this storm through the years, playing political games and viewing them as a necessary evil of ministry. It doesn't change the fact, though, that modern polity differs from the scriptural model. As the Church's makeup more and more resembles a business, we become less and less about the people, placing a greater emphasis on the corporate entity we've become. Calling out this grievance infringes on the comfort zones of many.

"The great American way of doing church these last ten or so years is to do church in the ways of the world and business community, and not in the way of God. In so doing, we have been crafting and creating our own problems and dilemmas,"[33] R. J. Krejcir Ph.D. of the Francis A. Schaeffer Institute of

Christopher Schmitz – Why Your Pastor Left

Church Leadership Development stated. Aspiring to do business like the secular world means we become more like the world that Christ called us *out* of!

This is not something that can be changed from the top down; it can only be rectified with a grassroots movement, led by Godly people. Because of the bureaucratic nature of the western church, and the autonomy that most churches enjoy when it comes to bylaws and self-governance, this change must start with the sheep. Authority claimed by sheep can only be rightfully returned by them.

It might sound morbid, but I don't believe this change will ever come. I grew up within the church; I've watched it for a long time. For all that scripture says regarding prayer, for all the preaching, for all the pleading from the pulpit, for all the flyers and bulletin inserts, for all the power available to a believer who prays, the most difficult thing for a pastor to do is get people to attend a prayer service. Changing the hearts and attitudes of the people in our midst from lukewarm to hot will take accumulated time in prayer: something American Christians have historically refused to do.

Our refusal to pray in spirit and in truth, (to actually listen for God's will rather than "tell God how it is,") has led to generations that are no longer able to understand or even recognize the voice of God. As we listen for that still small voice to answer our prayers, we are only able to hear our own nagging desires. It becomes easy, a habit even, to pray and immediately decide that our

---

[33] Krejcir, Dr. Richard J. "Why Churches Fail: Part I." Francis A. Schaeffer Institute of Church Leadership Development. 2007. http://www.churchleadership.org/apps/articles/default.asp?articleid=42339 (accessed August 2014).

Christopher Schmitz – Why Your Pastor Left

own inner-voice is a response from the Almighty. We don't even really pray. We rely on human logic and human reasoning in our selfishness and with our own plans in the front of our mind. God's wisdom makes very little sense to us—it confounds our own thinking. Those two conditions have bred a situation whereby we have thrust true prayer from our midst.

Because we have laid claim to His church and made it our own, we dare not give up our own control over the church's fate. We especially run from heavenly words that may move our spirit but not agree with our head. When faced with the quandary of reconciling the two, our solution has been to close our Spiritual ears against God!

In one particular all-church business session. The chairman of the church board stood up and addressed all attendees, of which about eighty percent were voting members. The meeting was called in accordance with the bylaws in order to vote on the continued service of the Senior Pastor at the end of every five-year term of service. Many churches, as did this one, have their own sovereignty so that they can control their own bylaws and church governance. Every few years, the pastor had to endure a popularity contest.

At the beginning of this meeting, the chairman spoke briefly and offered a prayer. His prayer was a plea that God would show those casting votes His will to either vote in support of him or for his removal. The pastor missed his two-thirds needed vote by less than one vote; (I believe it was .3% shy.) If this were a matter of human governance, I would understand. The leaders, however, had invoked God's presence and sought direction moments prior to a major vote; the evening before, the same person and those in his sphere of

89

friends personally telephoned other voting members to enlist their votes against the pastor.

That whole story is full of similarly messy details and dirt. My point is not the dirt; sordid elements surround all similar stories. I see spiritual trouble, though, when we invoke and invite the Spirit of God into our presence and then intentionally ignore what he may be saying to us. Do we ask God to make His will known but only allow Him to speak if it's in validation of what we've already decided?

Do we honestly believe that we are doing the right thing when we manipulate the will of a pastor or vote out/expel him or her? We rarely gut-check those decisions in our own prayer-starved lives. In that specific church, which I left soon after, I called out the remaining leadership on the fact of prayerlessness. I could have named each and every person present in the previous year's worth of regular prayer meetings, ticking them off of my fingers with less than two hands.

Our predisposition for self-governance joined with our reluctance to pray leads us right back into this cycle of Jeremiah. Our ticklish ears yearn for a Hananiah and we seek the leadership of an Ahab and Jezebel. We actively make ourselves easily swayed by another's "human logic." Colossians 2:8 tells us "See to it that no one takes you captive through philosophy and empty deception, according to the tradition of men, according to the elementary principles of the world, rather than according to Christ." (New American Standard)

Christopher Schmitz – Why Your Pastor Left

This cycle of self-reliance leads to one of two possible outcomes. First, for a variety of human reasons, we tend to emancipate ourselves from any authority in our lives. Chiefly in this context, that is our pastor; we often see ministers handed their walking papers and handled in a way that it villainizes him or her, or has/will discolor their future reputation.

The other possibility is that manipulation and demands of the politics excessively weary the pastor. All the games and politics lead to the breakdowns I discussed in my earlier chapter on disillusionment. The nonsense a pastor must deal with while trying to discern a middle ground between *OUR* directives and God's will either wear down a pastor so that they are ineffective or make him or her unable to perform at the expected level (even unable to bring the Word.) The resulting futility embitters them. Usually, this leads to disillusionment making the pastor dysfunctional. They are either asked to resign or he or she leaves of their own volition. A pastor should never have to compromise and bend to *OUR* wishes when God's desires have already been made plain. We ask too great a thing when we seek to compromise God's will with our own; Jesus did not only half-die on our behalf.

Either outcome results in the severed leadership. Particular circumstances are moot; it doesn't matter who or how—whenever a pastor leaves his position under any motivation other than divine calling (or disqualification by gross sin), the circumstances are the work of men. Despite of the intents of unruly sheep, there is a war raging between wolves and shepherds. Only the predators profit from a leader's *removal*. God will protect during the

91

interim if He redirects a pastor's call—but a sheep who postures as the shepherd will lead the flock into dangerous territory.

Friends, we must watch for signs of abuse from the lay leaders in our midst. It is hard to acknowledge it coming from them more so than the pastor because our deacons and board members usually come from our own ranks. Often, we grow up with them or have to face them in our own community, but a pastor who is forced out will almost always leave the community searching for a new appointment. This makes it hard to stand against any coup, but it must be done.

If we allow an abuse to occur because it's easier to expel a minister from the church than correct a harsh lay-leader, who does that show love to? It does not love our pastor—God's appointed proxy. It doesn't love the perpetrator because our nonaction validates their decisions and lets them remain in their sin. It does not love the congregation members because of the damage that occurs when a pastor is forced out or becomes dysfunctional. Further the world is watching; they see this and validate their own rejection of Christ with it.

Because of this refusal to self-correct on the church floor, we must realize that *we* are the dysfunctional ones. The dysfunction of a pastor is often born of our actions or inactions as we drag our leadership off of the pulpit and down into our midst. We must be willing to examine ourselves and be prepared to walk against the flow of popular opinion. It has been polled and found that people will knowingly join a crowd of those who are flat wrong and willfully violate their own conscience before they are willing to stand alone for their convictions.

Christopher Schmitz – Why Your Pastor Left

I can recall sitting in a coffee shop chatting with a unique individual. I'd asked him to confront a particular board member who'd been spreading dissention in the congregation. This unique individual was a former pastor in a different church of my denomination and had let slip some of the things being said about my Senior Pastor in the community. He unintentionally named the source. We'd assumed the source as a particular deacon, but could never directly attribute it to him until now; gossip and double-tongued manipulation had been a long standing problem in this assembly. The former pastor refused to step up. "I love your pastor," he maintained. "Pastor has a problem. Something needs to be done, you need a plan and a way to fix this, but I can't be the one to say anything. I live nearby; [this person] is wrong, but these people are my friends. I cannot be seen standing against them. If Pastor loses his job, he will move on, find a new community and a new church, but I plan on retiring here and being with these people the rest of my life." True to his word, he slipped away and let the situation remain the "pastor's problem." Less than two months later, the previously mentioned vote came and my pastor was forced out. The former minister, a voting member of our church, stated that he would vote in support of his pastor, but that was the limit of his willingness to act.

Is that the extent of our willingness to back God's chosen? Token support to which we are obligated because of our church membership? Are we really willing to do *nothing*? Standing against the flow is difficult, but sitting in the current might dash us against the rocks and break us.

Our culture needs an uprising of Josiahs and Jeremiahs. We need people willing to stand when it is unpopular and when it is difficult. Where are

Christopher Schmitz – Why Your Pastor Left

you? Are you edging your way to the back door of the church? Rise up. We need you to demand that the Word of the Lord be our first and primary source, a canon which trumps all others. It is a hard calling, but we will fail without you demanding a return to Godly authority.

Lord, I pray that you send us Jeremiahs. Place one in every congregation and give them the courage necessary to stand in the face of unpopular opinion; send them supporting Josiahs, men and women who partner with them, enabling them to stand in the face of those who oppose Your will. God, I pray that You are not lenient with your church; bless those who strive for You, and cripple those who seek their own gain at the cost of Your Kingdom.

Christopher Schmitz – Why Your Pastor Left

Chapter 6

(Ministry Incongruity, Ageism, and Faulty Expectations)

Firstly, I apologize if I come off as a bit jaded in this chapter as I have been on the short end of this prickly stick. I might be a little too close to this issue, having been burned in the past, so I hope you can read it for what it is, passion, truth, wounds and all.

Sometimes it may be ministry peers or staff who cause pastors to leave. Staff pastors can get sucked in and hoodwinked by a coup from within the body. (I mentioned this briefly in the previous chapter concerning church boards and people of influence). Sometimes, ministers are stressed and forced out by their peers.

I remember standing in the pastor's office, trying to reason with him, being keenly aware of how much we did *not* share in common with each other. He was seventy-three years old and had already told me in a previous meeting that he not only *did not* respect me, but believed I was "not worthy of respect." Those were his actual words.

Prior to our first meeting, we'd had a couple conversations on the telephone. Both of us understood that this could be a difficult assignment; he was taking over as interim pastor and was effectively saddled with me. I had a heart for youth and young adults and actively ministered on the high school and the local college campus. While not a trend follower, my ministry has been labeled as "nontraditional" by many people; I prefer the term effective. I've been compared to John the Baptist because, sometimes, the religious world finds they are not comfortable with me. My mandate and calling stems from 1 Corinthians 9:16-23, that I will become all things to all people in order that I might win some—I will do *whatever it takes* to win the lost. If they are valuable enough that Jesus died for them, then I can at least attempt to contextualize that message for them—help them hear it in their own language. I don't look like the traditional preacher—tradition doesn't save people: Jesus does. I merely present myself as a person who people might want to build a relationship with and in turn I can present Christ to them by example, (as well as testimony and scripture). When the interim pastor first came into my office, his usually chipper face fell visibly. I wasn't wearing a suit and tie. I had a long goatee and wild hair and there was modern music coming from the speakers of my laptop as I worked. I was not what he expected and he stated as much, publicly.

For several weeks I'd endured my questions being deferred and my time limit had expired: I needed answers on the details regarding the coming transition. I had six weeks prior requested a decision regarding a severance package and asked for a specific pay schedule and needed particulars on handling my accrued vacation time.

In the midst of all this, my life was in the upheaval that accompanies an uncomfortable and forced transition. The one thing I pressed for was a written agreement regarding the details decided upon by the interim pastor and the church board. This is the board which had already expelled my senior pastor and so I was on guard to make sure everything went smoothly and was done in writing. I needed to minimize the damage to my family at this point. I was told that I wouldn't be given anything in writing.

Christopher Schmitz – Why Your Pastor Left

Our discussion quickly broke down and the interim told me that I was being given more than I deserved (less than half of what I asked for,) and I was guaranteed nothing. He'd recommended I receive less and said I should feel lucky to get anything. There was a very real and concentrated effort to "control me" in the aftermath of forcing my senior pastor out—the intent of structuring a severance package that was both deferred and drawn out was so that the cabal in control of the board could ensure I didn't say anything they didn't like. Not things wrong or untrue, but an arbitrary and nonquantifiable disappreciation of my disposition. In short, I might get something, I might not, all depending on whether or not I could curry favor. Meanwhile, "church leaders" who lied to the congregation played an uncontested shell game with the facts.

This is probably a typical scenario, and I can appreciate the other side of the argument. The disturbing part of this, however, is the business tone it came in. Not from the interim pastor, his demeanor was angry—he actually kicked me out of the church as a way to end the meeting. The interim was upset because I told him I would under no circumstances obey an order to cease communications with any members of the church before or after my departure since many of them were on my prayer and financial support team for a mission's project I was fundraising for. Furthermore, many of these people were my dear friends, and while I would be relocating, they did not cease to be dear to me and I'd built relationships with them, which was foundational to my entire ministry. I asked him if he understood how fundamental that was to the well-being of those I had led to the Lord recently and those I ministered to actively.

Christopher Schmitz – Why Your Pastor Left

As he escorted me to the door he told me, "I don't care about this relationship evangelism thingy you're always talking about. It's a passing fad; I don't want you to tell me about it and I don't care about your ministry or how you do it. Now, stop wasting my time, I have important work to do." That's an exact quote; it's hard to forget something like that.

If I believed all senior pastors had that belief regarding younger ministers and modern methods of evangelism I would have given up on the church long ago. Unfortunately, not everybody understands that. Many younger pastors and parishioners have departed forever, believing this is our norm: a 73 year old man spouting trite clichés from a pulpit and crooning archaic hymns, directing all aspects of the church from his platform and driving home the feeling in a younger generation that any deviation would be discouraged.

Many churches are guilty of contributing to this monstrous church image that turns away younger people. This is the golden image of a church built of white bricks under a three story steeple. The attendees sit quietly during the hymn sing while dressed in their suits, ties, dresses, and flowery hats, each with rigidly perfect posture. There is no nursery because the babies never cry and their children never fidget. They only read from the King James version of the Bible (because that's the one Jesus wrote) and vote republican. These people hate homosexuals and rock music, always vote republican, love Joel Osteen and Bill Gaither. This "church" image is an idol that many older "saints" have devoted their unabashed love to, and claimed it's what Jesus would do. All the while they sacrifice the souls of the lost at the feet of this meretricious,

Christopher Schmitz – Why Your Pastor Left

manmade deity—after all, "If they would just bow before my plastic Jesus, they would be fine; they should all know better."

This interim pastor and I were both to blame for the incongruence between us. I apologized to him for my part in it before we parted ways. We each operated under a different set of expectations regarding the other's roles, duties and obligations. The interim expected that I would be just like the youth pastors he'd worked with through the previous four decades. At our first meeting, my appearance alone disappointed him and so he prejudged my character and my ministry. I wasn't what he knew by experience and so he didn't know where to begin with me, except to assume that I was sinning, unfit for ministry, etc. That's right, I was wearing blue jeans. Never mind souls won to the Kingdom through outreach ministries. Denim is sure sign of heresy.

Since he operated with the same expectations he'd always held, but never specifically told me what those were, I constantly disappointed him, usually resulting in multiple visits to my office and calls to my home each week. When leaders are unclear about expectations or don't thoroughly relate them to ministry staff, operating in unity is impossible.

I am sure that, while this is a book meant for church members and attendees, pastors will also read it. Perhaps some of them have lost staff and don't understand why. What senior pastors should know is that their staff members want to be on the same page, sharing a unified goal of lifting up the Kingdom. Communicate with them. They don't want to be compartmentalized, they want to see ministries overlap in regions that strengthen and solidify each other.

Christopher Schmitz – Why Your Pastor Left

D. Min. Randy Walls, director of continuing education at AG Theological Seminary in Springfield, MO writes an insightful article about this. Walls has some key insights.

In my conversations with young leaders, one thing they desire is a place at the table in the local, district, and national conversations about the mission and ministry of the [denomination.] To qualify this, a place at the table does not just mean an observer's posture. They want full participation; a chance to contribute their insights, experiences, and theological understandings of the work of God in the world today.

Since the demographic profile of current local, district, and national... leadership finds residence among the boomer population, there is often little room at the table for our younger colleagues.[34]

Walls goes on to ask his ministry peers to share their space, love, and influence so that an older generation can begin to empower and equip the next one. Walls recognizes that the failure to transfer ownership to the next crowd of leaders will be our undoing.

Mentoring has been a theme that has reached buzz-word status, but is truthful all the same. We need leaders who will pass on what they have, not forcing those they mentor to become clones, but leaders who will bring out the skills and talents inherent in their protégés and then give them the authority they need by passing the mantle to them, as Elijah did to Elisha.

George Barna writes, "The sticking point is our core value: power. We love power. We live for power. Power lunches, power ties, power suits, power

---

[34] Walls, Randy. "A Place at the Table." Enrichment, Summer 2010: 8. 8

Christopher Schmitz – Why Your Pastor Left

offices, power titles, power cars, power networks. Whether it is because of an unhealthy desire for control, a reasonable concern about maintaining quality, a sense of exhilaration received from making pressure-packed, life-changing decisions or due to other motivations, Boomers revel in power. The sad result is that most Boomers – even those in the pastorate or in voluntary, lay-leadership positions in churches – have no intention of lovingly handing the baton to [the next generation.] We must allow – and even encourage – the emergence of new models of ministry that either improve or replace what we introduced and nurtured... we must anticipate and support such progress even if it is not what we might have done. Scripture gives them, as it gave us, abundant leeway in methodology. Let them put their fingerprints all over the model they develop. Keep in mind that a great leader is defined not by the methods that he/she deployed but by their commitment to the vision that God has entrusted to him/her."[35]

American churches are dying off particularly because there is no replacement of those that we lose to death. I frequently hear older adults in churches complaining about their younger counterparts who have fallen away. The thing is, they haven't quite so much fallen away as they have been driven away. Not actively, perhaps, but an unused member will eventually leave. If you join a sports team that regularly competes, but are never given a chance to play, you will eventually quit—stop coming to the games—and eventually drop off the team, wholesale. Those feeling unneeded will find somewhere, something, better suited to their skills. We are all skilled at sinning and there's always room

---

[35] (Barna, Gracefully Passing the Baton 2009)

Christopher Schmitz – Why Your Pastor Left

to play; leaders who failure to empower those under them and release them to Kingdom work might as well overtly push them out of the church. The World offers them what you refuse to give.

Church buildings sit empty all across this country. Doors to vacant buildings remain locked on Sundays because of a lack of relevance, petered out dedication, and blatant disinterest. Leadership has consistently neglected to give ownership over to the next generation and this is the resulting fruit. As our culture progressed, humanity advanced to consume information differently. The human race is different now than it was generations ago. It is the duty of us who know Truth to find a way to still relate that. I've heard it said that we need to get away from this idea of "cultural relevance" because the Gospel is always relevant. This is true, yet we must always "contextualize" the message of Christ: Jesus did this often!

I have heard too many highly regarded preachers come against politics and science and medicine and psychology. "They don't need all that, they just need Jesus!" I've heard it from a number of pulpits, preached nearly verbatim. Don't you think that those people suffering from mental distress, illness, and bondage have tried that? This is the most proselytized nation on earth! The downtrodden have had enough of your Jesus—he didn't fix the problem. We have modeled a Christ that either doesn't have the power to save or one who refuses to save. Negativity has become the hallmark of our faith. I agree that Scripture is firm on many things, but like the Pharisees, we have begun to regulate everything else.

Christopher Schmitz – Why Your Pastor Left

The problem is that Christians come against everything. This is something that trickles from the top down. NPR reports on the author Anne Rice:

> The writer has had a fairly tumultuous religious history. Although she was raised Catholic, Rice rejected the church for the first time when she was 18. But in 1998, Rice — who's famous mostly for writing steamy, gothic, decidedly un-Christian novels such as Interview with the Vampire — had a religious awakening. She...began to write exclusively Christian-themed novels, like Christ the Lord: Out of Egypt.

> In July [2010], Rice decided she had had enough. She announced her decision on her Facebook page: "For those who care, and I understand if you don't: Today I quit being a Christian. I'm out. I remain committed to Christ as always but not to being 'Christian' or to being part of Christianity. It's simply impossible for me to 'belong' to this quarrelsome, hostile, disputatious, and deservedly infamous group. For ten years, I've tried. I've failed. I'm an outsider. My conscience will allow nothing else."[36]

---

[36] Rice, Anne, interview by Michele Norris. Today I Quit Being A Christian NPR. August 2, 2010.

Christopher Schmitz – Why Your Pastor Left

One pastor I worked with told me how easy it would be to legislate everything and make himself the standard. "I could tell everyone they aren't allowed to go see movies. I don't go see movies. I don't have a problem with them, I just don't do it as a matter of habit; I'm busy doing other things. But it would be easy for myself to take what I am comfortable with and what I'm not comfortable with and impose those as standards upon others." We need to be willing to open up and not hold such a death grip on social matters of right and wrong except where addressed to by scripture—if political correctness is any example, dictating the flow of culture and social morays is not something that can be done from the pulpit anymore.

Why do we try dictating to others how they should live on matters where scripture is silent? When you set yourself up as the new judge and legislator of right and wrong, you had better be prepared to also one-up Jesus in dying for me. I struggle enough to following Christ; I can't try to please *you*, *too*. We hold ourselves in too high esteem. God sees us as co-heirs with Christ—children of the King! We see ourselves as even higher than that, as superior to Jesus, when we refuse to accept people for who they are, who God designed them to be and let them operate within their own specific calling.

If you watch footage from conferences, gatherings, marches, simulcasts, etc. it doesn't take long to figure out that we "Christians," as a movement, like to "toot our own horn," and pat ourselves on the back. We enjoy hearing speakers who share our viewpoints and beliefs, who doesn't? Unfortunately, we are exclusive in that regard—we refuse to allow ourselves to

Christopher Schmitz – Why Your Pastor Left

be challenged and stretched. Anything beyond the self-set boundaries we've set has been precluded as sinful, regardless of a lacking Scriptural base.

This attitude has resulted in our culture progressing without us. That is why we appear as backward and irrational to the culturally savvy: we've been left behind by forward progress and have refused to catch up. We won't even try to see another's point of view: empathy is the devil's plaything.

The traditional and typical people will rarely vote in a pastor who thinks differently than the group, and so younger men and women called to Godly service rarely find positions as pastors. Eventually, they are forced out of that call because of the need to repay school debts or support their families, etc. This has robbed the ministry of called, Godly men and women. This is my explanation for the shortage of pastors that afflicts our country. A pastoral shortage does exist; despite the fact that we statistically close more than 3,500 churches per year (or as much as twice that by some studies). With the dropping number of available churches, pastorates should be harder to come by. Fact of the matter is, younger believers are passionate about following their Savior, but disenchanted with the institution of the "Church" and alienated by much of its "leadership." Enrollment is declining at Bible Colleges and seminaries; fewer people than ever are willing to sign on as members of "man's church," but many still feel the call to lead "God's Church."

If we, as leaders of the church, only pass that mantle, or only give place and ear to those who are already like us, we will never grow. As culture and humanity changes and transitions, if we refuse to move with it, we will continually find fewer and fewer new pastors entering the field.

Christopher Schmitz – Why Your Pastor Left

Cultural shifts and trends dictate the way we relate and process data. This mandates that we discover new techniques and methods to relate to a generation on its own terms and in its own language. One of the aspects that make up a culture is a generational factor. The culture of the Baby Boomer generation is vastly different than that of the Generation X group. They both live in America and are affected by many of the same factors, but have a fundamentally different way of thinking and processing logic, emotions, etc. They are moved by different things: their values are different. For instance, A study published in Science Daily found that individuals of the GenY generation viewed positive workplaces as somewhere they can perform something interesting and make friends doing it. Boomers and GenXers see the workplace as more of a "necessary evil," something centric to life necessary to afford the finer things. GenY places such a high value on relationships that they might change careers entirely based on how their workplace interacts with those around them.[37] A Christian's response, then, is to relate the "personhood" of Jesus Christ to them.

I'm astounded whenever I hear clergy or church leaders devalue the souls of the lost. I have heard on a number of occasions, and even worked under ministers, who have proclaimed as part of a pulpit rant that, "We don't need any methods or approaches to evangelism: we just need Jesus." Yes, I agree on the one hand. But I disagree on the premise that you are presenting only *your*

---

[37] Sage Publications. "Work, leisure attitudes of Baby Boomers, Generation Xers and Millennials compared." Science Daily. March 10, 2010. http://www.sciencedaily.com/releases/2010/03/100310083450.htm (accessed August 2014).

Christopher Schmitz – Why Your Pastor Left

Jesus—not the Jesus of the Bible, but your narrow view. I've debated this topic with folks ranging from church janitors to lead pastors and even college students. I once nearly shut down a twenty-four hour truck-stop and café with this debate. Yes, Jesus is the only answer—but we refuse to even allow the seeker to ask the question. We never show the lost that we care. In our eagerness to make clones of ourselves and "put another notch on our Jesus Belt," we skip over the Greatest Commandment (unconditional love) and *force* people to bend their knees at the altar of the Great Commission. "Turn or burn; don't you want Jesus to make everything so much better?"

Why do we focus on the church and on the witness/evangelist at all in this process? As Jesus hung on the cross, his entire focus was on the sinner, not on the saved. It was for the lost that He died, not the found. Traditional evangelistic mentalities blur the image and purpose of Christ. Our attention is not at all on ourselves when we lead a lost one to the cross—it must be only on that person: one hundred percent.

The magnitude of divine salvation and the Great Commission demands that we *go out* and rescue, not wait till the lost conform to acceptable standards. "Christian Culture" has habitually cloistered itself in an attempt to "avoid the appearance of all evil (1 Thessalonians 5:22.)" In taking Paul's command to new levels, we have made our very subculture that thing which we hate. We also forget that only in western, Christianized culture is our faith safe and secure and guaranteed to us by Constitutional right; we are not promised safety this side of heaven. Our cloistered, Christian bubble has made us irrelevant any but our own subculture—not only that, but it has formed a new and exclusive cultural niche

Christopher Schmitz – Why Your Pastor Left

which actually opposes Christians who operate outside of its graces. This is not real Christianity.

Real Christianity operates out in the open. It is transparent and not afraid of the marketplace—these believers are real and sincere. They are "Jesus Freaks" who love everybody. I don't feel a particular calling to major niche ministries such as XXX Church or Strippers for Jesus—that's not my call and I fear to walk where they tread, but I love and support those called to work within those ministries and advance the Kingdom of God in places where I will not travel. These unafraid Jesus Freaks, real men and women of God simply are who they are. They accept people, love people, and are thoroughly Christian and genuine. They are transparent believers, sin and all, while working at becoming a saint and taking as many along their journey of faith as possible.

That kind of raw personhood has no place in our own kingdom communes. We are too uncomfortable with that sort of person. Their passion and zeal for all that God wants to give us, all the change he calls us too, exposes the hypocrisy within our own hearts. To admit that believers sin, long-time Christians even, seems too much for us; it crosses the line of acceptability in the Church of Man where we have already proclaimed our own godhood. Rather, we expel any individuals whose sins are committed in or made public. *Our houses* become places of lip service to God. We maintain a comfort zone for members where neither sinner nor Christ may enter; both are too close to humanity to qualify for entry.

Christopher Schmitz – Why Your Pastor Left

"The story goes that a public sinner was excommunicated and forbidden entry to the church. He took his woes to God. 'They won't let me in, Lord, because I am a sinner.'

'What are you complaining about?' said God. 'They won't let Me in either.'" Brennan Manning[38]

At one particular church I staffed at, I realized that I was in exactly just such a church. I'd created too much of a stir and numerous complaints had been lodged against me. The very first room the traditional crowd had to pass beyond to get into the church sanctuary was the large youth room. The music style and dress style of my students was an affront to the sensibilities of the older saints. Many years later, I'm still flabbergasted how "mature believers" could be so misguided as to hold new believers and curious unbelievers to their own outward standards.

During the course of my ministry there, I'd increased the numbers incredibly and those born and raised in that church were increasingly uncomfortable with the appearance and the background of the newer faces. Interrupting my sermon on the "Love of Jesus" one of them stood and challenged my assertion that God loves the tattooed, pierced, blue jean and t-shirt wearing mass of humanity just as much as he loves those born and raised in the church. "I can understand them coming in here looking like that the first time they come. But for God's sake, we have a Wal-Mart in this town; they can afford to buy something nice! They should know what to wear."

---

[38] Manning, Brennan. The Ragamuffin Gospel: Good News for the Bedraggled, Beat-Up, and Burnt Out. Colorado Springs: Multnomah, 2005.

Christopher Schmitz – Why Your Pastor Left

I'm sure that the biggest reason Jesus picked his disciples was the quality of their garments. Miracles were undoubtedly performed for only the snappy dressers. Jesus died to rescue us from scourge that is ripped denim—oh how I wish that torn blue jeans didn't have the ability to damn a man's soul to an eternal hell of pain and sorrow. I hope my dripping sarcasm comes through. How is the outrageous, earth-shattering, mind-bendingly amazing love of Christ so overshadowed by such a petty and trivial, human concern?

It was but weeks afterwards that I found myself excused from my position. Rather than encourage and pull along the younger, newer believers into their faith and share with them a rich history of faith, belief, miracles, and personal testimony, I was told to cease my ministry, resign my position immediately, and relocate the contents of my office within the next twelve hours and lock my keys inside the building which I was no longer allowed to enter. I had been excommunicated and told I wasn't allowed to contact anyone in the community I'd had "church-related" contact with. Without the ability to label my sudden departure as calling, or expose me publicly as a sinner stripped of office, I was told no questions would be answered; it was as if I'd just disappeared.

What happens to the budding faith of young believers under circumstances like that? What becomes of those people who suddenly find themselves pastor-less without any explanation? I imagine them like small fish caught and held in a boat. They aren't big enough species for the haul so they'll get tossed back. But these are not fish. They are living, eternal souls: children of the eternal, Most High God who zealously desires them. Most of those "fish" are

Christopher Schmitz – Why Your Pastor Left

thrown back into an environment that will devour them merely because they were unfit for the sort of boat they'd been brought into.

Many churches are in love with the idea of reaching the lost, but they haven't prepared for the reality of dealing with them. Fishermen know that if you plan to catch fish, you must be ready to clean them. I've known many churches that take public pride in their youth program and brag about their church's tertiary ministries, yet refuse to then let it run properly or fund those programs so they are effective. Too many "Christians" just want bragging rights at the local café or PTA meeting. This is the kingdom of man taking precedence over God's Kingdom.

Any church that imposes a dress code, official or unofficial, mires the Spirit of God in human legalism. God is not concerned with how people look when they come to Him. There is no such thing as the "wrong-looking" sort of person in your church.

As another part of my expulsion, it was made expressly clear that I would have no opportunity to address any concerns or complaints levied against me, despite my willingness to find common ground with my accusers and history of taking corrective measures when I'd misstepped previously. I was not allowed to try and make amends of any sort or learn more regarding the "overwhelming number" of complaints the church office had suddenly received during my short family vacation. The entire scenario guaranteed anonymity and immunity to those who disapproved of my unabashed yearning that "unconditionality" be added to the "Love of Jesus."

Christopher Schmitz – Why Your Pastor Left

The "Cloistered Christian Sub-Culture" just about killed me. That's not figurative language either; the ensuing tailspin nearly broke me. In my darkest moments, I entertained thoughts of my family cashing in on my life insurance policy and thus regaining *some* sort of usefulness.

I mentioned disillusionment in earlier chapters. It took me twenty-five years in churches to realize that there's no such thing as love *or* forgiveness within the walls of many churches. Over the next half-decade, I began to discover that this was the norm in most church bodies, more often than the exception.

My heart breaks when I think how this is not an uncommon story. I'm too scared to research suicide statistics related to clergy. I'm scared that in my anger I might irreparably harm another of God's loved ones, rather than attempt an uncomfortable thaw of the "Frozen Chosen." I'm already incensed over the Church's inability to obey God's highest two commandments: Love Him with everything, and Love others as much as we love ourselves (in order that the world might be drawn to Him.)

We absolutely *must* get better at relating to our nonbelieving peers. This applies to both the church in general, and its members, pastors, leaders. We can't put the responsibility for the knowledge of salvation in the hands of the ignorant. We can't expect those who don't know the Lord to recognize their need for Him. Too much is at stake: an entire generation of souls! Churches: send your ministers to conferences with YOUNG speakers and with those who hold alternate or even opposing points of view—if nothing else, it will sharpen your pastor. We must get better.

I come from a very small town. My graduating High School class had fewer than thirty-five people in it. When I went to college to study ministry, another student I graduated with went to study medicine and become a medical doctor. Deep down, there was a vain part of me that compared the importance of professions. If the soul was eternal and infinitely valuable, did that make my call nobler than his? While my motivation was likely selfish in that period of my life, it did inspire me to study harder. The importance of such a mission was overwhelming and I determined that ministers should not be held to lesser standards than medical practitioners.

The problem of sin has been compared to a disease in countless sermons. As already noted, Jesus is the cure. Our "Christianized" culture needs to be made more aware of the application. A doctor will tell you it is foolish and even dangerous to swallow a skin cream to combat a rash or burn. Medicine comes in different forms, and just as one drug might be available in a number of routes (injection, topical, ingestion, etc.) to combat different symptoms, we must know our patient and determine the best possible delivery method to prevent harm.

Older generations used to just take whatever a doctor prescribed as the cure—they didn't need to know about the medicine, they trusted their care provider. Current generations have an innate distrust of authority (part of our molding at the hands of our Boomer progenitors, and also because of legal matters that guarantee data privacy and full disclosure.) Think of all the small print at the bottom of televised drug ads—all the side effects and detailed information must be made available to a consumer. It is important to know that

113

the drug works, but the consumers also want to know all the related side effects and possible interactions that might occur. Sometimes people feel the cure is worse than the condition, and that is an accurate picture of the world in regard to salvation. Clergy are no longer trusted by the world at large; the Church has consistently failed to produce results that the consumer group has confidence in.

Medical treatments change as technology and culture progresses; this holds true also for ministering to people. Allow me to confess here for a moment, I like to laugh and appreciate satire. I was always a fan of the satirized doctor drama Scrubs.

Oftentimes the show can get quite deep and introspective. In one particular episode (season2, episode 14), the hard-nosed Chief of Medicine (Dr. Kelso) has to confront his best friend (Dr. Townsend) because his friend had not kept up on modern medical procedures. The older doctor at one point refuses to let the younger doctor, played by Zach Braff, do a standard procedure and directs him to do an "old school," and risky IJ Cutdown during which the patient's artery is exposed and accidentally nicked by the scalpel, jeopardizing his life when a newer method would have been both more effective and much safer. Townsend was the most liked doctor on staff, but also the least versed in modern life-saving techniques, and by his own admission Townsend was "set in his ways." Ministers of older generations that refuse to find missional, contextualized methods of relating the Gospel of Jesus Christ to the lost also place their "patients" in jeopardy.

Being a doctor and being a minister are not professions of comfort. When we refuse to grow, advance, stretch, and meet the needs of others on *their*

Christopher Schmitz – Why Your Pastor Left

terms, people die... souls are damaged. Dr. Kelso tells his friend that, "This is not an age thing." He recognized that in the changing culture practices become obsolete. "Why do you think I spend every other weekend at a seminar in some hotel ballroom that still stinks of last nights prom vomit? I do it because I have to keep up." In a rare moment of compassion, Dr. Kelso reveals his passion for helping others. Townsend replies, "I just don't have the energy for all that stuff." In the interest of preserving life, Kelso has no other choice at that point but take his closest friend off the active roster.

A Christian's heartbeat must be for the lost. The best way for a pastor to meet the needs of his staff and congregation, as well as the lost, is to develop that missional heart that yearns to be as effective as possible in his or her field. We must stay current on the needs of our community around us. As George Wood, Superintendent of the General Council of the Assemblies of God has been quoted, "Our memories must not be greater than our dreams."

In her Ministry and Medical Ethics article, *Interpreting Research Results Related to Ministry*, Christina Powell, Ph.D., reports on the relevance of research in ministry and staying current on social and demographic trends. She writes:

> "Just as a doctor keeps up with the latest research
> findings in medicine to hone his diagnostic skills, pastors
> interested in church revitalization and transformation can gain
> insight from research findings related to ministry, for example,
> geodemographic research, which applies census data to maps,
> can help a church understand the needs of its surrounding

Christopher Schmitz – Why Your Pastor Left

community. Church attendance and membership records can assist a church—or perhaps an entire district of churches—to discern the changes most likely to enhance church health and growth."

"Surveys that reveal cultural trends can inspire new approaches to relating the unchanging truth to a changing world… We need to use the same steps that a doctor or research scientist must take to separate research gold from the dross and apply them to ministry research findings."

"Sometimes, the best way to determine what church research is relevant to your situation is to first conduct a little research of your own. Knowing the history of your church… will often provide insight into the life of your congregation."[39]

Powell reminds us that "those dusty church scrapbooks and records" can hold many insights into powerful moments in the churches history. It might also pinpoint hurtful situations with effects lasting years. I've seen several churches that keep framed photos to honor their previous ministers and their dates of service. Some churches have a full wall of them, each chronicling painfully short lengths. In other, very small congregations I have known "landmark" preachers who have been a fixture in the pulpit for many decades, complacently leading their atrophied congregations—if you can call going nowhere, leading at all.

---

[39] Powell, Christina M.H. "Interpreting Research Results Related to Ministry." Enrichment Journal 15, no. 3 (Summer 2010): 118-121. 118

Christopher Schmitz – Why Your Pastor Left

If you "just don't have the energy for all that stuff," then your passion for reaching the lost has been surpassed by your ability to effectively do so. It is perhaps time to switch gears in ministry. Fatigue and irrelevance may be accompanying a still, small voice that is redirecting a call to a niche of the Kingdom where the sheep still understand the language and methods you shepherd with. I believe that is why the Levites were required to retire from actively serving in the Old Testament worship in Numbers 8:25 at the age of fifty. They still had a part, but their active role was not leadership from that point on.

A 2009 Barna report finds that, "A decade ago the median age of mainline Senior Pastors was 48; today it is 55. That represents a shockingly fast increase, representing a combination of too few young pastors entering the ranks and a large share of older pastors not retiring. Another study by Barna found that an unusually high share of Boomer pastors are refusing to retire or plan to retire in their mid-sixties."[40]

Good pastors who cannot or will not tread into unfamiliar territory still recognize that need. They take on staff that is talented where they are not and have skill sets that complement their own, covering the areas where they are weak or blind entirely. They don't micromanage or dictate how their staff does their ministry, but they empower and release them to operate under divine guidance. They never write off a niche or people group; they might recognize a limited capacity and restricted ability to be effective so they may knowingly wait until they are better resourced or staffed to reach target markets. But they

---

[40] (The Barna Group, Ltd. 2009)

Christopher Schmitz – Why Your Pastor Left

don't expect that "The Church" is a "one-size-fits-all" entity and they act accordingly.

We need to show that Jesus it the real deal in *our own* lives. This isn't revealed by the fact that we wear a suit and tie on Sundays or weekdays or have a WWJD bumper sticker—the evidence is a changed life, and a life that is still relevant in that person's culture. We have been guilty of inoculating a generation against the cure by our claims that must only use it a certain way—people suffering from stomach pains intuitively know that a drop of ointment under a Band-Aid won't resolve their issues. The sick have observed regular users and don't see cured people, but rather addicts to something with side effects more undesired than the remedy.

Conversion to Christianity does not mandate a loss of identity. When a life changes and outsiders can no longer outwardly tell that it's the same person, they appear to have been body snatched—brainwashed by a cult. God gave us dispositions, personalities, and natural bents for a reason. Jesus does not wipe our personality at the cross; he changes our life on the *inside*, who we are to *Him*, but He doesn't make us Jesus clones and ask us to leave our self-image behind! Let's not tread upon the craftsmanship of the Creator.

In the Old Testament, the congregational leadership was frequently churned with freshness. The maximum span of a Levite's ministry was twenty-five years and could span only from the ages of twenty-five to fifty years old. This always kept the current generation in touch with their God. The theocentric society remained relevant to them, the culture, context, and language of their religion remain in *their* world and not their parents.

Christopher Schmitz – Why Your Pastor Left

I heard an argument about shortened lifespans, etc. in older days rationalizing this as an "old-age" retirement plan, and yet Moses was 120 when he died and over 80 when he handed down this particular command found in Numbers 8. Ages well beyond fifty were not uncommon in that era—mainly because of dietary laws and practices handed down by God. These are examples that He knows what He is doing. God also knows how young peoples' fire and passion can set flame even to old logs, possibly the reason for this Levitical requirement.

People, especially older people, take immediate offense when bringing up this passage from Numbers. I understand that it is an Old Testament restriction and not necessarily renewed under the new covenant with Christ; I am not suggesting that pastors be forced to retire at age 50. I wish we would entertain this *principle*, however. Young ministers, while perhaps not as experienced as their older counterparts, have something very vital that they bring to the Church. In fact, they bring vitality itself.

There is an underlying fear that letting the next generation handle the reigns of control in modern ministry will "destroy the church." Generational gaps being what they are, I admit that whenever I hear a person from an older generation make such a verbal claim, I interpret it as "change the church." I know that there is an innate reluctance to change (a factor that increases with age.) I also know that not all change is good. The common ground is somewhere in the middle if both sides will try to find it. I also believe, that many adherents in the older generation are more comfortable letting the church die than they are

Christopher Schmitz – Why Your Pastor Left

willing to adapt to change and progressively move towards seeing new souls saved and discipled.

In one church "Leadership Meeting" I attended, where all department heads gathered to develop a strategy for church operation and outreach, one of the most prominent heads, a female Boomer, stated, "Myself and the other women my age don't feel we should have to volunteer in those areas [children's ministry, nursery, Sunday School, Christian Ed.] We've already put in our time and paid our dues. I remember being a young mother and having to juggle kids and church and work. It was a struggle for me. The newer young ladies in the church need to know what that was like and pay their dues, too." I left the meeting resentful and upset with any who shared that sentiment. The Boomer plan was that younger moms, most of whom were single parents, come to the church with their kids and become believers in the one or two services they can attend monthly in between volunteering and teaching and staffing nursery and Sunday school rooms. Why would these women value and love an organization that does not reciprocate that love and ignores the demand that older women teach the younger women? What about discipleship? What about common sense? I pointed out that a new believer/nonbeliever was simply not qualified to lead a Bible study or teach children information that they simply did not yet know. Because I was too young (30) and "didn't know anything yet," my logic wasn't appreciated.

The disconnect between cultures runs deep, and not much has been done to cross that chasm. Minnesota Pastor Denny Curran presented a pamphlet titled "Church Planting For Dummies" at a conference I once attended. Inside was a chart that showed how the generational, disconnect gaps (the longest distance of things shared in common [i.e. life experiences, music tastes, cultural/generational issues, etc.]) are between older believers and younger nonbelievers. Older believers and older nonbelievers have culture in common, as do their younger counterparts, and those believers have a faith culture in common.

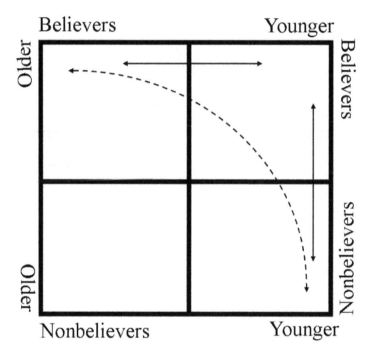

One of the things that a vibrant and growing church must do is win the mental game. We need to realize that older Christians have the least in common with younger non-Christians. That means older Christians need to work extra hard if they want to bridge that gap and relate their faith, life, experiences, and demonstrate love across the spectrum.

121

Christopher Schmitz – Why Your Pastor Left

How many nonbelievers do you regularly associate with? When is the last time you shared your faith with a member of *any* generation, your own or otherwise? Do we want to bridge that gap? We must understand that Christians, as keepers of the knowledge of Truth are mandated to be the ones making the effort to build that bridge. It is not incumbent upon the nonbelievers to seek their salvation. True, God will prompt and move many, but the onus of evangelism is on us, not them.

I hope I don't sound as if I'm attacking the Builder and Boomer generations, but generational studies and other surveys reveal such interesting data. One of the things I've learned (and experienced firsthand) is that both of these generations distrust each other. In the 1960s, the rise of the hippies and many other social-political movements demonstrated that the following generation wanted to be heard and demanded influence. They craved power: the ability to make decisions and take action, directing their own fates: autonomy and governance. Their Builder precursors loathed to relinquish any of their authority to the next generation (which was more immature at that stage in life than any previous due to psychological and social factors such as the validation of, and recognition of Adolescence as a developmental stage: teens were encouraged to "find themselves" and remain immature as long as possible as a way to better develop themselves.) This is the foundation that led to a consumer-driven, narcissistic, selfish culture that America has become, helped along greatly by an unhealthy preoccupation with celebrity (Boomers were the first to be exposed regularly to television and have technology readily accessible.) They also were "coming of age" when Credit Cards first became readily available,

122

Christopher Schmitz – Why Your Pastor Left

further encouraging them to get what they wanted now and think less about the cost. This is the mindset under which most current ministers were born from. Ironically, they also refuse to believe that they are aging. Their marketability and buying power is the main impetus driving lines of herbal supplements, age-defying skin creams, and new kinds of cosmetic surgery.

It is my belief that integral to "Peter Pan" syndrome is a genuine belief that they cannot, in good conscience, "pass the mantle" of their leadership down to any of the younger generations. In their collective mind, most of the Generation X is unqualified or too fickle to lead; they are too small—there exist far too few of them who maintain a respect for God's Church—many of them have expressed a blatant disinterest or destructive desires/radical change for it. Yet, we hold that in common. The sixties were known for Boomer's demands to institute "radical change" and their desire to "be heard."

They are so easily offended by the growing pains of the younger generation and so the younger generation is held back and not able to mature themselves. Psychologists have identified this also as a contributor to "failure to launch" syndrome where young adults are just big kids living at home—they were never given duties and responsibilities and is easily seen in the contemporary western church by its many immature believers—Christians who refuse to take anything beyond the "milk" of a new believer, as described in Hebrews 5:13,14.

I don't have the answer for how to fix that disconnect. But I'm pretty sure that the Bible agrees with the theme from the sixties, as sung by the Beattles, "All ya need is love." If we could all operate with a 1 Corinthians 13 mentality, we'd be able to overcome our differences and strive together in unity. So, while I don't have the answer, I do recognize the problem, and that's half of the battle.

History, especially Biblical history, is so often doomed to repeat itself. America was once this bastion of Christian influence, "One Nation Under God." The "roaring twenties" came in an era that followed on the heels of one this nation's greatest spiritual awakenings. The revivals at Azusa Street sparked the renewal and planting of churches across the nation. Missions and evangelism became priorities for people and first-generation Christians (new converts) boldly took their faith out into the world.

Many of the new converts (or those newly ignited by the preaching of Pentecostal preacher William J Seymour,) were on the "cutting edge" of the 20th Century's Christianity. Many of those newly baptized believers did not fit the die-mold which the church had cast; nonetheless, the global impact that these believers had is still being charted by historians. As time progressed, many of these believers settled into churches and their lives settled down. They had families of their own, assumed parental roles, and took church leadership positions.

I applaud these believers. Wisely, they raised their children in the church and instructed them in the ways of the Lord; they mainly did church as they saw demonstrated by their parents and peers. Likewise, many of their grandchildren were also brought up in the church (this would be the Baby Boomer generation.) Oddly enough many of the Boomers resented church and many failed to go as adults. Some of those who did attend only did so for the benefit of their children, wanting them to also have a foundational, deified belief system. The GenXers are mainly beyond all forms of education and the colleges and grad schools now mostly hold GenY/GenMe students. As you look at this brief history we can easily see the rushing river of spiritual fervor in the early 1900s crawl to a trickle by the dawn of the twenty-first century. Pollsters reveal that about four in five "Christian Students" (i.e. kids raised in church) leave their faith behind them entirely after they depart for college, mostly this happens within one year of leaving.

What does that mean? Well, the impact is huge (a second grade math student can tell you it isn't long before the church numerically bleeds to death.) It also shows us that many of our children and grandchildren attend church in an effort to make us happy. It has been that way ever since Azusa Street and has remained a current factor all through this time. Should we then give our children the option of attending? That's like giving a chimpanzee a revolver and a Redbull! What we have been missing all throughout this time are opportunities to engage future generations in the work of the Lord.

I call this the Judges 2:10 effect. Starting in verse 8 we find that Joshua dies. "And Joshua the son of Nun, the servant of the LORD, died, being an hundred and ten years old. And they buried him in the border of his inheritance in Timnathheres, in the mount of Ephraim, on the north side of the hill Gaash. And also all that generation were gathered unto their fathers: and there arose another generation after them, which knew not the LORD, nor yet the works which he had done for Israel. –KJV."

Christopher Schmitz – Why Your Pastor Left

We discover in Judges 2:10 that third generation beyond the great revival and redemption in Moses' time wanes into a complete wash. The first generation walked beyond the Red Sea and fed on Manna, followed the pillar of fire. Their children, the second generation, marched around Jericho with Joshua. Their grandchildren, the third generation, completely forgot about their God and followed after personal pleasure and the foreign Gods of other peoples.

Only foolishness says we can rely on the faith of our grandparents to save us from our sins or circumstances. We cannot blame our parents for our own apathy and lack of faith. It is the responsibility of every generation to claim their faith for their own, to leap in face-first into the presence of God. What every generation needs are parents and grandparents that will dare the next two generations to do bigger and better things in the interest of advancing the Kingdom. That is where we have failed since Azusa. Too long have we looked back at the previous generations as living in the "good old glory days" of Christianity and tried to emulate that. The only thing that does is alienate the next generation as we try to cram the entire body of believers into the way-back machine.

We do not need a restoration of the "good old days." We need a new, fresh outpouring of the Spirit of God. We need to catch a new, corporate vision of unity and advancement under the banner of Jesus, something that impacts the culture and creates a new "First Generation" of believers—a passionate group of people that truly understands what it is like to be lost in sin.

This is the attitude that the church must have. Its prayers must cry out for the lost. It must respect and love them regardless of who they are and it must

Christopher Schmitz – Why Your Pastor Left

leap across all barriers of disconnection in order to raise up Christ. Most of the truly dynamic and inspirational pastors that I know harbor a heart that beats for the unloved and the unsaved. We need to partner with members of all generations in order to see the greatest impact upon our culture, which is a multi-segmented organism. No part is more important than the other, but many parts are larger and require more concentration and dedication to work within, thus demanding greater resources and attention. Don't write anyone off.

Every person must have his or her own awakening. They must individually possess their faith—they have to own it. As long as their faith belongs to their Grandma, it will only have validity in their grandmother's sphere of influence. A person's faith can never truly operate, and never really save, until it is real to the individual.

The church (this includes pastors,) needs to get better at making opportunities for its members to make their own faith alive and active. This goes beyond knocking on doors once a year and handing out pamphlets. This goes far beyond attending potlucks or church picnics. We must partner with each other and empower each other with encouragement and opportunity. We must communicate clearly and effectively so that we are unified, but also remain open to the idea that God operates differently within each and every culture and sub-culture.

We absolutely must have unity in the ministry—that means respecting each other and building relationships with each other so that we can effectively work towards a common purpose. Disjointedness must be combated, and this starts at the base level within the body of the church. Pastoral staff relations

127

should be a shining example to the rest of the congregation and a model they should aspire to.

One of the reasons that pastors, especially ministry staff and associate pastors, leave is because they are so disconnected from the ministry that they burn up, burn out, or self-destruct. Stretch and educate your lead pastors so that they learn the best way to empower and release their staff, thereby growing the Kingdom of God. Support them and encourage them and publicly validate and affirm the staff and ministry associates, but do so without instilling jealousy or causing possible division and segregation.

Chapter 7

(Money Issues)

I'm a registered Kansas City Barbecue Society judge and member. I love eating good food. I've had some amazing stuff, but I've never eaten off of a king's table before, not like the biblical Nehemiah.

Nehemiah is an amazing book. Nehemiah was the cup-bearer to Babylonian King Artaxerxes. Essentially, he spends every meal with the King and tastes everything first. If Nehemiah doesn't keel over from poison, the King knows it's safe to eat and drink. His character as a child of God makes him a joy to the King. When Nehemiah learns of the desolation of Jerusalem during the Babylonian captivity, he becomes sorrowful. Artaxerxes recognizes his subject's depression and desires to make him happy. The Babylonian King allows Nehemiah to return and rebuild Jerusalem, and even foots the bill for it. It's pretty amazing stuff.

At one point, after much of Jerusalem is rebuilt, Nehemiah is called upon to report back to the King for a period. When he returns to Jerusalem after, he is distraught to find that the Temple worship has been abandoned. The ministers who carry out their duties had not been given their scripture-required allotment; they had not been given their due pay for performing their duties and so they had to find other means of support.

Nehemiah 13:10,11 reads, "I also learned that the portions assigned to the Levites had not been given to them, and that all the Levites and musicians responsible for the service had gone back to their own fields. So I rebuked the

Christopher Schmitz – Why Your Pastor Left

officials and asked them, 'Why is the house of God neglected?'" Basically, when the ministers and church workers were not paid, they all went home to work the family farm in order to make a living. They stopped "pastoring" and got jobs flipping burgers just so they could feed their families.

I know pastors who have given up on the ministry because of the financial pressures that accompany it. In my experience, financial burdens are one of the biggest killers of minister's aspirations. Balancing college loan repayment, providing for a family, and meeting the bill requirements of an American family often suffocate a pastor's effectiveness. In 1 Timothy 5:18, "For Scripture says, 'Do not muzzle an ox while it is treading out the grain,' and 'The worker deserves his wages.'" This directly follows a key passage telling us that ministers who preach the Word are worthy of being honored by even receiving up to twice a typical wage. Underpaying a pastor steals that minister's honor and is a very common ministry-killer.

The mentality of many average people is summed up in these statements, many of which I have had said to me:

- Things are tight enough already; the pastor should be a "tent-maker" and be more like Paul (receive no money for the ministry and get a second job for all income).
- Our pastor doesn't have kids/is single/is retired so he doesn't need as much.
- Our pastor is young, we had to struggle for a while too when we were young.

Christopher Schmitz – Why Your Pastor Left

- I remember when I only earned $X.xx a week... and I survived: he or she can too.

- We give him a parsonage. If I had free housing I could live on a fraction of what I earn.

- If we pay him too much he won't need to trust the Lord.

- A pastor doesn't really work more than a day or two a week; they should be more grateful that they receive what they get.

- Pastors are not supposed to be rich; being poor keeps people humble.

These statements reveal hearts that do not value their pastor, and by extension his or her ministry and the God who the pastor represents. I chose to honor God's calling when I first entered the ministry, really when I changed my major in college. I took a vow to be obedient to God's *calling*, not a vow of *poverty*. We should never place our pastor in a position or lifestyle that we, ourselves, are unwilling to live in. Congregations should also remember that ministry is a life-style career; it's not just a job. If possible, a pastor's salary package should include the forethought of retirement options and the pastor's future, not just enough to "get by in the here and now."

The most appropriate metaphor for the biblical pastor is that of a shepherd. David says in Psalm 23:1, "The Lord is my shepherd, I shall not be in want." In regards to the financial state of shepherds in biblical times, I uncovered some interesting information. After the exile, Pharisaic rabbis degraded the role of the shepherd. Pharisees forbade pious Jews to purchase wool, milk, meat, etc. from shepherds because they, by nature of their profession, had little income. Talk about a vicious cycle. Essentially, shepherds

131

were *suspected* of a thievish and dishonest nature because of their vocation. Shepherds were loathed by the public, similar to New Testament tax collectors. In commentary on Psalm 23, the Midrash states "No position in the world is as despised as that of the shepherd." Are modern churches guilty of despise/pharisism? Does your congregation "despise" its pastor?

While in a church staff meeting, one pastor I worked with liked to frequently ask us what we learned each week, what God had been revealing to us. When it came my turn to answer this question, I responded, "This is not my church." My response surprised the pastor and he asked me to explain.

"This is God's church, not mine," I explicated. "I'm finding that I worry less and release control more freely when I realize that this is not *my* church. God owns it and He is powerful enough to make sure that things go properly." That's not to say that things never go poorly; I realized that pastors should not be dictators, but rather leaders under God as the head. I am an under-shepherd appointed to lead this flock, but these sheep do not belong to me. The Church is God's.

Greg Hickle, Secretary Treasurer of the Minnesota District of the Assemblies of God tells a story about church ownership. He was called on as a consultant in a church board meeting because of his experience and qualifications regarding church financial matters and church polity. The board had called his office and asked, "How do we know if we are paying our pastor too much?"

This particular church was like many others and had monetary problems and difficulty meeting all of their financial needs. In a meeting, the board expressed their concerns that they were overpaying their pastor in lieu of shrinking offerings. Their methods were modeled after the business world. The thinking was that if the money was not coming into the coffers, the pastor, as the head of the company (this man was referencing a sole-proprietorship type of small business) should make less money in times of hardship (or no money at all if there isn't any income after expenses). To those without a comprehensive knowledge of ministry, both Scripture and experience, this might seem like a very valid point.

Hickle offered a guideline for using that business model in the context of the church. "If the money does not come in, then the business owner receives no paycheck that week and I'm in favor of you using that model," he said. "So with your current expenses, etc. your pastor takes a reduced wage or forfeits it entirely." Ears on some of the board members perked up at his seeming agreement. "But who exactly is the owner, here? It's the whole church, and as examples, you all share in that leadership position. So Pastor receives no paycheck this week. But next week, you get no paycheck and Pastor gets yours. The following week the pay schedule shifts again down the line and so every week you get the next person's wage or lack of it and every six to eight weeks you will get no income." That idea was never implemented and the church reworked its finances in order to compensate their pastor. Nonetheless, it's an interesting look at merging a business model so that it aligns with the early church's principle of believers "having all things in common." I suspect that, had they gone to it, the pastor would have received a comparatively significant raise in wages.

133

Though you might sometimes read otherwise, the fact of the matter is that most pastors are underpaid. I recently read some interesting articles that published the exorbitant incomes of church pastors. The figures were skewed, however, basing the average income scales on wages of ministers staffing at American and Canadian churches with attendance counts from 1,000 to 15,000. (Hartford Seminary Sociologist Scott Thumma who compiled the 2005 "Megachurches Today" survey defines a megachurch as a congregation with at least 2,000 people attending each Sunday.)[41] The vast majority of churches, however, are rural churches with small congregations. Despite the increasing trend of the megachurch movement, most church attendees on a Sunday morning attend a smaller, rural church. Surveyed findings on megachurch pastor salaries hold very little context for the typical pastor, whose attendance is 2-10% of his megachurch peers.

In 2010, the typical pastor barely made more than the national Census Bureau's official poverty guideline. On average, a pastor serving a congregation of less than 1,000 attendees received a median salary and housing package of $31,234, according to a study by sociologist Jackson Carroll.[42] Taking into account factors such as family size and insurances for medical and other typical benefits, plus possible tax filing status as self-employed and paying necessary taxes on church-owned property such as a parsonage and a typical minister

[41] Thumma, Scott, Travis, Dave & Bird, Warren . Megachurches Today 2005 Summary of Research Findings. Survey, Hartford: Hartford Seminary, 2005. 1
[42] Carroll, Jackson W. and Becky R. McMillan. God's Potters: Pastoral Leadership and the Shaping of Congregations. Grand Rapids: Eerdmans, 2006.

Christopher Schmitz – Why Your Pastor Left

could easily be living below the poverty line, and this is before the skyrocketing, mandated health care costs imposed in the mid-twenty-teens.

No *good* pastor enters the ministry with the sole purpose of personal profit. It's true that Godly men and women don't seek personal profit in the ministry; we don't do this to get rich. A minister must do his or her job with excellence, but how much better is the job done than when the pastor is free to concentrate their full attention to the ministry? I've nothing against those who prefer to function as bi-vocational ministers, but that should be the choice and calling of the pastor. Let's look at scripture. 1 Corinthians 9:14 says, "The Lord has commanded that those who preach the gospel should receive their living from the gospel." (New International Version.)

How much should a pastor make, then? Many qualified advisors have all made the same assessment. A minister *should* be paid according to both the local economic factors *and* their qualifications: their education, skills/duties, and experience. As a general rule of thumb a minister requires education and skills on par with a school Principle. They will each deal with administrative aspects of the facility and staff, deal with people, study, speak publicly, operate on a community level, and minister didactically (have some teaching capacity).

Hickle made this recommendation to a church board. The reply was, "Well, we can't pay that much! Principals and Superintendents of local school districts make more money than we can afford." That's an idea here that is easily overlooked when we concentrate on the nickels and dimes. Our attitude needs to be right: it's not so much about what we can afford to pay a pastor as much as it is about what we *should* pay our pastor. In 1 Timothy 5:17 Paul

135

writes that a pastor is worthy of a double portion/honor. He is not talking about respect and goodwill—a Greek word-study, or even simple context of the following verses reveal that Paul is talking about actual wages. While it's not common that a church can bless its leader accordingly, Hickle says, "I believe that God would not be displeased with paying your pastor twice the going rate in order to honor him."

A church Hickle spoke of had fallen behind in its bills. The pastor took a pay cut of $1000 a month to help the church try to meet its commitments. After eight months, they were still falling behind. Another pay reduction was likely forthcoming. The pastor could not keep his family financially stable with another reduction; they had already trimmed all the fat off their personal budget and tightened their belts as much as they could go.

The pastor was expected to sacrifice his own livelihood in order for the rest of the church to continue, and the congregation was content to let him be the only contributor to that problem, and still, that wasn't enough. If the church belongs to the congregation, then so do the burdens of the church. I cannot fathom a pastor remaining long in a similar situation before meeting financial ruin. Can you imagine playing a game of Monopoly with several other people, but every time you pass go you *do not* collect $200 while everyone else does. How would you feel? Even if you *really* loved Monopoly, could your heart stay in it for long?

Churches don't understand what a pastor sacrifices if they are asked to give up extra time or income beyond that expected of anyone else. Pay-cuts and shortages are equivalent to the pastor contributing the difference out of their

Christopher Schmitz – Why Your Pastor Left

own pocket. This pastor I mentioned essentially gave an extra $12,000 dollars by years end to the church (beyond his tithe and any offerings, benevolence, and missions giving). Can you imagine suddenly living on $12,000 dollars less, annually? More devastating, think about percentages, could you survive on a sudden 40% pay reduction? Could you happily remain in your employ?

How would you adjust your lifestyle to meet a demand for an extra thousand dollar monthly requirement? Would you get a second job to make up for the shortfall or seek a new job entirely? In almost every case I've known, pastors switching from full-time employment to a bivocational role have transitioned fully out of ministry or quickly sought ministry elsewhere.

This pastor tried to help meet those financial needs. As a shepherd, his sheep didn't follow, and so he walked forward with his entire flock strapped to his back. Pastors are shepherds that lead by example, but they are also partners in ministry *with* the congregation.

With this concept of sharing the load, I've heard it commonly stated across denominational lines that people think their pastor should neither be the highest paid member of their church nor the lowest paid person in their midst. That statement doesn't really help anyone determine what they should pay their leader, but it can help determine if your pastor is grossly underpaid. If he or she is below the median income line in from your membership's roster, consult the church board, or whatever your denomination's method might be, regarding how you can increase this amount.

One local pastor from my hometown region was on a mission trip in Ireland. While touring there with an Irish minister, they were forced to stop on a

Christopher Schmitz – Why Your Pastor Left

road while a flock of sheep crossed. Like the majority of American pastors, he had never actually seen a shepherd and their flock; he only knew about shepherding from books, study materials, and Sunday School flannel-graphs.

The sheep crossed as a large, amoebic mass with a man at the back who pushed the sheep forward. This picture puzzled the American minister.

"I'm going to have to restructure the way I understand the picture of a shepherd's leadership," he told the Irish pastor. "I've always thought that a shepherd led from the front and the sheep followed him—that's the picture we've always been given. This shepherd is *driving* his flock across the road."

"You're picture is correct," the Irish pastor told him. "That's not the shepherd pushing them forward. That's our butcher."

Sure enough, on the other side of the road was the slaughterhouse. Shepherds lead; butchers drive.

Scripture also reflects that there is a difference between true shepherds and hired hands. A shepherd is worthy of their wage (even up to a double portion of that) but their focus is on the flock rather than on that wage. A hireling cares only for the financial gain. As a church, we must beware that the right sort of person is hired initially. We must also be mindful that we can turn the heart of a shepherd and transform them into a hireling by underpaying a pastor or asking/forcing them to sacrifice until their focus shifts from the flock to their own immediate, pressing needs. This happens easily as a pastor tries to balance the requirements for good Christian leadership. A pastor must be able to meet the requirements of a deacon; this would include managing their own household well. An underpaid pastor struggles to meet this foundational requirement and the stress can eventually bleed over and disrupt his ministry. An improperly compensated minister easily becomes dysfunctional, disillusion, and burned out or burned up.

I want to make sure that I distinguish the role of ownership here and the clear roles of pastors; many call them under-shepherds. Prior to the crucifixion, Jesus clearly states that *He* is the shepherd and that the Shepherd owns the sheep and loves them. Others will flee because they are merely a "hired man" and don't place the same value upon the flock; their love and commitment to the flock is different.

After the resurrection, Jesus eats with most of his disciples in John 21. In this passage, Jesus commands Peter to "Feed my sheep." This is the portion of Jesus' life where he established his church. He had already told Peter that He would build His church upon him. Knowing that the ascension was near, Jesus empowered Peter with authority and released him into ministry. John 21 is replete with interesting Greek word studies, usually centered on the theme of love and the varying terms used (*agape* and *fileo*.) The apostle's love for Christ binds him to Jesus' command to "Feed the sheep." Jesus uses the word *bosko* in two occasions; *bosko* literally means to bring them to graze or put out to pasture, to actually give food to the flock. On the other occasion, Jesus uses the word *poymaheeno,* which means to tend as a shepherd.

What does this word study teach us? As a matter of calling to those who love the Lord and are called into such a position, Jesus transfers his authority as the Shepherd to his chosen "stand-in" shepherds. As a side-note, I've been often told that all authority is responsibility based. Pastors bear all the

139

responsibilities of the Shepherd, while not actually possessing ownership of their sheep. Love is the key. Do you love Jesus? The amount for which you love Christ is reflected in your obedience and actions toward your pastor. Jesus loved you enough for the cross; I know many pastors who strive every day to love their flock with such a self-sacrificing love.

"I am the good shepherd: the good shepherd giveth his life for the sheep. But he that is an hireling, and not the shepherd, whose own the sheep are not, seeth the wolf coming, and leaveth the sheep, and fleeth: and the wolf catcheth them, and scattereth the sheep. The hireling fleeth, because he is an hireling, and careth not for the sheep. I am the good shepherd, and know my sheep, and am known of mine. As the Father knoweth me, even so know I the Father: and I lay down my life for the sheep." John 10:11-15 KJV

It's been said that a pastor "works doctor's hours, has the equivalent of a lawyer's education, and has as many bosses as there are members in your church." I would add to that statement, "and takes the wages of a burger flipper." If I took a nonministry job with similar requirements I would want the wages of a doctor. Calling and love are the primary factors which motivates a man or woman to assume the mantle of shepherdship.

The question, then, is do we treat our pastor like a shepherd or a hireling? I've known so many pastors who have been treated like a hireling. In many churches the pastor's duties are dictated by a board or by other quasi-political sub-groups in the congregation through whatever pressure they can assert. The board/elders/deacons have a certain amount of qualifications they must meet for such a position. A pastor's qualifications exceed those, as so should his authority (and thus his or her responsibility). Treating a pastor like a hireling is like making a kindergarten teacher take orders from his or her class. Consistent under-compensation translates to a minister as non-appreciation.

Most of this is directly applicable to senior or lead pastors, but it affects staff ministers as well. In some cases it affects them even more so since most staff pastors are even more grossly underpaid than senior leadership.

Many denominations encourage the recognition of a pastoral/clergy appreciation Sunday or month, even. This is a great idea, though it's often poorly implemented. One pastor friend of mine was on staff at a church that honored their ministers one Sunday for "Pastor Appreciation Sunday." They took a moment to acknowledge and bless their senior pastor with a nice financial gift above and beyond his salary. Then, they recognized the pastoral staff and had them stand in the pulpit for recognition and appreciation of their ministry. They honored them with thirty seconds of uninterrupted clapping. Not only was it awkward, but practically insulting. The congregation just made the subtle statement that only the senior pastor has real worth.

Is your pastor a shepherd or a hireling? Do you follow his leadership and support him or her, or do you or others try and "back-seat" drive the church? Only the pastor should be at steering the wheel; using the map (scripture) you can always feel free to make suggestions, but the pastor is the shepherd. He leads; sheep follow. When the sheep are in the front, the destination is likely the butcher's shop.

Greg Hickle, with his unique position in state-district leadership, has added insight. He spent many years in pastoral ministry and also in an

141

administrative capacity over many other ministers. Essentially, he is a "pastor's pastor," but on Sunday morning, he sits in a church pew like any other churchgoer; he is subject to his younger pastor's leadership. He says that he doesn't always agree with choices and decisions that he's seen made while in his pew, but recognizes that it's not his role to pastor this church. He follows a rule that should be made the standard. "Regardless of my agreement or feelings about a pastor's decision, if it's not illegal, if it's not immoral, and if it's not unscriptural I will support my pastor's decisions." This is a direct result of understanding that authority is responsibility based. It's like school sports. Parents on the sidelines scream at the coach because their child isn't in the game as much as they'd like. These parents aren't in a position to make that substitution—they are not the coach. Parents who have actually volunteered to coach and put time and energy into that role often see a different side to the whole equation.

I've known one particular church (and many others that have seen this scenario as well) where the most prominent givers in the church dictate their preferences to the pastor. If suggestions for service order, music styles, or sermon topics are ignored, they withhold their tithe. This church in particular barely paid its pastor; if the sermon went a few minutes longer than the congregants preferred, or if they felt convicted by Sunday's message instead of championed, the minister literally went unpaid that week. In *every* case in *every* church that this happens, it is a violation of God's will and those who withhold the tithe forcibly remove any chance for God to bless them. Read Malachi. Refusing to give God worship (that's what our giving is—essentially

Christopher Schmitz – Why Your Pastor Left

worshipping God with our wallets) is like a child refusing to tell his parents that he loves them because he didn't get his way. It's immaturity. Mature Christians never attempt to financially manipulate their pastor.

While the church in its current incarnation tends to run itself like a business, we need to recognize that this is not the model Christ established. It was not the structure practiced by the early church.

One church board I'm familiar with ran into financial problems during a transition period. The staff pastor recognized that the budget didn't allow for adequate payment of both positions. The staff pastor had been offered a part-time job a local Christian School; the pay would provide nearly equal compensation if this pastor surrendered a portion of his current wages. The staff pastor could work part-time at the church and also at the school.

A financial advisor to the church board presented this plan and it was determined that the staff pastor would taper his hours and pay accordingly. Soon after, two members of the board were in the business office to write out checks for wages and bills. They suddenly found themselves confused over the issue of paying for medical insurance on the staff pastor. One deacon strongly expressed that the church should stop paying it because, as a business owner, he doesn't pay insurance for part-time employees. They figured they would pay the current month and take the issue up at the next meeting.

At the next board meeting, the discussion ensued and the member presented a strong argument, that, "In the real world, businesses don't pay benefits to part-time employees." The advisor interjected, "*This* is the 'real world.' We should not model our actions after the principles of worldly

Christopher Schmitz – Why Your Pastor Left

business; if anything, *they* should want to model the way we do things, here. I had considered the option of stopping the benefits, but I didn't bring it up because I didn't think anything should change. This pastor recognized that the a senior pastor would need to receive a higher wage than we are able to afford and volunteered to take a pay cut so that God's will can progress in this body." The staff pastor continued receiving medical insurance.

Secular business models mandate decreased costs (wages being part of that) while increasing revenues. The cutthroat nature of free-market business has bred an atmosphere where people are routinely stepped on in order to get ahead. It's like war; all is fair and justifiable as long as costs go down or sales go up. The church is called to be something that the rest of the world aspires to emulate, not to expertly perform the standards of the secular world. If the secular world is sinful, let us not be experts at sinning. We must renew our minds and aspire to a higher principle.

Shepherdship is a principle for how we do "church business." "The *real* world" model is not the proper model for the church. Trying to reconcile the Godly methods with those of the world will always fail. The church only taints itself when it aspires to Donald Trump's standards. We must recognize that this is a fundamental issue of proper "value/worth" setting.

God doesn't view value in the same ways that people do and this leads to frequent inconsistencies in the church. While we claim that we love God with all our hearts and minds, we continually commit the sin of Cain, offering God the things of lesser value and call it "sacrifice." Scripture is full of instances where God's anger burns against His pseudo-worshippers who love Him

Christopher Schmitz – Why Your Pastor Left

outwardly but inwardly hide their valuables beneath their tent. King David does a good job of recognizing the need for value in 2 Samuel 24:24. He is prepared to make a sacrifice to God on the threshing floor where the Death Angel stopped. The thresher wanted to *give* the king all that was required for the sacrifice from his own possessions. David replies, "I will not make a sacrifice that costs me nothing." David recognized a primary principle behind assigning value: value costs something. Jesus did not clap for thirty seconds to free us from sin and death: He laid down His very life because He *valued* us.

How do we value the things of God? Have you ever been to a "church rummage sale?" Nowhere else exists such a collection of unwanted garbage. Whenever a "rummage sale fundraiser" is announced, laity tends to look for things to donate that are broken, unwanted, or are on their way to the dumpster otherwise. Some see it as a convenient way to avoid paying fees to the city dump by dropping items off at the church. What a horrible way to "raise money." I've wondered if bringing my bagged trash to the church donation bin for such an event and putting a $5 sticker on it would make my point. *God doesn't want your refuse.* If you want to honor God, bring in your *good* TV and sacrifice it for Him; *you* keep the thirteen inch black-and-white model as *your* main set. Would that be hard? Of course! It's supposed to be; that's what sacrifice is about!

I met Duke Edwards a couple times in my ministry. He is a respected church planter and missionary to the US as well as a former rodeo rider. At one point in his ministry, he ran a Christian summer-ranch where kids could come

Christopher Schmitz – Why Your Pastor Left

and ride horses, camp, etc. They were always in need of donations and resources.

One day, a woman pulled up with a horse trailer and a donation of two horses. She told Duke how she was moving and didn't have room to take her prized horses with her in the relocation but had heard about the ranch's ministry to children and teens. She went on and on about how she loved the Lord and was so happy that her animals could go somewhere that they could be of great service and kids would be able to ride them. She was giddy with the thought that she could bless his ministry, and the ranchers thanked her profusely for her gift.

While a ranch-hand gave her a tour of the ranch and explained how they ministered to kids, Duke unloaded the horses. The first horse made a terrible clomping noise as it walked. It wasn't until he'd got it out of the trailer and into the nearby riding pen that he noticed this horse only had three legs!

Maybe the horse has learned to compensate for its condition, Duke thought. *She'd said it was intended for children to ride.* He got up on the horse. It took a step forward and tipped over under Duke's added weight. The horse was a danger to any who rode it.

Duke took out the other horse and led it into the arena. This horse had cloudy eyes. Looking closely at it, Duke realized it was blind as a stone. Still operating under the donor's premise that these horses were to be used for ministry—to be ridden by kids—he saddled up. *Maybe they operate in tandem,* he figured. *I've heard of blind horses able to follow wherever a lead horse goes. Maybe the blind one follows the three-legged horse.* He climbed into the saddle and the horse bolted into a gallop and crashed into the fence at the edge of the

146

arena, spilling Duke over. Neither horse was rideable. Both posed dangers to children. Such was this woman's "generous donation."

Showing the ranch-hand the condition of the horses, Duke's friend burst out laughing. He shared a scripture that perfectly the situation.

Malachi 1:7b-8a(NIV) "you ask, 'How have we shown contempt for your name?' By offering defiled food on my altar. But you ask, 'How have we defiled you?' By saying that the LORD's table is contemptible. When you offer blind animals for sacrifice, is that not wrong? When you sacrifice lame or diseased animals, is that not wrong?" The horses fit this description exactly: one was blind, one was lame, and the donor thought this would bring joy to the Lord.

People often donate to pastors figuring that any poor ministers will be happy with any gift they receive, in fact, they have be grateful in order to have Godly character. It's a common cliché, "God, you supply a pastor and we'll keep him humble." Duke's new horses had no value. If anything, they would actually cost the ranch money. The "gift" was useless, but still required the food and maintenance of any other animal.

What is your pastor worth? Doug Self, in Pastoral Ministry Newsletter, calculated the rough dollar value of a typical preacher, albeit tongue in cheek.

- A professional motivational speaker gets $1,500 per speech. Multiply that by the 50 Sundays per year a pastor preaches to get $75,000. (Raise this number accordingly for additional sermons on Sunday evenings and Wednesdays.)

147

- Workshop leaders get $350 a week, which would add another $17,500 per year for pastors who lead classes or teach lessons.

- If you calculate a counselor's fee at $50 per hour, the average pastor's five hours of counseling per week is worth $12,500 a year.

- For home visits, doctors get $62.50 an hour, plumbers $35. Average that to about $50 per hour. A pastor who does fifteen hours of visitation a week should be worth another $37,500 per year.

- For administrative services, a grade-school principal makes around $20 per hour. Thus, a pastor giving fifteen hours a week to administration merits another $15,000 annually.

- All told, the typical pastor should get a yearly salary of about $157,500.[43] (It may be worth noting that this figure was published in 1988; the inflation rate has increased by nearly an additional 51% since that time making the modernized figure over $311,000.)

That's not likely to happen in most churches. The figures above also leave no room for actual sermon prep or developing materials for study or classes. Neither is there room for prayer and personal study or conferences. A typical pastor works far more than forty hours. This is not just a job. It is true what some ministers say, "Being a pastor is the hardest, most under-appreciated,

---

[43] Kessler, J. "Being holy, being human: Dealing with the expectations of ministry." The Leadership library, 1988.

Christopher Schmitz – Why Your Pastor Left

most underpaid job that you will ever love." I once, on a whim, calculated my hourly wage while on staff at a church while receiving what I considered to be a decent wage. It turned out that my wages were on par with local waitresses' hourly rate—except that waitresses also got tips. I was never upset about that; I could truthfully say that I was not ministering for the money but because of the call.

Here is a finding referenced in Leadership, Fall 1992[44]

- 70% indicated their compensation contributed to marriage conflicts
- 22% feel forced to supplement their church income

Current Thoughts & Trends, May 1992[45]

- Over the last 3 years, a typical pastor's salary increased less than 1/2 the inflation rate
- Average increase for 1988-1991 was 7.4%
- Over 40% of single staff pastors felt they were underpaid
- 33% of senior pastors felt they were underpaid

By and large, our culture at large has dishonored and devalued pastors. Because very few pastors publicly speak of this, and because both the survey data and scriptures could argue for a wage increase, this silence is a credit to the general character of pastors.

---

[44] (Wheeler 2012) 37
[45] Ibid.

Christopher Schmitz – Why Your Pastor Left

The common belief is that pastors are/should be poor and should be happy with whatever they get. People forget the danger in invoking God's wrath (God decrees a death sentence for the "Sons of Belial in the second chapter of 1 Samuel because they brought dishonor and resentment to the sacrifice—Verse 17.)

Money is such a touchy issue when we discuss it in the church. Isaiah 1:11-16 says sacrifice is a matter of the heart—even giving good/valuable sacrifices with a wrong heart blemishes that sacrifice. What do you truly value—show your pastor that you value him. Honoring your pastor honors God.

People watch the church; nonbelievers are scrutinizing us. At one church I staffed at, a parishioner actually reached over the pew during worship time and stole my wife's purse. A first-time visitor was the one to witness it and he told me what he'd seen; my wife and I were busy serving during an altar call, forty feet away when it happened. That person never came back.

The church should be the standard that the "real world" desperately wants to emulate. Friends, let's show our faith, respect, reverence, and appreciation in all areas of the church, not compartmentalizing the mission of the church into different boxes: ministry and business, respectively. Rather, our *faith* must impact *the way we "do business."*

Christopher Schmitz – Why Your Pastor Left

Chapter 8

(Ministerial Jealousy)

One of the easiest places to develop a prideful spirit is on a church worship team. People with the gifts and talents to lead public, corporate worship well often find themselves in the crosshairs of the enemy and the weapon is jealousy. All eyes are on that leader and each set of eyes sees someone other than the real person actually leading. They often see a person incapable of having problems, perceiving only his or her incredible gifts and talents. Some will see a person who's as close to God as any human can be. Worshippers who focus on the leader rather than the object of worship tend to see the leader as an archetype of Christian perfection. As time progresses, worship leaders find it easy to subconsciously take those projections onto themselves and assume that same belief.

It is similar for a pastor. Pride can creep in if we don't call it out early in our lives. I frequently satirize this point with a monologue. "You will never find anyone more humble than myself. I'm definitely more humble than *you* are. That's what makes me so great. I should probably win an award for my humility, in fact. I deserve it; someone needs to recognize me for my great achievement in humbleness. I'm so humble that I deserve a trophy, or maybe a medal. Yeah, definitely a medal, then I can wear it around so everyone can see how humble I am."

Christopher Schmitz – Why Your Pastor Left

Pastors can become prideful. We work as leaders of men in a position that demands respect. The job demands talent and skills beyond many peoples' understanding and we daily face situations that scare the daylights out of lesser folk; public speaking alone is cause for trepidation in most. Like worship leaders, because our intents usually start with our hearts focused and centered purely on God, the seeds of pride are usually by some subconscious devil.

Never does jealousy arise so powerfully as when a person has developed a prideful spirit. Jealousy is the explosive reaction we get when prideful expectations do not align with the reality of our daily lives.

I previously mentioned the problem of the nine-month stay. This won't be the last time I reflect on that number, it is one of the things that molded my outlook on ministry and motivated me to write this book. As I prepared in college, I sat in a lecture when an older pastor shared his experience during his younger years. He'd come face to face with jealousy during his internship decades previous. He stated, "I pray that none of you wind up serving under someone like the pastor whom I interned for. He almost ruined me for the ministry."

This pastor came on staff as a ministry intern to work in the church temporarily. As people typically do, the parishioners did their best to make the intern feel welcome and appreciated, perhaps even fawning over the new staff in that "honeymoon period" that typically accompanies a new office.

Whether it was his normal nature or some specific quality in the intern, the pastor became very jealous of the attention given to the new guy. He micromanaged, verbally cut down, and devalued the intern who unwittingly

152

stole some of the pastor's glory. The intern, now a veteran pastor who was preparing others for ministry, speculated that pastor probably felt like an older model in the eyes of his congregation and a side-by-side comparison might reflect poorly upon him. This is what pride can do to a pastor.

The class lecture was directly related to the damage that inter-staff jealousy can do to a ministry. A number of ministers he'd known and even taught had fallen victim to that nine-month statistic, a full-term ministerial abortion, because the hiring pastor was jealous of new staff's skills or other features.

As pastors, we need to know exactly who we are in Christ. We need to understand our calling and know that ministry is not a popularity contest. It is a good pastor that recognizes how every member of his staff or team fulfills a different role, doesn't feel it necessary to be the "best at everything," recognizes his own weaknesses, and who actively seeks to surround himself with people who are better than he or she is at certain aspects of ministry. Doing so brings excellence to Kingdom work.

Good pastors recognize the need for an arm bearer or armor bearer. In the Old Testament we see that Aaron and Hur held up Moses' arms when he was too weak and tired to continue. We also have the example of a king's armor bearers. The armor bearer helped prepare the king for battle by dressing and strapping him into the armor (a feat impossible by oneself.) The armor bearer was also present in battle to guard against attacks to his king's blindside.

Insecure pastors will seek to make themselves the king in their surroundings by refusing to hire or utilize talents of others more skilled than

Christopher Schmitz – Why Your Pastor Left

they in certain areas. When this happens, Kingdom growth is stymied. I've heard of this happening in countless churches, seen it in action, and have been so fortunate as to never have staffed under such a pastor.

Regarding this, both discernment and discretion is a must. I almost did staff under a pastor like this, but felt a check in my spirit and declined a position that was both well-paying and had been my "dream-job" ever since college. After a positive interview, my wife and I had lunch with some of the other staff pastors. Some of the things they spoke about felt divisive to me. They didn't agree with the pastor's direction and methods and felt it incumbent to "warn me" about a few character flaws in their leader, since it looked by all accounts that we would be joining the staff. I really wanted that job, but felt God warn me it would not end well if I took it. The situation was clear: there were too many personalities at work to their own ends, boundaries were not respected, and the pastor didn't "have his house in order" when it came to staff relations. I couldn't bring my family into that scenario and so we declined. Within a year, the entire staff had turned over, and the church had restructured many of its ministries. That specific position turned over at least twice again in the next year and a half. Even had I weathered those storms and retained the job, the position eventually morphed into one that I would not have enjoyed. Spiritual discernment and logic often work as complementary forces.

Pride can be a real ministry killer. Pride is typically self-destructive; when it shifts to a more outward mode, it usually operates through jealousy. God wisely directs pastors to live with a heavy dose of humility. The position I could have taken came with a bit of prestige; it would have boosted my own pride to take the job. I understood that part of declining that offer served to prepare me for something in the future. Perhaps God knew about my secret "superhero-complex," and the position presented itself to me purely for the purpose of future preparation. I don't know. But it humbled me… and I'm still waiting for my trophy/medal, just in case you're wondering. I still have more pride to surrender, but I'm getting there.

Pastors sometimes live life on a pedestal; sometimes our culture thrusts us onto this pedestal. Regardless, we have a natural predisposition to the green-eyed monster. Typically underpaid and over-skilled, we find jealousy can come easily—sometimes the only real, tangible thing our church position provides us is that platform, and so we heavily guard it, keeping close watch over seats of influence. This is *usually* a good thing; we are the gate keepers of the pulpit.

"My church," is a commonly used phrase, but with more than its surface meaning. It is easy for a pastor to begin thinking of their appointment as "his or her church," and forget that role as an under-shepherd. I mentioned earlier how an older minister once asked me what I'd learned through a difficult period I'd endured in a ministry as I prepared to leave. I truthfully replied, "This is not *my* church. It belongs to God, only." Pastors sometimes grab a hold of their office and the duties so fiercely that they lose sight of all else, including God's very will and design.

Jealousy is a monster that every pastor must deal with on his or her own terms. Of course, recognizing that we are susceptible to it is the first step to that end. At a local level, it is natural for a pastor to covet the seeming success that another area minister might be having. Special events and prominent

Christopher Schmitz – Why Your Pastor Left

community interactions can, under the guise of aspiration, entice a pastor to compare oneself and his or her ministry and eventually lead to either prideful vanity or burning jealousy. Of course, the grass is always greener, as the cliché goes, and *from the outside*, another church always seems a better picture of perfection. Coveting the success of another pastor is unwise; the success is likely less than imagined and inheriting their success also means taking over their problems, too. At the onset of ministerial disillusionment, jealousy finds its first foothold.

At a more national level, countless pastors watch the success of prominent ministers with perfect hair, manicured looks, and movie star glamour. There seems no end to their book deals, national influence, and media attention. Pastors from every walk watch and observe these elite. Every house of worship aspires to be the next Mars Hill or Saddleback church, rising to success and impacting a broad area for the good of Christ's Kingdom. For some pastors, their observation goes beyond observing successful, savvy pastors in an effort to glean useful techniques that they can assimilate for their own uses. Some pastors, especially disillusioned pastors, find that jealousy of successful ministers, either local or national, can give them a bitter spirit, especially when mimicry and imitation of the pastoral stereotype fails to achieve the success they dreamed of.

There is a difference, mind you, between jealousy and striving for greater effectiveness. The line between jealousy and a minister's desire to implement techniques and methods that are working effectively for other pastors is a broad, gray line. Don't assume a license to accuse a pastor of jealousy or

Christopher Schmitz – Why Your Pastor Left

"trying to be like" every other pastor whose had success. As a pastor, I could only interpret such a claim as disgruntlement with a new direction or method and a resulting refusal to follow Godly leadership.

Only the pastor, or person, can realize when they are genuinely jealous; never make such an accusation, but allow the Spirit of God to work in their life. It is not the duty of another to point out jealousy in their peers and leaders. Because jealousy is rooted in pride, the bearer of such an accusation, true or not, can only damage themselves. The proper course is to pray and expect God to make a radical change. Just beware that it might be yourself that God asks to change and not the object of your intercession.

For those of us Walt Disney Generation pastors out there, we find it especially easy to succumb to the green-eyed monster. WDG pastors typically want their success now. We've been told that we are going to do great things, prayed over, prophesied over, trained, and equipped by human standards, but we do not like our forty-years in the desert. Moses did his time in the desert before the big showdown in Egypt. Joseph waited in the prison. That seeming obscurity drives us nuts.

In my first ministry I had to face my own prideful nature. Luckily, God always knows just what we need and he dealt with me privately during some personal Bible study. Reading scripture can actually save you a lot of embarrassment.

My first ministry was as a youth pastor, and no matter what I did, I couldn't grow my ministry past a certain point. Every time we started to increase numerically beyond my core group of teens, a portion of them would

157

depart and become a permanent part of a different ministry that was literally "just down the road."

In the neighboring town, just a few miles away, another church of the same denomination had a massive youth group. In fact, the group was so large that it created a bit of a vacuum in the community. The church happened to be run by a guy I'd met just once or twice in college and happened to be a part of the same denomination I was affiliated with. Because the group was large, it was well funded, which made the cycle continue. Most teenagers in the area that attended youth group were somehow connected to that ministry.

As kids came and eventually went, it was hard not to feel as if I was in competition with the other youth pastor. Of course, we both operated within the same denominational lines and so we often did joint events and attended the same camps and conventions, which ensured that I couldn't get away from the fact that, by way of direct comparison, his was bigger. To be perfectly crass, the secular world calls this "penis envy." It's rarely a matter of actual anatomy, but the analogy is apt. We always have some reason for insecurity, whether it's the size of our truck's mud tires or breadth of our own library: analogous comparison breeds envy.

I wondered how my peer had been so successful. He'd been in the area a couple years before I'd come. I wanted to discover what he'd done in those years so that I could learn how I might employ similar success, so we had some conversations. Of course I came to discover how God took him deeper before He took him wider. My peer's first ministry there grew from large numbers down to a handful as he adopted a missional, sincere attitude to ministry. Only

158

then, on the proper foundation, did the ministry grow with stability. The fun, games, music, and other things that accompany a dynamic youth ministry came again, but later, after the focus was proper. Teens were drawn to a sincere ministry that was growing because it grew you. That's a lot to learn—and it takes time to incorporate.

About that time, I was reading in the Gospel of John. I've always been a bit of a John the Baptist sort of character, so I often gravitate to scriptures surrounding him. In John 3:22-36 we find that both John and Jesus were baptizing people in the same area and John's disciples began to get jealous, seemingly offended by the turf war. Specifically, they were irked that more people were going to Jesus than to them (verse 26) and after all, wasn't John first?

John wisely points out that God gives each their own ministry and it's not their business to dictate to God how things should be. A truly Kingdom-minded approach is to recognize that they were both on the same side, working towards the same goal. John understood that he and Jesus were ministry partners, each doing what was appointed and allotted to them in their specific roles.

While I didn't grow by leaps and bounds after incorporating that epiphany into my ministry model, I did feel more stable as I found my own place in ministry. My ministry grew, but it was mostly internal, and God always wants to take us deeper so that he can take us broader. Jealousy was not something I wanted within my own life, so I'm grateful that this realization came early in my career.

Christopher Schmitz – Why Your Pastor Left

Jealousy creates pastor-dictators who compulsively grab and hold onto more and more, constantly trying to amass the power that they need to maintain their position and authority. Pastor-dictators see strength of character and vibrancy in other ministers or leaders (in their own church or outside of it) as potential usurpers to their throne.

Only in recognizing what John the Baptist did can we avoid becoming a Darth Vader. In Star Wars (IV) Princess Leia tells her captors, "The more you tighten your grip… the more star systems will slip through your fingers!" Releasing ministerial purpose and destiny into God's hands is freeing.

Holding onto jealousy and pride with human authority takes such constant vigilance that it wears out a pastor and can burn him or her out or cause disillusionment. Disillusionment only feeds the cycle.

Jealousy-based disillusionment or resentment is explosive in all situations. When it goes off in the close-quarters of a ministerial team, there are bound to be multiple casualties and injuries. As much as I've laid out demanding support for the lead/senior pastor, sometimes your beloved staff pastor(s) left because their superior forced them out. As wrong as that can be, it is still incumbent upon you to support your senior pastor. Pray for them, talk with them, encourage them, and understand them and the burdens that accompany ministry. When insecurity is removed, those problems can be rectified and the balance of ministry can be restored. Any insecurity that your pastor might have cannot be dissolved if he does not have your personal support. A ministry can only begin to become healthy and balanced from the top down.

160

So how does one refocus a jealous staff pastor? Loyalty and stability are primary keys. A shepherd can make better time and more accurately chart his course if he doesn't have to divert and chase down sheep that have wandered off and if he isn't constantly watching over his shoulder for signs of a coup.

One of my pastor friends recently called me after being fired from his church staff position. He told me about what had happened and how he'd upset a couple of key people in his church by preaching the offensive Gospel of Christ (much as I had done) and standing on the solid word of God. Because he'd caused some discomfort in their midst by opening his Bible, he paid for his "mistake" with his job. His senior pastor didn't have his back when it came to those key people in the velvet pew.

I advised my friend the best I could when he told me how many members in the church wanted to meet together and storm the pastor's office as a group and express their anger. "Do all you can to distance yourself from that," I advised him. "It doesn't matter how much they love you or how wrong your termination might have been. Really, angry mobs can only plant seeds of division at this point."

I told him that he should probably do whatever he could to discourage his supporters from meeting together under this angry agenda. Their point would be best taken if each supporting family met separately with their pastor to express their concerns. Not only does this stop a witch-hunt, but only in smaller numbers can anything actually be accomplished. A large group with an agenda becomes an unyielding witch-hunt and is hard to reason with.

"At this point, just do your best not to do something really bad. Kick the dust off your feet and look for where God would have you next. You just don't want to be responsible for something that can damage your reputation further down the road and limit your future in ministry." That was the same advice that I had been given by an older, wiser minister.

So far, this entire chapter has been about jealousy on the part of the senior pastor. The green-eyed monster is not limited to pastoral fallout from the office of a senior pastor, however. Staff pastors have been known to succumb to the seductive words of insurgent power seekers in the church or grasp power themselves and grasp at the office of their superior.

Jealousy isn't only wielded by members of the clergy, either. We've all had to grapple with this at some point in our own lives, but it can easily infiltrate a church and damage it incredibly when it's not handled properly.

What happens when older members harbor excessive pride for their own "glory days," or maintain the belief that "God's presence just isn't here like it used to be?" Because God is life, moving, active, always relevant, the pride and longing for the "good old days" can cause resentment and jealousy on the part of older believers (or long time believers) and a newer generation of Christians. This plays directly into those "worship wars" and tension that sometimes exists between those factions within a church body. Truthfully, there should be *no factions at all*, with our call to unity. Don't compare or pursue those days long gone! His presence is always more alive in the present. We cannot gain more of Him by going *back*, where he cannot operate except via nostalgia.

Christopher Schmitz – Why Your Pastor Left

Pastors operate in a precarious place. They are called on to stand in a public, visible stage and live transparent lives under a solemn call. Their followers call on them to operate continually at high levels beyond human capacity—hence, no person can truly perform this task except by the grace of God. As ascetic as it sounds, ministers covet more duty, more responsibility, a grander stage, a taller pedestal. Help your pastor out; be on task—build that relationship to help safeguard his or her spirit from jealousy.

Just because a pastor finds himself on a pedestal in the public world, it does not mean that this pedestal should be a lonely place. Pastors need to be affirmed, encouraged, and followed. Love and support your minister. Help him or her bring balance to his or her ministry for your sake, their sake, the sake of the church staff, and the sake of the Kingdom.

Chapter 9

Respect in the church

I can't seem to ask myself the definition of *respect* without hearing Aretha Franklin belting out those lyrics in my mind, "R-E-S-P-E-C-T! Find out what it means to me." For me, the idea of respect is burned into my mind with thoughts of fire and the concept of *the fear of the Lord.* I can remember being taught as a child in a church service that we need not cower in fear or experience terror from the Lord, but that *fear of the Lord* means having a healthy respect for Him, like understanding the power and heat in a curling iron or an open flame. Fear, or respect, is recognizing boundaries and authorities for what they are and bearing in mind the consequences of disrespecting that boundary. Grabbing onto a curling iron as a kid taught me something: respect it, know it, use it properly.

Respect is all about properly balanced *love* in unity with *boundaries.* It's the love that is sincere enough to give a firm, negative reinforcement when needed. I can remember being spanked as a child; as clear as day I recall my parents telling me that they loved me too much to *not* punish me. I certainly didn't feel it at the time, but I understand that as a parent, now. It is a disservice to a child when we warn him or her against some action and then spare them the rod. It irks me to see parents count, "One… two… two and a half… two and three quarters… two and thirteen sixteenths…"

We are probably all familiar with daytime television shows like Dr. Phil and Montel Williams. Regularly, these shows feature a panel of teens that are simply out-of-control and also their parents who have no idea what went wrong or how to fix it. Sadly, this can sometimes be the picture of the church as well. I've witnessed both sides: pastors who abuse the sheep and sheep who walk all over their pastors. Abusive ministers don't last long; they acquire a reputation and fade into the shadows. Pastors who let their sheep take advantage of loose boundaries can be found frequently.

Admittedly, weak pastors are partly to blame for laity that walk all over the clergy. Two factors largely contribute to a ministerial predisposition to this leaning. Firstly, our culture inclines us to be push-overs. Ministers are often judged by quantifiable means (number of new converts or attendance counts) and that, combined with the seeker-sensitive movement, have geared us to be "nice" at the cost of our own boundaries and core values. (We bend over backwards to make visitors want to come back—but face it, only God can draw them back… the church can't compete under human power; we don't stand a chance against televised football, Xbox, and Facebook.) Secondly, I don't see enough of an effort to train our leaders in how to handle conflict. Interpersonal conflict is an elephant in the room/pastor's office. Conflict was addressed, but were I advising Bible Colleges and ministerial training programs, I would emphasize a need for intensive training in this area.

165

Researching stress in the ministry, I was reading a textbook geared for ministerial conduct. I came across a brief paragraph regarding conflict. The advice was simple: get professional training! I think too many pastoral training programs assume that everyone in the church treats each other with basic human decency. Conflict training should be a mandate; we live in much less friendly times than those gone by—human decency is an oxymoron anyway. My personal training came from a combination of bivocational sales techniques and working with incarcerated teens (where they actually taught techniques to diffuse tense situations.) I've actually used many of those techniques that I learned in that setting, where I would deal with potentially violent adolescents, in church situations. Who's to say that violence can't reach inside the walls of a church? I personally know at least two pastors who have been assaulted on church grounds by their parishioners. We are, after all, assemblies of human beings and that means we bring our own set of emotions into the body with us.

Boundaries are everywhere. I learned at one institution that a person should stand perpendicular to any person that might be hostile—this posture minimizes your profile, making you appear slightly smaller, and can help diffuse hostility. On the other hand, squaring up your posture to them makes it seem as if you are trying to make your profile more imposing, asserting dominance. I've used this advice a lot, it can affect the tone of a conversation, and it's all subliminal. Utilizing body language is part of being an effective communicator. Church leadership

Christopher Schmitz – Why Your Pastor Left

should understand that physical boundaries have implications to mental ones. One of the things I learned in cultural studies is that everybody has different physical boundaries. In some ethnic groups, people will carry a conversation with their faces hovering inches away from each other. I've known people from other ethnic groups where physical boundaries are substantial. For example, the Hawaiian men that I've known get uncomfortable if you interact with them while any closer than arm's length.

Knowing and respecting both physical and mental boundaries are very important in the ministry. I've known many pastors who never take a day off, they drop everything to address an "emergency" that turns out to be nothing more than Anxious Annie needing her pastor to hold her hand. Sometimes pastors need to draw a hard line and cut that cord. Jesus should be that lifeline to security; a pastor who constantly assumes that role can actually stymie Annie's faith and reliance on the Lord. It also crosses boundaries for the pastor's family. The family of a pastor (spouse and children) that is consistently "abandoned" because of the needs of others will grow to resent the ministry, the church, parishioners, and even God at times. Pastors, and their families, need those times together. The pastor needs regular time off. While matters of life and death are always priority, parishioners should consciously respect a pastor's days off. (Don't worry, giving him or her a day off won't allow them to "abuse the time-clock." I consistently took a regular day off in my last pastorate and still worked too much; I averaged over seventy

167

hours a week and turned off my phone on Thursdays and every-other Saturday.)

Part of pastoral burnout and blurred borders is because modern shepherds are too afraid to use the rod to make a sheep mind the boundaries. Shepherds possess both a rod and a staff. The staff is for gentle guidance; the rod is basically a club. It wasn't only meant for warding off predators; sometimes positive reinforcement isn't enough to get the point across. I know that I risk coming off as a harsh, villain of a pastor who wants to beat on sheep—but this is untrue of me. I want to establish boundaries. How do we reassert our boundaries to swing the pendulum back to the proper balance of power? Ask teens who've had total freedom if a parent seems harsh or restrictive when they start asserting their boundaries with negative reinforcements (punishment). Sometimes the club is mandated; it's another one of those uncomfortable scriptural directives. But once a boundary is allowed to be pushed back it is difficult to ever regain it.

That said, pastors should be mindful to pick their battles and not need to come down on every issue. Really, this is helpful advice for anybody *not* living the life of a solitary hermit. Also, clear boundary violations should always be addressed in the same forum that they came in and a person's boundaries should be made clear so that people know where they begin and where they end. Clear, unimpeded communication is the goal and boundaries are critical to that. Basic, dignified respect is the vehicle that travels within those boundaries.

Christopher Schmitz – Why Your Pastor Left

Soccer moms and hockey dads need to remember their place and check themselves at the door. Throwing gas on a fire always has a way of coming back and burning your own eyebrows off. There is a clear and distinct difference between fans/cheerleaders and a team's coach. Remember that authority is tied to responsibility—the cheerleaders share no blame in a team's loss or performance. I write this after NFL head coaches Brad Childress and Wade Phillips were fired as Head Coaches of the Minnesota Vikings and Dallas Cowboys, respectively, amid seasons plagued by shoddy performance. *They* shared the brunt of responsibility for the team's performance. I'm not aware of any pro or amateur sports teams ever firing their cheerleaders for losing seasons. If you are not the coach and not a player, you are a cheerleader. You may make noise, but you have neither responsibility nor authority.

What does respect entail? Specifically, in regards to ministry, what is different than being a CEO or business leader? There is only one real difference and that is the divine calling of God. Ironically enough, despite being hand-picked by the eternal, almighty God of the Universe, Pastors typically get less respect than corporate leaders or business officials. Honor a pastor (even a staff pastor or ministry associate) at least as much as you would the head manager of the bank you utilize or the superintendent or principal of the school your child attends.

I know that it seems blatantly obvious to respect a pastor, but disrespect has become a cultural norm—not just in the ministry, but everywhere authority exists. Often, disrespect comes from within a

Christopher Schmitz – Why Your Pastor Left

church or community. Sometimes it comes from other "competing" churches or ministers because of doctrinal chaffing, personal conflict, jealousy, or downright meanness. While the necessity of respect is palpable, it's easy to overlook it in everyday situations. I've made a non-exclusive list of *some* of the areas where it's easy to violate that boundary and either purposefully or unwittingly disrespect your pastor.

Respect in Financial Areas of Ministry. A pastor should be expected to be able to handle his administrative duties. Those duties typically involve handling money or at least overseeing the overall accountability of the church's finances, even if he is not the person writing the check. Many churches utilize other methods, utilizing the skills of deacons, elders, secretaries, other paid staff, etc. Like all things in life, finances are a necessary part of keeping a ministry moving. A pastor is responsible for the overall health of his or her ministry and thus is a critical component to the financial structure of a church or ministry.

Pastors are placed in a position of trust. Some surveys have pointed out that ministers were once the most trusted people in a community; that status has radically changed in the past five decades so that bankers are now the highest trusted professionals. Don't let the secular standards discredit the pastorate. Money is critical, but it's God that makes the church advance. If not the highest authority in a ministry's financial flow-chart, a pastor should be in the top-tiers. Staff pastors, likewise, need a certain amount of control over the budgets for their ministry areas.

Christopher Schmitz – Why Your Pastor Left

Many people have confused the idea of accountability with blatant mistrust. I am in favor of various systems of checks and balances, but a pastor without budget input/control over key areas (direction) becomes nothing more than a spiritual public speaker. Finances are a key rudder to a ministry's direction; a pilot can't fly an airplane anywhere but into the ground if a passenger in the rear is controlling the flaps.

Respect in Authority/Judgment Decisions. A pastor is someone who has been trained to lead. Essentially, they must lead. It sounds stupid that I'd even need to make that point, but people from outside the ministry "chain of command" frequently restrain a minister, hijack the decision making process, or criticize/undercut a pastor's judgment.

A pastor makes decisions for very specific reasons with the good of the ministry being prayerfully considered. It is an objective role that a leader must take, putting aside personal concerns in pursuit of the vision that has been cast. Pastors must plan a strategy to bring their ministry to the place that they envisioned.

In his *The Character of Brother Lawrence*, the author and friend of the seventeenth century French monk shares the story of how Brother Lawrence handled his disagreement with his ministry superiors. "I remember telling him without any forewarning that a matter of great consequence to him, and one, on which he had set his heart and long labored for, could not be carried out, as the superiors had made up their minds against it… he replied, 'We must believe they have good reasons for their decision, and our duty now is to obey…' he had many occasions to speak of it afterwards, he not so much as opened his mouth thereon."[46]

Oftentimes, other people wish to purposefully insert themselves into roles they desire for personal reasons. For example, one day I had the president of the church board and his wife in my office; they were livid. Their daughter and son were not on the Youth Group's worship team. I faced all sorts of accusations and resentment. The deacon and his wife insisted that my decisions, (based on the college training which prepared me to arrive at my conclusions,) were, *just plain wrong*." All the money and years I studied in university were an apparent waste since they taught me to arrive at a different vision for the youth ministry's worship team. It's funny that the most qualified person to make those decisions, one who's responsible for the whole of the ministry and is the closest to the situation (the parent/deacons had never attended a parent-meeting, a youth service, or met for a private meeting or even coffee despite my requests,) so often has their decisions challenged. In this specific case, I had already asked their daughter to join the team and she had, unknown to her parents, declined. People often jump to conclusions and villainize/criticize a leader without ever communicating with him or her directly.

This sort of situation is extremely common. Disrespect by undercutting a pastor's authority is even more common when the pastor is younger. Ministers must rely chiefly on the support of God and not

---

[46] (Lawrence 2009) 93, 94

Christopher Schmitz – Why Your Pastor Left

their human experiences, which is why Paul could justly advise the young pastor Timothy, who was about thirty, "Don't let anyone look down on you because you are young," (I Tim 4:12a). *Jesus* was only about thirty when he began *his* ministry. Remember, if you're not the coach you are a cheerleader. Cheerleaders don't call plays.

Respect for Personal Boundaries. Pastors are people too. All human beings deserve a basic modicum of respect. This is sometimes overlooked for pastors because of the thought that he is "everybody's employee." That's simply not true; he or she is God's employee. However, there is a general attitude of ownership out there that says: "1. We give money to the church. 2. Pastor receives a wage/parsonage from the church. 3. Therefore, we are his/her boss. Especially when the pastor receives a parsonage is this felt. I've heard many stories of pastors coming home and seeing nosy parishioners inside their home snooping around in their absence, or they're inside the ministry home in the morning when the pastor wakes up. Given the above, the invasion is justified because "this house is the really the church's so I'm entitled access." That is a huge breach of personal boundaries

Countless other personal boundaries exist. Some of them include the pastor's family, how a pastor raises his children, what the pastor drives, the pastors chosen hobbies and peers/friends, and private data including personal retirement, investment, medical treatment choices, legal, and banking data. If your pastor is comfortable sharing this data, or wants you to know it, that's his or her prerogative.

173

I've never felt a bigger attempted intrusion into my personal boundaries than when a church secretary insisted I turn over my personal credit card information to her in order to receive a reimbursement. I'd floated several thousand dollars' worth of annual convention registration fees on my personal credit card because the church's account had limits lower than needed and all prepaid registrations had to be made via credit card. It wasn't a worry to me because we had a process in place for paying reimbursements and all these registration funds had been deposited into the churches' general account already. I'd already utilized this system many times for reimbursements. The secretary insisted it would be easier if I inserted her as a middleman in my personal banking procedures and would give her my account numbers, etc. so she could access them and make payments directly. I told her, "I'm uncomfortable giving you that information and just want you to cut me a check for personal reimbursement, as usual." She requested my info on at least three separate occasions, sidestepping my request for the check I was owed. Finally, in my absence, she approached my wife and asked her to turn over that information so that we could be repaid. That's intrusion, manipulation, and blatant disrespect. Never put your pastor through that. From then on, I felt that I must always have my defenses up in the church business office.

I've heard it said that, "If your pastor wants to drive a Mercedes and eat nothing but Mac and Cheese, that's his decision to make." I've let that be my guiding principle on how I view *my* pastors. I assume that their priorities, while different, are balanced in their own life.

Remember that he or she is human and deserves those same respects as others. Would you treat your close, personal friends in the same manner as you would your pastor? Choose to honor them *at least* as much as you do your closest friends, as a general rule of thumb, and you should be fine.

Respect Their Personal Life. This is similar to personal boundaries, but I consider it different because the focus is different. Personal boundaries can be moved at a person's discretion and personal comfort levels. It is good sense to always consider the fact that pastors have their own lives separate and distinct from pastoral duties. His or her identity as a minister is unchanged, we are representatives of Christ wherever we go, but pastors do have their own lives and families.

A pastor must be free to live that life outside the beck and call of parishioners when he or she is "on their own time." While a minister might lay down some of their personal time or hobbies to meet a need of their congregation or deal with some "emergency," there are some areas that they should never be asked to compromise. We live in the "microwave generation" in America. This is not a generational factor but a cultural attitude of instant gratification. What seems, in a moment, to be so urgent can usually wait for your pastor's attention until his or her next scheduled business hours begin. The exceptions, of course, are for

175

matters of life and death. It is only narcissism that could demand we dictate *our* schedule to the minister.

A pastor's family should never have to take a back seat to the flock of sheep. Such a position de-elevates the importance of a pastor's family. This always hurts the pastor's family members and stresses a pastor's marriage (assuming a spouse, if married).

1 Timothy 3 gives us a list of qualities and character traits that should be inherent or previously developed should one aspire to the role of overseer or pastor. These are each aspects of his or her personal life; you should never intrude on situations involving maintenance of those aspects, especially involving the upkeep of a healthy marriage (verse 2) or the maintenance of his family (verse 4). Never interrupt pastor's date night, and never, ever take a pastor's time away from their kids. The church does not own a pastor or his or her schedule. Be sure to award them vacation and scheduled time off.

It's such a simple thing to check your pastor's agenda in advance and request meetings as needed; they will make room if they can. If it seems like an emergency, and some things really are, try waiting until the next day. It won't likely kill you and you may find you've found deeper perspective—even discerning the will of God on your own overnight.

I once had a church board schedule an impromptu church work-day at the parsonage that my family lived in. The meeting was scheduled on Thursday for the coming Saturday. I was expected to lead the effort, contacting people in the church to come and help. My schedule was

176

already full, however. My presence would have required canceling a ministry event that had been scheduled six months prior, was a keystone event in another person's ministry, and in which I'd invested many, many hours of preparation—far more hours than it would take to pull weeds from the parsonage lawn.

It may sound like my ministry is full of bad experiences. That isn't the case. The good has far exceeded the bad, but these stories from my personal experiences prove that seemingly little issues are *easy* to overlook, but have huge cumulative, detrimental factors. On their own, they are minor irritations, but collectively they become ministry killers.

Respect Their Ministry. It has become a modern cliché that we recognize the 80/20 rule. The generalism is that twenty percent of the people do eighty percent of the work. Of course the point is that everyone should have an active part in the church, not just show up. In our consumer culture (not just Americans as buyers, but people who simply consume and take, take, take,) it has become the nature of our majority to make demands for satisfaction while offering nothing in return. The Bible calls these people Sluggards (read Proverbs 21:25; 26:16; and 18:9) and the statistic begs the question: if the majority of churchgoers are sluggards, what does that say about the church as a whole? Also, remember that "sloth" is one of the so-called "deadly sins." I think the statistics are worse, personally. In my experience, about five to ten percent of a congregation does ninety percent of the work.

Christopher Schmitz – Why Your Pastor Left

People don't typically like to do work, or sacrifice. I get that. Only the psychotic and the masochistic willingly subject themselves to personal displeasure. When our eyes are on the future reward in heaven, however, we see that sacrifice is meant with a higher goal in mind: one that pays off in the end. Human nature, that comfort-seeking part of ourselves, makes it easy for us to find excuses for joining the eighty percent crowd and shirking. I remember one older minister lamenting that he desperately craved revival and the congregation publicly huzzaed the aspiration, but the prayer meetings scheduled to birth the seeds of revival consistently numbered single digits... usually needing only part of one hand to count attendance. Another pastor I spoke with charted his attendance records versus his annual calendar. Attendance increased roughly four hundred percent the weeks surrounding big, fun events and fell to abysmal levels when they had regularly scheduled service projects; nobody would work. They offset both events regularly, and held them on a quarterly basis, so his graph showed: summit, grave, Everest, Mariana, Wenzhaun, Death Valley, mountain top, canyon. The line never plateaued; he had four peaks and four pits because everybody scrambled for the door when the four-letter "W" word came up.

It is a sign of an immature, weak Christian if you only attend the "fun" events and refuse anything that will stretch or grow you. Ministry is not entertainment! This is one of the major downfalls that the seeker-sensitive movement has injected into the subculture of Christianity. The stress inherent in many ministries today is not the preparation of a

178

Christopher Schmitz – Why Your Pastor Left

message or planning a smooth and orderly service: it's getting people to show up, especially if it's any service or "extra event" beyond a Sunday morning worship service.

If you want to demonstrate respect, here's my advice: show up! Get involved in ministry. The 80/20 rule stresses pastors out. In a calendar year, I scheduled 3 meetings for parents of teens, sent letters, advertised, gave personal invites, promised food and childcare, begged and pleaded. I never had a single parent show up (and these were done on my day off/evenings after I was told by some parents that it would be the only time that would work into their schedule). Make your presence known! A shepherd with no sheep is just a lonely guy with a crooked stick.

Partner with pastors to make them more effective. Don't expect your pastor/shepherd to lead you anywhere if you refuse to follow! If your pastor has been accused of being ineffective, the usual culprit for his ineffectiveness is the refusal of his or her sheep to cooperate. Remember that shepherds tend to the flock. Shepherds shepherd; sheep make sheep. Both roles have a distinct and separate calling. Ministry cannot happen without *you*.

Other pastors also need to respect their peers and should always strive to respect those serving under them. Narcissism is rampant in America; with programs meant to turn us all into WDGs and give us obscene self-esteem boosts, most everyone in America believes that *they* should be in charge, rather than their current boss. Typical American

Christopher Schmitz – Why Your Pastor Left

pride means it is never easy to take a "back seat" role to the senior pastor's ministry. Tension or resentment can be the result of "micro-managing" a ministry peer.

I remember working on a construction crew that was run by a wild-eyed, foul-mouthed micro-manager. He showed me exactly how he wanted each siding shake placed and hung—but he insisted on a method that was irregular, slow, illogical, and inefficient. In fact, I'm pretty sure that the packaging itself advised a wholly different method. The boss stood there for four hours watching me work to ensure that I followed his procedure, and cussing up a blue streak because it was taking too long. The other workers walked back and forth chuckling to themselves because they had all taken their own turn in similar situations. I guess it was too much; most of that crew walked out on him one day, abandoning him (only the foreman and I were willing to stay).

This is similar to the picture of David in Saul's tent before the battle with Goliath. Saul tries to fit David with his armor. I like how the Veggietales version puts it when Dave says, "You know, I think I should just be plain old me." People in managerial roles often dictate not just what to do, but exactly how to do it. Sometimes this is necessary, but it's not always the best method when you have qualified people working under you, people who have the training and education to see them through.

David couldn't be God's man if he went into battle trying to be Saul. Staff pastors are an extension of the senior pastor's ministry, but need to be themselves while doing it—they can't do it looking just like someone else. If someone else could do that particular ministry better, then God would have called that person to the office instead. Empower your ministry peers and release them to do the work of the Lord.

Respect Their Calling. A church in Fargo, North Dakota has a youth pastor on staff, Cal Thompson, who has been a dedicated youth minister for over twenty years. His ministry has been earmarked by some incredible events over the years, such that he was invited as guest on a nationally syndicated morning television show. One of the things that Youth Pastors will inevitably face is the attitude and belief by parishioners that people only assume a job as a Youth Minister as a stepping stone to garner ministry experience before he or she decides to pursue a Senior Pastorate. Ministers such as Cal Thompson in Fargo break that mold and prove that ministry, all aspects and roles, are a matter of calling, not of convenience or rungs on a ladder.

The ministry is full of niches and sub-groups where God will specifically gift and call people. In my experiences, I've seen a great deal of disrespect given to staff pastors because they "aren't a real pastor." The thought is that, since a staff pastor/youth pastor/worship pastor/etc. is not the senior pastor, their call is of a lesser nature or they are worthy of less honor and respect. In fact the belief that these are just "stepping stone" positions has created a culture of temporary stewardship in America.

Christopher Schmitz – Why Your Pastor Left

People within a church congregation don't always understand the traditional training for most ministers. It had always been my intention to work in Youth Ministry forever; ministries like Cal's were the ones to emulate. At a collegiate level, in order to pursue this, I received the same basic training that any other graduate would receive who was pursuing a role as a Senior/Lead/or only Pastor. At the credentialing level, I passed the same tests, interviews, and peer reviews as any other minister including senior pastors. On top of that, I received additional training for the specialty work of youth ministry. If anything, specialty pastors often have additional education to prepare them for their roles. Scripture reveals that there are a number of different callings, giftings, etc. While some of them include extra responsibility (and hence authority) none of them should be less respected or less desired.

One of the differences in roles is that of social groups within the church structure. The group at the "top of the food-chain" has more interaction with the senior pastor than with staff pastors. Logically, those with greater financial influence in the church will be drawn to greater interaction with the Senior Pastor; the next generation of these people, however, are currently being formed and molded by the Children's and Youth Pastors. All of these people, child to adult, are of equal and infinite value to the Lord. It is not the value or importance of the people a minister works with that dictates the degree of respect and honor is due a pastor—it is all equal. There is a difference in responsibility and authority (which is tied to wage and Kingdom reward). The calling of a pastor to

Christopher Schmitz – Why Your Pastor Left

greater or lower offices does not affect the respect and reverence due that minister. My spirit aches whenever I hear a ministry peer referred to as, "Just the Youth Pastor," or hear that someone is, "only the Seniors' Pastor."

I'm merely pointing out the importance of calling is not lessened by the role within the church. The Senior Pastor is obviously of paramount importance and has full authority over his ministry staff. He or she is also worthy of a greater wage, as scripture would recommend. But both ministers serve the same Master and the same kingdom and both work towards the same goal, yet fulfilling different functions.

Any vocation in which a person works in the full-time service of the Lord is worthy of respect: from the Senior Pastor to the Church Janitor. This is a lesson that even many older ministers need to understand. I believe that the loss of respect of a much younger or much older pastor's peers is the reason they leave vocational ministry. Younger pastors refuse to meet this human notion of the necessity of "putting in time" to be worthy of consideration (especially since it was God who called them and not a man.) Many elderly ministers who haven't had the call of God lift from their lives have been made to feel as if they have nothing left to offer. Both are false.

I confided in one ministry superior I'd been struggling to please that, "I feel like you don't respect me." To which he bluntly replied, "You're not worthy of my respect." In an instant, the cohesiveness of the ministerial staff was shattered. I asked why not and he replied that he'd

183

ministered through the 1960s and that there was a movement which formally stated we will not trust anyone over thirty. He stated, "You're not yet thirty." The pastor didn't realize or remember that he'd actually been at my thirtieth birthday party. I quoted 1 Timothy 4:12 to him, an effort to plead my case. He quoted Jack Weinberg/Jerry Rubin, hippie activists, as a valid response to overrule the apostle Paul.

Respect is due across the board—and it is a two way street. I, for one, am utterly and sincerely thankful for those who are called to serve where most dare not. You nursery workers and church custodians: I tip my hat and salute you. Age, gender, calling, I don't care; I love and respect any minister that stands on the Word of God—and even more so those who do so in sacrifice.

Respect Their Sacrifice. No job demands as great a sacrifice as your pastor's. Pastors give up a lot in order to acquire the proper training and education required for such a position. Oftentimes, those taking pastoral jobs turn down more prestigious job possibilities earlier in life in order to pursue the calling to ministry. It's a great sacrifice and not one that ends there. Often, a pastor finds that later in life they cannot get out of the ministry if they want to because they are basically unqualified for anything else. Pursuing pastoral ministry is like jumping off a cliff; a pastor holds faith that the plunge will be appreciated, that they will splash down in the water as intended and not crash down upon the rocks. Scripture talks about stumbling blocks. It's hard enough to leave everything else behind and hurl oneself over the precipice without others throwing boulders into their path.

Pastors, by necessity of maintaining their authority, are sometimes called upon to draw a hard line in the sand. There are some situations in which a pastor must call people out on their sin or lead an initiative for change. A minister without that authority has no real way to lead: all his or her pleas, revelations, convictions, and ultimatums from the Lord will fall upon deaf ears if the line between authority and obedience has been blurred.

When I was studying in college, one of my ministry professors spoke extensively on this topic. Because we humans are creatures built for relationships, one of the greatest sacrifices a pastor will make is in the area of intimate relationships. "In order to maintain those boundaries," the professor told us, "you won't be able to have as many close friendships as 'regular people.'" I can tell you that his words were true. Usually, the only other people that understand what it is that a pastor does are other fellow pastors in similar situations.

People will often try to manipulate others for their own personal purposes. Pastors are not immune to this. Others may try to work their way inside the pastor's inner sphere for various purposes; thus, ministers often need to assert boundaries more rigidly than others. A minister's sense of boundaries must be acutely clear to his or her parishioners because of the necessity of authority inherent in the call.

185

Relationships are just one of the areas where people sacrifice if they enter the ministry. Understand that your pastor bears a burden in prayer, in thought, in time and energy, all borne in support for the flock. By the very nature of the call and the duties demanded, pastors work longer, harder, and for fewer wages than any comparable position. Few people sacrifice like a pastor.

Chapter 10

(But On the Other Hand…)

I hope that I haven't come across to heavy handed through the last couple chapters. A one-sided argument is rarely the complete and accurate picture of any scene. As I've stated before, my only real intent is to share personal stories of things I've seen in ministry in order to cast a light on an area that has been ignored. I do want to sympathize with some of those situations that I have addressed.

Because some of those stories are deeply personal, I found myself having difficulties stepping outside of myself at times to really look through the eyes of an opposing side of view. Empathy is a necessity for any pastor. Until we can empathize with the situations and aches of the hurting, we can't ever truly help them.

There are multiple sides to every story. A situation is never as black and white as it might appear on the surface. One might think, the church, of all places, would have distinguished grades of black and white, but this is rarely so. One would also think that there should be no dissention, no opposition, no factions, no cliques, and no "sides."

When a new pastor comes in, he may step into a scenario where rival factions are fighting over the color of the church carpet. During the "honeymoon period," he won't see how the strong personalities vying for one color or the other delve much deeper than they appear. Certain people will have held grudges against another for decades—and the root of the problem isn't simple

187

pettiness, but rather old bitterness that has been allowed to ferment through the years.

Sister Martha hates a carpet pattern because it used to be in her old home, decades ago, and Sister Ethel tracked mud on it. The incident led to a personal battle of pew squatters that raged for years before it seemed to die. Sister Ethel, now part of the decoration committee chose that same pattern for the church's foyer remodel; of course this seems a purposeful insult to Martha. It might be Ethel's subconscious revisiting an old sin; it might be deliberate. Neither is the point.

Pastors cannot be expected to know these minor, personal details. They shouldn't even be an issue—but they so often are. When a pastor, in his ignorance and/or indifference is asked his opinion on that carpet, he is drawn into a battle he or she is unaware of. Either decision makes the pastor somebody's enemy while they, obliviously and unintentionally picked a side.

Grow up people! These childish arguments hurt the body as much as they hurt the lost. These petty arguments have eternal consequences. When toddlers can't get along and share, decide who gets to play with the doll at the moment, the wise parent takes the toy away. Nobody wins. As the pastor, rip the carpet out! It's better to have the situation out in the open and resolve it than let a cold war brew. Carpeted churches are not necessary to disciple people or mandatory for a soul's salvation! Get your eyes off the petty and the temporary and understand that it is better to enter heaven with only one eye than to have let the other eye drag you into sin—that is the original intent of the passages in

Matthew 5:30 and Matthew 18:8. *This message is so important that Jesus preached it twice!*

The unfortunate reality of our churches is that these sorts of situations exist, or have existed, in almost every western church with any sort of history. *Really* good pastors have an added measure of patience and discernment that helps them perceive that these things are going on and so they can take steps to gently disarm these situations. Some pastors can discern them, but don't have the skill set to neutralize this bomb; I imagine that pastor feels a little bit like riding shotgun in a car with a crash-test dummy at the wheel. These situations, in particular, I am very blunt in addressing. Pastors who can gently love their sheep into the proper course are amazing. My first instinct is pull out my shepherd's rod and whack some sheep (if my preceding paragraph wasn't enough of a clue.) Every pastor has his or her own different personality and approach. I work intentionally to love those who sin while remaining purposefully ignorant.

A gentle shepherd is a thing to cherish. My personal leaning is to defend the flock from threats and expand the grazing territory. That's how God developed me. Other pastors are far gentler, always ready to embrace a member of the flock. Every pastor must be able to exercise both love and defense because the spiritual war is very real in America and it has breached the defenses of many western churches.

Earlier I stated, "It doesn't matter who or how—whenever a pastor leaves his position under any motivation other than divine calling (or disqualification by gross sin), the circumstances are the work of men. Despite of the intents of unruly sheep, there is a war raging between wolves and shepherds. Only predators profit from a leader's *removal*. God will protect during the interim if He redirects a pastor's call—but a sheep who postures as the shepherd will lead the flock into the miry clay." When sheep usurp control only predators win. But what about the rare circumstances when God might be calling a sheep to do just that? Could such a thing happen?

The elevation of a lay leader to a pastoral role must be possible. Remember that every shepherd began as a sheep somewhere, either lost, or in some flock somewhere. God is sovereign, so He may operate this way. I cannot imagine the heaviness of such a calling. I cannot imagine such a situation where the right thing is to do anything other than pray until the pastor or God acts. Scripturally, God has acted in these situations by sending discomfort or ailments to redirect his unwieldy tools; people are sometimes struck down and die in many Biblical cases of men contending with the will of God. Because of the potential damages inherent to the body and the individual, prayerfulness and accountability to other elders is an absolute must. NEVER, NEVER seek this solution and never decide that this is God's will.

There are many pastors whose time has come and gone. I've even heard other pastor's admit that they should have retired long ago, but their failure to plan for a future retirement has left them with no options but to remain in a pastoral role, just barely getting by as the church languishes. Such is a difficult situation.

I have encountered pastors who have not recognized this, but in my own spirit, I have felt as much and know of others who recognize those same

Christopher Schmitz – Why Your Pastor Left

things. While that might even be a properly discerned bit of knowledge, there is nothing we can do with it but pray for God to open doors and open the eyes of such a pastor. Anything else is human effort: division, bodily damage, and the appearance of pride.

When I worked as a carpenter, one of my coworkers used to ask subcontractors on the job site who seemed to take an abnormally long time, "Are you gonna retire on that one, or what?" It was a half-jest, only, a colloquial way to encourage them to speed up. The implication of the phrase is that they were stretching out a simple job to continue earning an hourly paycheck.

Some pastors need to give up the ghost and leave. Some won't relinquish the stranglehold on the pulpit for fear of their future or for lack of faith in their successor. Some pastors drain a church because they did not plan for retirement; they were sure that the Second Coming would happen in their lifetime. These pastors plan to "retire" on a church. Churches feel too guilty to cut that cord. Truth be told, I don't think that I could do it. I think the proper way is to pray them out and let God do it. Before any outside action is taken, though, an honest discussion between the pastor and the board would go a long way. Remember to always give a pastor respect, regardless of differing opinions.

There is another sort of person that shouldn't be in ministry. Pastor-dictators often find pulpits to occupy. I've mentioned them previously, too. While neither situation is entirely ethical on the part of the pastor, this is not some sin that is hard-coded and easy to identify. Nobody can know the heart and situations he or she is in except the Pastor and God. The only recourse we have

191

is to pray and let God change either the Pastor's heart, or yours! It sounds like I'm a broken record—but prayer is the only valid solution! God knew what He was doing when he designed the system! He wants to be involved in His church, to be consulted in every day-to-day decision. It is only because our culture has drifted so far away from a regular habit of prayer that we find revolution preferable to prayer in intra-church conflict. Trust me, whenever conflict is brewing the pastor lives in the crosshairs, and he or she knows it.

Conflict surrounds humanity; as a whole and as individuals we bathe it, are birthed in it, and struggle until we die. We must endure it, but we can also do our best to see other points of view. In one message I preached, I boldly proclaimed, "I am not a pleaser of men." I described a scenario in which a person might try to manipulate me into backing down and relenting in my radical pursuit of an empowered life lived for Christ. I used the words, "I don't care what you think. I am not a pleaser of men; I only live to please God." Conflict ensued.

I saw one specific person bristle. He had already disagreed with me on a number of occasions. My radical passion needed to be tempered, in his opinion. Ironically, he was not a church member, but visited occasionally. He'd taken to "sharing" his disapproval of me with specific, key members in my congregation. I'd already met and spoken with him about my meaning. The funny thing about people is that they tend to only hear a part of any given message—they often only hear what they envision you might say, rather than the words you actually use. What this person heard me say was, "I don't care about you—you are always wrong and I am always right." My intention was to

192

reflect that I stand only on the Word of God—because it alone is truth—and you (congregation members) should too.

When we know we make these errors, it is necessary for us to find ways to bridge whatever breach is holding us apart. Sometimes it only takes little things, small sacrifices to bridge big gaps between personalities. Make a plan and stick to it. I tried to complement this person every time I had some sort of interaction with him over the summer. The first thing I did whenever he entered the room was smile and I intentionally greeted him. One of the areas he had publicly criticized me for was music style preferences and how I had implemented it into my ministry niche. At the end of the summer, a situation came up where musicians were needed and he was asked to play guitar and lead worship for an evening. I surrendered my preferences and let my personality take a backseat enabling him to pick songs, dictate the style and flow of the worship. We played together, and it was good—there was unity, a bridge was established. I never had another problem with this person. I didn't change and neither did he, but we respected each other and built a relationship that I wouldn't hesitate to label as a mutual friendship.

Despite the superiority of God's will and message, we need relationships to gain that authority and permission to speak into someone's life. I will preach Him always; I don't spew feel-good "Reader's Digest" sermons that may validate a brother's sin. That was the point of my "I don't care" comment. Pastors, by their nature, care. But we also stand on something, for something, greater.

Christopher Schmitz – Why Your Pastor Left

A pastor who is incapable of preaching unpopular messages is not able to bring the whole word of God. Mankind's sins are progressively worse as we become more and more like the people from the days of Noah—it's prophetic, and obviously happening. Scripture teaches us that even those in the church are being fooled (even in the early church) and so we must hold on to the Word more so than ever and not be persuaded by the words of man or even an angel. With that expectation, we can assume that more correction is needed and that, more than ever, biblical messages will become unpopular and difficult for a sensual/pleasure-seeking (hedonistic) culture to accept. This affects both pastor and layperson. Check your pastor; double-check their scriptures. Hold them accountable to a Biblical standard and hold yourself there too, maturing in sanctification. And above all, love.

Empathy asks you to put yourself into the shoes of another. When you do so, to the best of your abilities, ask yourself if you feel genuinely loved. This is one of those things where the eye of the beholder holds more truth than a bucketful of intent.

Another area where pastors (and those concerned) should examine the other point of view is in the area of hardships. The Bible is full of instances where God puts His chosen ones into situations in order to test and refine them. He certainly calls pastors, at times, directly into the fire. He might direct us into the path of different Ministry Killers so that we can gain a resistance to them or be trained and prepared for future encounters and our past experiences have refined us for future ones.

The story of Abraham and Isaac is the classic story that is usually used to demonstrate tests from God. Joseph's many trials over his life are another example. The hardships from these tests are not necessarily from God, but God can use them in order to bring about something good. This is a concept that goes all the way back to the free will debate. It is a fundamental way we see Scripture as a whole. God does not cause evil or dictate our decisions, but He will sometimes take the evil caused by men and turn them into a greater glory. Why am I bringing this up? Because I want to point out that, while God brings about a greater thing, uses hardship to prepare and advance His chosen ones—that does not justify the sins of the person causing the hardship.

Here's a common scenario. A person's doctrine deviates and the pastor privately calls him on it. The person causes a church split by slandering and accusing the pastor. The church is in shambles, as is the emotional state of the minister. The offshoot church eventually withers and dies and the church languishes for a long period before fully recovering. The pastor writes a book about his experience and is able to help many of his peers work through similar troubles. The church becomes very successful and instrumental in bringing about an area-wide revival.

A greater ministry is birthed in this painful situation. But do the ends justify the means? Even though it took a hardship to bring about this good work, a hardship birthed by the sin of a person, that does not mean that the sin is justified. To use the potential good caused by a sin as a rationale for character development or a divine test dismisses the notion of sin entirely and even endorses it; every sin from gossip and white lies to murder and pedophilia

Christopher Schmitz – Why Your Pastor Left

become justified and ratified by God. Romans 6:1,2 states, "What shall we say, then? Shall we go on sinning so that grace may increase? By no means! We are those who have died to sin; how can we live in it any longer?" (NIV) What if people didn't sin? Without that hardship to act as a catalyst, would God's same plan come about? We humans like to justify our sins, preplan them even! If we chose not to sin and didn't force our pastors to walk through those trials, God would use another method to bring about His perfect will. Perhaps He would use more miracles to bring about His plans in the absence of such readily available crucibles. How easily we forget the omnipotence of God.

God certainly does steer people into certain hard paths in order to develop their character. He uses the spinning of the potter's wheel and gentle redirections to steer us through a process that feels violent to the clay in order to build something good and useful.

I've shared some personal stories in this book. Some of them are intensely personal and so my passion inherently bleeds through, but there is no bitterness. I hate none of those people who have caused me pain in the past. I think that many of those hardships were specifically undergone so that I could write this book. It is all a part of what God has called me to, how He has developed me. Of course, I'm not ready to hold hands and skip to the petting zoo with those who have done me great harm in the past. God gave me enough of a brain to memorize useful clichés such as, "Fool me once shame on you; fool me twice, shame on me." I have common sense enough to learn from the past mistakes and inclinations of others in addition to my own.

Christopher Schmitz – Why Your Pastor Left

I also recognize that I'm not without my own faults. I can be a difficult guy to minister alongside, as well. No person is perfect.

I've worked alongside ministers who see the world through Gaither-Vision. Usually, such ministers frown upon ministers like me—mostly this is because we are called to different segments of the human population! It's not a matter of a different Gospel or a different God—it's about the precontext we view scripture under in order to present it most accurately and effectively to our audience. There shouldn't be this animosity between us: we worship the same God and work for the same Kingdom. In fact, I've had to apologize to a couple of ministers for my own attitudes and judgments. One of these pastors stated, "It takes different types of bait to catch different kinds of fish." Even though he refused to free me up to minister effectively, it didn't make him any less passionate and called to his own ministry—the onus of the situation was on me. My job was more difficult, but not impossible. My lack of bridging that particular gap is perhaps a validation that my thoughts and ways are not always the best, either. I've yet to corner the market on effectiveness and methodology.

My generation sees things radically different, but when I try to empathize, I understand that the heavy responsibility of pastoral leadership and years of experience color the lenses one views the world with from the behind the pastor's desk. After all, my generation's Christianity is full of seeker sensitive fluff, overly emotional hyper-spiritualism, and a drift from sound Biblical foundations just as much as it is hooked on corporate revival, personal sanctification, and a missional movement unlike anything since the haystack revival. Foundationally, we are the same; fundamentally, we are different; graciously, God transcends.

Because I can empathize with my ministry peers, I can sympathize with their decisions and points of view. Because of our shared vision for the Kingdom, I can overcome those areas of broad differences. I can't agree with all our previous generations' precepts and methodologies, but there are many points that I *can* agree with, specifically fundamental, scriptural truths. If all parties would strive to find those common grounds, we could relate cohesively under the same eternal Truth that is God's Word.

In this type of scenario, empathy and sympathy don't mean that we necessarily agree with the methods and beliefs of the other party. We don't need to be in total agreement over every minor detail as long as scripture is not violated. There are so many areas that are left up to personal preference. In a clash of music style preferences, one parishioner complained about the type of music being played in the youth group worship telling my Senior Pastor that we needed to change it (even though, as an adult, the music was not intended for him and he had never been present through a worship service.) In the absence of a scriptural reason to complain he said, "Well, Pastor, you just have to hear it." My Pastor wisely informed him, "I have two degrees in music. I've studied music through cultures and time and discovered that no generation has ever really liked the music of the generation that comes after it. I don't have to go listen to it to tell you that I probably won't like it… *but it's not about what I like*. It's about reaching the teenagers letting them worship God in their own element."

Christopher Schmitz – Why Your Pastor Left

I so appreciated my pastor when he shared that sentiment with me. I agree, he probably wouldn't like the music, but I'm thankful for Kingdom minded ministers who know how to step out of their own preferences and let the Kingdom advance in areas that they are unable or uncomfortable in pursuing.

Music genres, clothing styles, minor denominational differences, these are all just different approaches to common problems. God doesn't condemn the girl in blue jeans for freestyle rapping a worship lyric sung from the heart any more than He loves the three-piece suit wearing backup singer in a Gaither-Tribute vocal group. These things are all transcended by God's love. So many of the reasons that we judge our fellow man are merely matters of personal predilection and they have no place in the ministry unless you are willing to die on a cross to prove those preferences are the new canon—even then, I won't enforce them unless you can resurrect yourself as well.

Newer converts might have different revelations on scripture, even. As we go through experiences, walk in our Christian life, and study the Word, scripture comes alive in deeper shades of personal meaning and self-application. It's like an onion; the whole thing is an onion, but you have multiple layers that you can peel away. Every set of preferences is like another layer of the onion. While different, it's all exactly the same. All generations should be willing to expand their options and learn how to contextualize their faith to those around them, regardless of which "onion layer" they might be in.

God uses our personal and shared cultural experiences to impart personal revelation, too. While truth is there, many people have dissimilar leanings and a different understanding of how God operates today, and through

Christopher Schmitz – Why Your Pastor Left

scripture. These minor theological leanings have different applications in various segments of the population. These matters of personal preference, be they educated belief, clothing choices, music penchants, or a host of other minor things, should not be reasons for conflict. If it doesn't violate some scriptural standard, it's not going to damage you. If your brother is not condemning himself (that standard being blasphemy of the Holy Spirit/the Unpardonable Sin) then he merely holds a different worldview. This is a strength we must stop treating as a weakness. If we harnessed our diversity we could better reach our communities and subcultures with the message of Jesus.

Every worldview has its own strengths and weaknesses and it's natural for the different generations to have their own gaps buffering them from each other and causing some initial mistrust. As I said, conflict is everywhere. It's up to all of us to empathize with our peers and bridge those gaps.

What we truly need is unity. The body must be unified with its head and the leadership must work harmoniously.

Truly Godly leaders and elders will lay aside their own kingdoms, little castles made of sand, in the interest of the Kingdom. In the interest of unity and a bigger, corporate vision, pastors understand that they must not be pleasers of men. The men and women of the church will follow their pastor who pursues God.

Unified churches are full of love and respect in the absence of sin. The headship knows when it's time to multiply, time to step down, time to birth, time to die. Everything works: if we could only be genuine in everything and love genuinely.

Christopher Schmitz – Why Your Pastor Left

I understand that the problems I mention in this book might not be *your* norm or your experiences or observations in ministry; they are mine. The things I've said are unpopular; I know this with certainty and even during the course of writing this have been attacked and insulted by friends. Few people like a boat-rocker.

Even if I am wrong, however, in the extent of these problems, these problems *do* exist. It is the obligation of the Church, as God's chosen vessel to represent His message, to correct herself. It is scriptural and it is common sense. Many self-governing churches harbor an innate resentment to their liturgical brothers, especially towards the Catholic Church, because of their position that they have never erred, despite recorded history of redactions and various, deliberate sins committed by the greater church during the darker ages of the past. Many modern churches are often no different; a refusal to consider correction translates as a refusal to acknowledge imperfections, or a contentment with the status quo. God wants so much more than that, he desperately desires His *unblemished* bride.

In "Second Choice: Embracing Life As It Is," Viv Thomas writes about the condition of America. She compares it to Judah, prior to the Babylonian captivity. God's chosen ones had wandered away from Him, choosing instead to remain in Jerusalem, ruling over themselves as *they* saw fit. Judah ignored the prophets sent to her who, for years, forecasted her doom and preached repentance.[47] Detailed accounts are found in Ezekiel and Jeremiah. Jeremiah

---

[47] Thomas, Viv. Second Choice: Embracing Life As It Is. Crown Hill: Paternoster Press, 2000.

Christopher Schmitz – Why Your Pastor Left

shows us that the country even invoked the protection of Yahweh God, making a twisted concoction of idol worship and Hebraic law; they listened to demonic prophecy and claimed it in the name of Jehovah, calling the prophets liars and reveled in the torment they inflicted upon them.

Not every person in Judah was a wicked sinner or had bent their hearts and knees to Baal. Many within the country were still Godly, but they were carted off to Babylon and punished with the rest of their peers. Daniel and the Hebrew boys were all carted off into captivity due to the sins of their rulers and their countrymen.

We must listen to reason. It is the obligation of the Godly to rescue their nation from bondage. Be faithful like Daniel, Hananiah, Mishael, and Azariah.

Be an agent of change when called upon and pray for the failing strength of your countrymen.

Chapter 11

(When God Does Call People Away—The Right Way to Leave)

Hopefully your last pastor left under the best of circumstances. Even in the best ministries, there are times when God divinely calls a pastor away, usually to either continue developing the church, or to continue shaping the pastor for another work. Often it's both. Growing a church is a developmental process.

Dan Secrist writes, "Pastoring a church necessitates constant paradigm shifts... because the church is changing often. If you do not continue to grow and change, the church will stop growing and changing. All change is perceived as loss to someone, and loss is typically met with resistance and anger. We must recognize that all of our planning, labor, and innovation can never replace the truth of 1 Corinthians 3:6,7: I planted the seed, Apollos watered it, but God made it grow. So neither he who plants nor he who waters is anything, but only God, who makes things grow."[48]

There is a logical process that God takes a pastor through before He moves a minister onward. Sometimes, because ministry can have unique hardships, a pastor needs a certain amount of confirmation that God is, indeed calling him or her to a new ministry or releasing them from their current one. Like Gideon's tentative tests, a pastor wants to know for sure he or she is in

---

[48] Secrist, Dan. "Growing From a Pioneer Church to a Multistaff Church." In The Pentecostal Pastor: A Mandate for the 21st Century, edited by Thomas, Goodall, Wayde, and Bicket, Zenas Trask, 482-491. Springfield: Gospel Publishing House, 2000. 490, 491

Christopher Schmitz – Why Your Pastor Left

God's will and not merely giving up on that which God previously called them. In times of turmoil, it's easy to give up and pass the buck to God; saying that He has called a minister away is such a simple solution, but a good pastor waits through the difficult times that accompany any transition. A good pastor will make sure that his or her spirit is satisfied in the clear knowledge of a new calling.

Sometimes people from outside that process (friends of the pastor, visitors, other clergy, and lay people) think they saw the resignation coming long before the pastor did. They might have seen some indicators. Those signals, however, are often the same signs that accompany spiritual attack, the chaos of birthing revival, and fallout effects from interloping human manipulation. Plainly: we cannot judge or truthfully say, "I told you so." It's all God; anything else is mere opinion or speculation.

I wrote previously about certain types of pastors who refuse to recognize that God wants them to move on. Some pastors actually hinder the ministry, but the only way to properly deal with them is on your knees in prayer. God will call them away and birth new life with a blessing to make up for what was lost ("I will repay you for the years the locusts have eaten" Joel 2:25a NIV.)

Secrist tells a story of a church he encountered in Madrid, Spain. "There were large spikes sticking out of the door from top to bottom, it looked like a fortress! Evidently children used to pound on the door during services and disturb the small band of faithful worshipers. So they drove huge spikes from the inside of the door clear through the wood, and the sharp points greeted you as you approached the door. Then a new pastor came. He didn't just take the

Christopher Schmitz – Why Your Pastor Left

spikes out of the door, he opened it and welcomed the children. Before long, there were kids clubs, crusades, Sunday school, and other activities that attracted those 'little nuisances' right into the kingdom of God!"[49]

Whether your previous pastor was a great pastor or not, sometimes God calls a minister away and replaces them because of a need for a shift in ministry dynamics. This new pastor in Madrid came with a new philosophy and solved the problem of kids banging on the door while infusing a kingdom-minded growth into the DNA of his church.

I was looking though a website which posted church position openings. One of the ads said they wanted someone to continue in the same manner and vision as the previous pastor who left for some different ministry and departed under good circumstances. I wondered if this church was holding God back from doing something new in their midst by requiring their new Pastor to be essentially the same. Remember what Secrist wrote: change will typically be perceived as loss and meet resistance and anger. At the very least, something new will encounter some amount of resentment.[50]

It may be that God has developed the church to a certain level, and wants to take them to another level by changing everything, developing something new within them. We should never expect someone new to do the same old-thing people are used to, even if that same thing has been working. We need life and freshness, and God is constantly remolding us and encouraging us as we grow—because we are not perfect yet!

---

[49] Ibid. 486
[50] Ibid. 490

Christopher Schmitz – Why Your Pastor Left

Sometimes, in developing the character of a pastor, God needs to take them in a new direction. This might even mean a departure from "traditional," vocational ministry. Moses spent 40 years in the desert for *his* preparation for something new.

Leadership guru John Maxwell says, "No man can measure the burden that God has given him; he can only respond to it. When God gives you a burden you must stay at work because it is God who has given you that burden; but when the burden leaves, it is time for you to leave. However, just because the burden is beginning to leave does not mean it is time to leave. Before a leader begins changing his location, he must examine why his burden is leaving."[51]

In his article, Changing Pastorates, Ron McManus addresses this question of determining God's will. He reinforces what Maxwell postures regarding the release of divine call. "If God has brought you to a place of ministry, you are...in the will of God; to make a move, then, will require God's releasing you from the original vision...or assuring you that you have fulfilled the mission He called you to accomplish."[52] McManus also poses several questions to help determine the pastor's motives in accordance with God's call, or the release of it.

Two of his questions get straight to the point. *Have I fulfilled the vision God put in my heart when I came here?* This answer is a major factor in

---

[51] Maxwell, John. "When to Quit." Vols. 10, no.1. El Cajon: Injoy Life Club, n.d.
[52] McManus, Ron. "Changing Pastorates." In The Pentecostal Pastor: A Mandate for the 21st Century, edited by Thomas, Goodall, Wayde, and Bicket, Zenas Trask, 514-521. Springfield: Gospel Publishing House, 2000. 515

Christopher Schmitz – Why Your Pastor Left

discerning that release of the ministerial burden—a necessity for a good transition. *Am I allowing my emotions to dictate my decision to leave?* This second question is an indicator of possible burnout or a disillusioned pastor.

A disillusioned pastor is worn out, depressed, pressed and wounded in battle—but certainly not done with the fight. Athletes know the expression "hitting the wall." Disillusioned ministers have hit the wall; they feel they can't continue, like they have nothing left, but persistence sees a "second wind" and a redoubled renewal of the effort as the pace becomes easier and the worst of the pain has passed.

When disillusionment sets in, the first thing to go is the pastor's assuredness of calling. I've always known to guard against this, even since my early days studying in a university. I think God instilled this in me, knowing that it would be challenged vehemently in the years to come. I took steps to refresh my sense of calling whenever I felt it weaken; a pastor should frequently remember it, hold it dear, and find sources of personal encouragement so they don't succumb to self-doubt. It is so easy to forget what was once so vividly clear. Given the chance, time will wash everything away in tones of sepia.

I've never doubted my personal calling, not seriously anyhow. When I lost a ministry job in one community, some of my peers questioned me, perhaps unsure what to think about their own relationships in ministry. Had I mistaken my calling to assume that pastorate? Answering their questions made me, for the first time, really think long and hard about free will. Was I wrong in my call to partner with that church for ministry, or was my removal an act of choice, a

Christopher Schmitz – Why Your Pastor Left

decision made by a person not involved in that communication between God and myself?

God calls and opens doors, but there is a human component somewhere in it all. I'm not a closed-minded Arminian, and I'm not leaning towards Calvinist doctrines either. The truth is in the middle somewhere. I do believe that it is the call of a preacher (any Christian, really,) to present the Gospel to whomever we can. It is still up to that audience to accept Christ's free gift of salvation or reject it. Likewise, God can open those doors and avenues to ministry and call us to positions and places, but there is a human component to even that. Sometimes people are able to close doors to places God desires his mouthpiece to enter. There are doors that God will open which no man may shut, but in the physical world, He has given us a certain measure of control over our own surroundings and circumstances.

In college, I worked with teens in a live-in counseling center. I had opportunities to share my faith because it was run through a Christian organization. At some point, though, my boss became uncomfortable with the openness of my beliefs. At first, I thought it was because she held a different denominational doctrine. I soon realized that she refused to examine even her own beliefs. She held views that didn't agree with her own denomination's doctrines, and she told me I couldn't talk about faith issues around her or she would fire me. God wanted her to examine herself and open her life to Truth, but she held enough control over the situation to close a door. I respected her request and kept my job by not pressuring her to respond to God's prompting.

Christopher Schmitz – Why Your Pastor Left

People within the church have certainly done the same thing to many ministries. Many churches have histories of specific, recurring problems, often stemming from problems in the past, usually problems that somehow involved the leadership. The issue can manifest itself as a cycle of short-term pastoral stays, a series of ministries, which only last for short tenures. Often, because of the initial problem, the churches' lay leaders determine that they will not let themselves be hurt in that way again. Healing can only be achieved by a solid, grounded ministry that is earmarked by love and patience; it must be an enduring ministry that puts in time.

Pastors must resist the urge to move on to greener pastures; they should only consider a change if they know they have achieved the vision God called them to. Disillusionment and emotions, or the desire to "upgrade" their ministry position needs to be avoided; the stepping stone mentality of many ministers needs to die. The culture of temporary stewardship that we have created has given the secular world sufficient reason to discredit the message we bring and has damaged the general trust people have had for ministers.

A statewide youth director I know shared a story with me after I'd been a staff pastor at one particular church. She was a counselor at a Bible camp in her earlier ministry in the state. One of the girls in her cabin had been from my church. The girl needed some guidance but refused to receive it from the counselor. Her feelings of pastoral abandonment reached to deep. "I've had three Youth Pastors in just the last couple years," she vented, "and I will never trust another one."

Christopher Schmitz – Why Your Pastor Left

Before I had taken that staff position, I spoke to one of my ministry mentors who pastored a church in a nearby community. He told me, "Make sure you stay put—show them the love and patience of Christ. They've had so many pastors in the last few years at that position; they really need someone with patience and longevity." However, the interim leadership informed me that my resignation was required, (a polite way to fire someone under the guise of protocol.)

When it came time to make my impending departure public knowledge I was told to say, "God has called me out of this ministry." I replied that God had not released my burden and I did not feel that was true and I refused to make that statement. I disagreed when I was told that it was the fact of the matter. "If you can't make this your statement of resignation, then you won't be allowed to speak publicly about the matter at all, and we will be watching you," was the final reply. With a ministry that centered on a genuine witness, I agreed to take the silent approach. To the interim's credit, they didn't claim my relocation was a matter of calling, but made a statement matter-of-factly. I didn't want to obstruct the church's authority or progress, but the only thing I was able to depart my position with was the knowledge of what I had accomplished in my tenure and the testimony of my character. I wasn't about to leave my ministry under false pretenses.

We must make every effort at openness, honesty, and sincerity of motivation. We have to kill the culture of temporary stewardship and reclaim our trustworthiness. Western Christianity's loss of credibility has impacted countless ministries.

Christopher Schmitz – Why Your Pastor Left

Properly handling ministry transition is so critical. The possible emotional trauma transitions can create (for both the pastor and those in his past ministry) is high. McManus warns transitioning pastors, "Any emotional baggage you carry into a new pastorate will immediately influence and cripple your effectiveness."

Those mature lay-leaders in the church should prepare to counsel their peers through any periods of grief that will inevitably follow any transition. The next thing they must be prepared for is guiding their peers through the murky waters of resentment that the following pastor might find himself or herself in. A church's elders and deacons are instrumental here; they will be the ones the laity looks to as a new pastor takes over.

Resentment can sometimes gain a foothold when a new pastor is compared against the former. The comparison is unavoidable. Where the guidance must come in, is in recognizing that the results of such evaluations don't reveal anything but differences. The disparity is neither good nor bad; it is simply different. Every minister brings his own philosophy, style, and character. These are the things that compose the distinct make-up of a pastor as an individual and no two persons are alike. If you can see it or not, differences are bound to be a good thing; embrace these changes and follow God's plan as he grows and stretches the ministry of such a church.

As much as it may feel like an internal betrayal to "let go" of your previous pastor, it is exactly what a good transition needs, and good pastors know this. When the Kingdom is clearly in focus, everything works perfectly! We must not follow mere men as we do Kingdom work; people come and go in

Christopher Schmitz – Why Your Pastor Left

our lives but it is Christ who is at the center of our faith. 1 Corinthians addresses this issue—twice, in fact.

What I mean is this: One of you says, "I follow Paul"; another, "I follow Apollos"; another, "I follow Cephas"; still another, "I follow Christ." 1 Cor. 1:12 (NIV)

When one of you says, "I am a follower of Paul," and another says, "I follow Apollos," aren't you acting just like people of the world? 1 Cor. 3:4 (NLT)

The surrounding verses give the context. This is not a Kingdom centered on the personality in the pulpit. Understand that it's all about God and less about the pastor. Paul states in 1 Corinthians 3: 5,6 "Who then is Paul, and who is Apollos, but ministers by whom ye believed, even as the Lord gave to every man? I have planted, Apollos watered; but God gave the increase." He recognizes that the pastoral leadership, however great, is still composed of ordinary men. It is God's Church, not mine.

Hopefully your pastor transitioned well and left the new pastor in a position of strength, for Christ's sake. There are many ways a pastor can make the transition smoother for the future minister as he or she steps out. A transitioning minister should prepare detailed finances and ministerial overviews, schedules, calendars and traditional events that might be a part of an individual church's rich history. These things give a heads up to the next person and help them in their effort to concentrate on learning the people and building relationships. A pastor can make efforts to praise his coming replacement, giving the congregation every reason to place their faith and trust in the skills

212

and vision that the next pastor possesses. I have also seen a number of pastors officially install their replacement, similar to Elijah passing his mantle of leadership and position to Elisha.

If the pastor has been unable to make these things happen, the lay leaders in the church should make every effort to achieve the same end result and *equip the pastor, prepare the people, and pass the mantle.* This was a three-step plan that I developed to ease the transition of my replacement in my last pastorate. While a pastor is the best person to accomplish this, any leader in the church can help accomplish these tasks and a unified leadership team, partnering with the departing pastor can make the final weeks of a ministry a celebration of unity birthed in expectation for a movement of God.

The goal of a good transition should be to form a launch point from the ceiling of success of the resigning minister. The new pastor should be able to launch off of this success, discern God's vision for the church, and advance the Kingdom with freshness and power. The goal of a good pastoral transition is to set up the new minister for even greater success than what the previous pastor enjoyed.

Chapter 12

(The Pastor's Wife and Family)

The struggles in this chapter chiefly concern the *wives* of pastors. Pastors' wives face unique struggles that are not typically shared with male husbands of female ministers. Husbands of pastors don't seem to share the same set of congregational expectations as the more common example of male pastors with a female wife. Typically, churches understand that he will have his own full-time employment outside the church.

A Christianity Today article states, "The call of the pastor's wife is both consecrated in its place of privilege and complicated in its emotional ambiguities."[53]

In her article, "Ministers' Wives: The Walking Wounded," Mary LaGrand Bouma discusses the loss of identity of "Pastor's Wives" (or PWs,) or how they can't "be themselves."[54] Typically, PWs are introduced as "the minister's wife," a rare distinction—it's uncommon for other spouses to be called "the plumber's wife" or be introduced as "the librarian's wife." Pastor's wife/author/and minister at large Jill Briscoe states, "She has a name—and it is not 'The Pastor's Wife.'"[55]

---

[53] Zoba, Wendy Murray. "What Pastor's Wives Wish Their Churches Knew Part 1." Christianity Today, April 7, 1997.
[54] LaGrand Bouma, Mary. "Minister's Wives: The Walking Wounded." Leadership, winter 1980.
Lawrence, Brother. The Practice of the Presence of God. 24th Printing. Grand Rapids: Revell, 2009. 63
[55] (Zoba 1997)

Christopher Schmitz – Why Your Pastor Left

In the wake of ministry expectations, her husband's calling, family issues, and personal struggles common to humanity, it isn't any surprise that most PWs encounter an identity crisis. She typically hears something like, "The previous ministers' wife was president of the Women's' Ministry," and, "Our last Pastor's wife managed to play piano *and* supervise the nursery." She typically finds it difficult to "be herself" when nearly every other woman in the church is telling her exactly *who she should be.*

Sometimes pastor-husbands fail to inform "search/call committees" that their wives should be treated like anyone else. Like any other lay-person, a PWs ministry can only succeed if she's acting within the range of her own gifts, personal limits, and calling—not anyone else's. "If this is 'pulling rank,' then so be it," writes Mary LaGrand Bouma.

Many churches look for a "pastoral team" in the hiring process. I've heard countless stories of pastors hearing in the interview process how they would only be considered for candidacy if their wives had certain talents; right at the onset of this relationship between church and minister, outside expectations are set upon his wife. Sometimes, in their desperate need to do the work of God, pastor-husbands fail to correct this notion that a married pastor is a "two for the price of one" worker package.

I applaud the pastor who can walk out on a pastoral search committee. "It seems to me that you care less about hiring a quality pastor and more about a church pianist. Feel free to call me when you realize that my wife is not a 'free employee.'" That's the gutsy and admirable road. It's unfair to commit a spouse

Christopher Schmitz – Why Your Pastor Left

to a role that she might or might not volunteer for. We need more husbands who protect their wives like that.

Too often people speak for each other and commit them to things without their input. Just recently, after a heavy snowstorm, I overheard my father volunteer me to clear my schedule to give free computer tech/support. Thanks Dad... I then volunteered *him* to plow the person's driveway. Pastor's sometimes do this same thing to their wives.

Because of their high calling PWs are distinct from other people. I hesitate to use the word "different," but sometimes, extra factors inherent to ministry amplify the struggles and emotional trials they endure.

Dennis Rainey points out the need to balance ministry life with personal life. "I can think of no other profession where the demands of the job can enter the home with such ease, frequency, and intensity. If a pastor is successful in ministering to the needs of his people, then the demand for meeting more needs will increase. If husband and wife fail to understand and regulate this, their marriage may become a casualty."[56]

Ministry is a life of sacrifice. Truly, people have no idea how much a pastor's wife can be made to suffer. It is a doubly hurtful thing for a wife to watch her spouse endure the pains of this sacrifice. As the pastor-husband's helpmate, all of the pastor's concerns and trials might become *her* pain as well, in addition to her own stressors. (All the ministry killers and stressors that can

---

[56] Rainey, Dennis. Ministering to Twenty-First Century Families. Nashville: Thomas Nelson, 2001. 14

Christopher Schmitz – Why Your Pastor Left

affect the pastor, from disillusionment and jealousy to finances and boundaries, can also adversely impact the pastor's wife, and thereby hinder the ministry.)

Because the ministry family finds themselves living in the confines of a "glass parsonage," they have unique stress beyond the problems of the modern family which, (according to countless surveys, personal observation, and any television viewing shows,) is grossly dysfunctional. It's easy for a ministry family to be overwhelmed by outside factors—traditional (non-ministry) families find it hard enough.

I know what this book is about. The title is on the cover. I want to provide advice on how to retain/protect your pastor. Speaking from personal insight as a pastor, there is no better way to show love to your minister than to passionately love his wife! Let her be herself; love her on her own terms.

A radio host once asked a guest what she thought would be a wonderful way to minister to the pastor's wife. "Maybe offer to clean house for her, or something like that," he replied. Remember boundaries! Most PWs have had their fill of snooping people. The last thing you want is for your "blessing" to become an even greater burden. All PWs I know would be mortified by the thought that people in her church think she can't keep her house clean which could be implied with the offer. This sort of gift might be used manipulatively (I can tell you—it has happened,) by church members as a way to shame or "correct" her behavior. Make sure your "gift" doesn't impart extra expectations upon her. This radio host stated, "If that's something [you] want to do, it would be best to pay for a cleaning service to come in." That variation on the idea respects her privacy and doesn't hint at condescension.

Christopher Schmitz – Why Your Pastor Left

The pastor's wife is both her own person and an extension of her husband. You may love and respect your pastor, even treat him like a king, but if you mistreat his wife, it's as if you'd abused *him*. I consider myself tough. I admit to a bit of a superhero complex. I can handle mistreatment and I can endure unfairness; I can bear it all—but when I see my wife my children in the crosshairs I come out swinging. Nothing gets me more ready to fight than the need to defend my beloved—it is my duty as a husband and father.

Everything a pastor endures could be considered amplified in the PW, both the love *and* the hurts. They all translate back to your pastor.

Sometimes, when I see my wife getting frustrated with the expectations of being a PW, I ask, "Whatever happened to the green-haired wild-girl that I fell in love with and married?" Encourage your PW to remain genuine and unique; don't force her to fit the "traditional" mold that religious people expect. God calls *all sorts of people* to reach *all sorts of people*. A lady with green hair and a nose-ring can get into places and love people that are unreachable by those riding out the cardigan and denim smock.

GRID (World Vision's Christian Leadership Letter) invited pastors' wives to tell them how they felt about their role and calling. With all major Protestant denominations represented, most letters just talked about wanting to "be themselves."

Sometimes, the parsonage kitchen gets a little too crowded. The old cliché is "too many chefs spoiled the broth." There's good advice in that statement that the church must heed. The ministry marriage is a bit like that kitchen—there are many personalities, strong cooks in their own right, but there

218

must be a chain of command. If your PW is a leader along with her husband, she is a head chef; *let her lead*. Empower and release her into leadership; respect her just as you would her husband.

Understand that with so many cooks, the kitchen gets overcrowded quickly. Don't be particularly offended if she cuts down on traffic, especially when it's in areas of her comfort and control, such as her house and family. In fact, I frequently advise reducing "kitchen traffic."

I was involved in an emergency counseling session with a pastor friend of mine. He offered a great piece of advice to the "husband," (I use parenthesis as the couple was cohabitating, and the advice essentially became a pre-marriage counseling crash course in relationship boundaries.) He said, "As a man in this committed relationship you should never, ever have a friendship with any woman to rival her (the wife role.) *She* should be your closest female friend; in fact, she should be your closest friend of any gender." Too many chefs easily topple those boundaries. Spouses should regard each other with the highest value possible—not even Church business is allowed to intervene. Mark 10:9 says "What therefore God has joined together, let no man separate." (KJV) "Church Business" has certainly become an extension of our humanity in the American church; the fact that it so often encroaches when God's Word would seem to cloister is evidence of that.

Lastly, we can't expect to please everyone. A Bill Watterson *Calvin & Hobbes* comic strip quipped, "A good compromise leaves everyone mad." That notion has always stuck with me. I promised one church (where I successfully candidated,) "I guarantee that I cannot make all of you happy—what I *can* guarantee is this: if I tried, I could make all of you upset with me." Don't expect that your PW can please every person in the church. After all, some people are downright impossible to please.

Scripture is laced with symbolism represented by the union of marriage and the example of family. When the clergy marriage is strained, the church suffers. PWs often struggle with having to "share their man" with other women. Often, pastors are expected to do "home visits" which sometimes include women alone in their homes; that creates unique temptations and pitfalls for the pastoral marriage. One pastor I know shared the story of a home visit he went on. A ministry peer happened to drop in on him before a scheduled home visit and so he invited his friend along. The pastor rang the doorbell and waited on the stoop with his friend; the woman answered her door completely nude, intending to seduce the pastor. He was grateful that he had an alibi to vouch for his purity. Sometimes those extra chefs in the kitchen accidentally violate boundaries; sometimes it's more intentional than that.

It is common for female parishioners to judge their pastor's wife; taking on the "other woman" role common in affairs, they believe his wife fails to "measure up" to expectations they secretly expect of her. While that awkward relationship dynamic doesn't (hopefully) include the sexual aspects, it certainly breeds a certain tension between Pastor's rightful wife and certain congregants. Read about Hagar and Sarah in Genesis 16 to get an idea where this type of animosity can go.

A survey taken by Leadership Journal in 1992 reveals that 94 percent of ministers feel pressured to have an "ideal family," while 77 percent said their

Christopher Schmitz – Why Your Pastor Left

spouses felt pressure to be "an ideal role model for the Christian family."[57] It may be an old figure, but I don't suspect that it has changed much. If it has, I suspect the numbers have increased as quality role-models disappear from a public stage now dominated by broken, dysfunctional personalities from Lindsey Lohan to the Kardashian family. The Cleavers and the Bradys are long gone. Most modern families are entrenched in the influence of reality television shows featuring superstars whose outrageous outbursts and celebrity sex-tapes regularly make headlines. One network runs a popular show on primetime called *Modern Family*; it features a gay couple, extremely dysfunctional familial characters, and endorses so many immoral behaviors.

Here is some data taken from a 1991 Survey of Pastors from the Fuller Institute of Church Growth.[58]

- 90% work more than 46 hours a week
- 80% believed pastoral ministry affected their families negatively
- 33% believed ministry was a hazard to their family
- 75% reported a significant stress related crisis at least once in their ministry
- 50% felt themselves unable to meet the needs of the job
- 90% felt inadequately trained to cope with ministry demands
- 70% say they have lower self-esteem now compared to when they started in ministry

---

[57] (Zoba 1997)

[58] London, H. & Wiseman, N. Pastors at Risk. Colorado Springs: Chariot Victor Publishing, 1993. 22

Christopher Schmitz – Why Your Pastor Left

- 40% reported serious conflict with a parishioner at least once a month

- 70% do not have someone they consider a close friend

        Focus on the Family Survey

- 1 out of 4 pastors do not have a trusted friend in ministry

- Only 20% of churches have 2 or more paid staff members

The pedestal can be a lonely place for both the preacher *and* his wife. For all the previously mentioned Ministry Killers, their wives also face that added burden of "measuring up." Isolation is a constant companion for the typical PW. Here's more poll data regarding wives:

Wendy Murray Zoba discusses this problem and more in "What Pastor's Wives Wish Their Churches Knew." Zoba writes:

> Many pastors' families, when they move into a community to assume a call, are perceived as outsiders. "Everyone else was part of the history of the church and the traditions," says one wife, adding that among the deepest struggles attendant to her husband's call was the "intense loneliness" she felt for the "first five to seven years." "We had families who went back years and years. When we came, we were outsiders and newcomers. And there was little sensitivity to the fact that we seldom saw our families."

> Another told me how she and her husband and children would leave immediately after the Christmas Eve service to drive all night in order to spend Christmas with her

Christopher Schmitz – Why Your Pastor Left

parents in the South. ("We had one Christmas dinner sitting in our car, eating 7-Eleven pizza," she said.) Once, when they returned after the holidays, they learned that there was a movement afoot in the church to disallow the pastor any travel during the holidays. "They have their families right here in town and so are never alone on the holidays," she said. "But they resented our wanting to leave so that we could be with our families." [59]

It is only seldom that other women within a church congregation can truthfully and realistically identify with the isolation that the resident PW(s) feel. The sad realization is that members of the laity who *do* honestly sympathize with her are themselves former PWs/ministers that have "taken a break" from ministry, permanently or as a sabbatical. The circumstances often necessitate that your PWs closest friends are other PWs, even if those who belong to another local church of differing denominations.

PWs are far too valuable to be neglected, and they must be able to have their own confidants and friends. An unfortunate trend in recent years has been the discouragement and growing depression that overshadows the American pastor's wife. This can usually be traced to isolation factors which affect her. Isolation is usually one of the greatest factors leading to suicide. In the age of touch-screen, instant, personal networking, Americans find themselves more isolated than ever. In my personal observations, Facebook has been more responsible for intra-church anxiety than quality relationship building for PWs.

---

[59] (Zoba 1997)

Christopher Schmitz – Why Your Pastor Left

Dr. Cecil Paul surveyed a sample of PWs at Eastern Nazarene College during a Pastors' Wives at a mid-west retreat. When asked open-endedly what they disliked most about the ministry, 47% mentioned expectations others have for them. The top two things that bothered them most were people who reject God after all their efforts, and not having enough willing workers. Their biggest discouragement was unresponsive people (44%).

Eighty-eight percent of Cecil's respondents answered yes to the question, "Have you ever experienced periods of depression?" Of those polled, 23% said this occurred once or twice a year. For most, the time of onset was within the first 5 to 6 years of ministry. When asked to describe this experience, the terms "general discouragement and mild depression" were used 77% of the time. Seventeen percent of suggested "deep depression" described their experiences; of those polled, 17% had thoughts of self-destruction.[60]

I think these statistics reflect local and national headlines. I've read stories of PWs who seemed to have every gifting and blessing necessary for success who have died by their own hands. Those cases are extreme, but I'd rather be overprotective of our pastor's beloved than wave off her concerns and further contribute to her fragile mental state.

Emotional PWs rarely make national news. Sometimes things send them reeling over the brink, however, and the country is suddenly caught up in the fragile makeup of the ministry family after a suicide or homicide. Depression and abuse, whether at the hands of her husband or others, has

---

[60] Bordelon Alder, Donna. "How to Encourage Your Pastor's Wife." Thriving Pastor, 2005.

Christopher Schmitz – Why Your Pastor Left

resulted in national headlines surrounding mentally broken PWs such as Mary Winkler who killed her pastor-husband with a shotgun, Kristen Lawson who attempted to drown her children in the family bathtub during a bout with severe depression, and other similar cases.

It's clear that discouragement and disillusionment affect our pastors' wives just as much as they affect the pastor. I think Dr. Paul's survey reflects a fragile psyche, made rawer by the expectations other people place upon them, and coupled with certain unresponsiveness to her personal pleas, and the lack of notice or recognition. Dis-appreciation will weigh heavy on *any* mind.

Growing up, my father worked out of town, giving my mother a sense of isolation during those four days or so that my father was regularly absent. I don't think my parents fought all the time, but I do remember something my mother constantly vented when frustrated. Whenever she felt overwhelmed she'd lament, "I feel like I'm the only one in this family!" That is how PWs can feel—alone, on an island, just needing a response to prove that somebody cares.

Statistics certainly reveal that depression affects PWs. Many survey groups have tracked relevant data over the last few decades. Here are a few excerpts:

> "Our surveys indicated that 80 percent of pastors and 84 percent of their spouses are discouraged or are dealing with depression." August 1998, James Dobson's newsletter.[61]

---

[61] (Wheeler 2012) 35

225

Christopher Schmitz – Why Your Pastor Left

Blackmon & Hart, Clergy Assessment & Career Development

- 12% of ministers report they were depressed "often or always in their ministry"[62]

Malony & Hunt, The Psychology of Clergy

- 60% of clergy wives hold full time jobs or are involved in careers
- Some studies suggest 70% of clergy report experiencing major distress
- 33% have considered leaving the ministry[63]

From "Marriage Problems Pastors Face" (Leadership, Fall 1992)

81% insufficient time together

71% use of money

70% income level

64% communication difficulties

63% congregational differences

57% differences over leisure activities

53% difficulties in raising children

46% sexual problems

---

[62] (London 1993)
[63] Ibid.

Christopher Schmitz – Why Your Pastor Left

41% Pastor's anger toward spouse

35% differences over ministry career

25% differences over spouse's career[64]

Syndicated columnist Terry Mattingly wrote in the late 1990s that the divorce rate for U.S. pastors had risen 65 percent in the past 25 years.[65]

The statistics are fairly consistent from survey to survey. Most PWs feel that the ministry has been hazardous to their family. One in four PWs wishes that their husband did something else for a living. I stated earlier that laity rarely understands how much a ministry family sacrifices—especially the pastor's wife. Four out of every five PWs continue doing ministry, despite the fact that they believe it damages their family. They are placing such a high value on the work of the Lord that they sacrifice the good of their family in order to do the work of the Lord. *That* is how much your Pastor's wife loves you! Never take advantage of that.

Pastor's wife and professional counselor Gabriele Rienas offers advice to PWs. She says there are three primary things minister's wives must remember. "She needs to use her life to glorify God. She needs to serve her husband and family as her first calling and priority. She needs to maintain visibility in *some* area of congregational life." There are a lot of gray zones

---

[64] Ibid.
[65] Zoba, Wendy Murray. "What Pastor's Wives Wish Their Churches Knew Part 2." Christianity Today, April 7, 1997.

Christopher Schmitz – Why Your Pastor Left

between those three needs where a PW can find her identity and be herself, free of the expectations of others.

Luckily, Rienas believes that the old paradigm is fading. "Not so long ago people expected a pastor's wife to play the piano, teach Sunday School, and run women's ministries, while at the same time hosting guests in her home. She was to accomplish all of this while raising her children as perfect angels who could be an example to all. She was prim and proper, did not speak out of turn, and was always kind and submissive to everyone. And, if the church bathrooms needed cleaning, she did that too, with a smile."[66]

I'm a pastor. I'm not cut out to be a pastor's wife. I'm just not strong enough. Meeting those expectations take either superhuman skills or an unprecedented amount of deception.

"I have great news," Rienas writes. "The well-defined image of the typical pastor's wife is fading. Ministry wives are entering a new season of liberty. Unfortunately, the old, preconceived ideas still live with us and in us."[67]

Jesus was both fully God and fully man. He was literally "Super-human," and yet, Christ was subject to his own humanity. Sometimes the rigid set of standards we expect of our PWs can only be attained were she were more than human; we cannot demand more from the pastor's wife than we did of Christ. I pray and hope that this freedom and liberty Rienas anticipates takes hold soon.

---

[66] Rienas, Gabriele. "Q & A For Ministry Wives." Enrichment, Winter 2011: 128-129. 128
[67] Ibid. 129

Christopher Schmitz – Why Your Pastor Left

H.B London, a Focus on the Family director of a ministry to pastors and their families said that the most important thing a minister can do to encourage strong families and good marriages is to "model a strong marriage. Model attentiveness. Model Intimacy. Model loving parenthood. That's the first thing. Remember that your marriage and your family are more important than your ministry."[68]

Let your Pastor's Wife be just that. Let her be a wife first and foremost. Understand that she is not Superwoman; she cannot be since you just might be her personal kryptonite. Just allow her to love her husband and love God with all her heart.

---

[68] (Rainey 2001)

Chapter 13

(Owned By the Church—Life In the Fishbowl)

Gillette was a goldfish I'd bought for an illustration I used in one of my earlier ministries. I let the kids in my youth group name him (it?) We were discussing the topic of boundaries one night after some casual conversation about rules and other parental ideas that the teens resented. Without warning I reached my hand in, grabbed Gillette and yanked him out of the water and set him on the floor. The poor fish lay there gasping and flopping. Teenage girls shrieked and screamed. "Put him back! Put him back, Pastor Chris! He's going to die!" One girl had even broken into tears.

"Gillette doesn't want to go back into the bowl," I said. "He hates all these rules, like, 'only stay in the water' and 'don't go beyond the glass walls.' I'm pretty sure *he doesn't like his curfew either*. Look at him flip around there on the ground. He looks like he knows what he's doing. He's fine on his own. He just felt so confined within these boundaries; they were cramping his style. It's not like those boundaries were meant to keep him safe or anything, right?"

Don't call PETA on me. The fish was only out of water for a few seconds before I returned him.

Boundaries are a good thing. They can keep us out of dangerous areas and they can prevent other forces from entering where they don't belong and doing damage. Human skin is exactly such a boundary. Skin keeps out harmful diseases and toxins but it also has methods that it can allow things to be passed through the barrier to let in good things, such as topical medicines.

230

Sometimes things try to rip through those barriers, even using the pretense of obeying scripture, etc. in an effort to subvert a pastor's boundaries. Specifically I mean the family/home life of the minister. "The fishbowl" is a dangerous place—the stress is a major factor in clergy burnout and the overwhelming transparency of it all is a breeding ground for character assassination.

Even if those trials are overcome, the stress certainly impacts the pastor's home. Here are some findings from Leadership, Fall 1992 "Marriage Problems Pastors Face."[69]

- 81% insufficient time together

- 71% use of money

- 70% income level

- 63% congregational differences

- 57% differences over leisure activities

- 53% difficulties in raising children

- 35% differences over ministry career

- 25% differences over spouse's career

Current Thoughts & Trends, December 1992

- 28% of pastors said ministry was a hazard to family life

- 94% felt under pressure to have the "ideal" family

- Estimated 20% of clergy suffer from long term stress

- One year the Southern Baptists paid out $64 million in stress related claims, second in dollar amounts only to maternity benefits

---

[69] (Wheeler 2012) 36

Christopher Schmitz – Why Your Pastor Left

Peeping toms love big windows. Most people will acknowledge that gossip is often a problem in our churches. Too much forced transparency is kind of like forcing your pastor and his family to dress and undress in front of their windows for the whole congregation to witness.

There are some places within the boundaries of the ministry family that don't have any real bearing on the effectiveness of the pastor. Some people (usually of the nosier, inquisitive sort) claim access to criticize and scrutinize the pastor's family because of the mandate that the pastor must be able to manage their house well (1 Timothy 3:4). The problem with that idea is that "managing well" can be a subjective idea that places the pastor under judgment. That is not the intent of this verse, and with the problems inherent in human free will, we cannot use this verse as an excuse to violate his or her boundaries and force access into a place where we do not belong to exercise judgment that we are not entitled to pass. Besides, scripture is filled with Godly leaders, prophets, priests, and kings, who did amazing things for the Kingdom but had family issues (Eli, Daniel, Josiah, just to name a few).

Keepers of pet fish are advised to very seldom use dip nets and such tools to chase their fish around the bowl; it stresses the fish and can damage them. Being a part of a ministry family has been compared to living life within a fishbowl. Any entity on the "outside of the fishbowl" is a person who does not have a relationship granting them internal influence. Before you think that you are in such a role because you serve on a deacon board, understand that this relationship is not gained by position or title; it can only be granted by those on the inside. Entities on the outside have no justifiable reason to try and manipulate what is inside it. Please, don't tap on the glass. It agitates the fish.

Stress added to the fishbowl from an outside, uninvolved source only pressures the family and stresses the pastor's marriage. The biggest result of "fishbowl intrusion" is an ineffective, worn down, and distracted pastor. In his book "Confessions of an Insignificant Pastor," Pastor Mark Elliott writes about how the ministry (and the people in it) damaged his family.

> "I can still remember the day that I had to tell my church that *my kids were off limits!* Come after me but it's not fair to come after my kids.
>
> My prodigal is a casualty of his personal choices and the unfair, unpleasant expectations the church has placed on him. All of my kids talk about how hard it is to be a [Pastor's Kid]. I've tried to always stress the many benefits of being a PK. I've lovingly confronted my prodigal. I continue to show my love and try not to push him further away. I still pray and hold onto God's promises that my child will one day return to him."[70]

The lack of boundaries and good judgment by the people within the church contributed to this prodigal's departure. Ultimately, it is the conscious choice of the individual making a decision to do such; we cannot be held accountable for the actions of others, but God will judge us for those. Can you

---

[70] Elliott, Mark. Confessions of an Insignificant Pastor. Lima: Faithwalk, 2009. 206,207

Christopher Schmitz – Why Your Pastor Left

imagine if the role was reversed, though? What if the words or actions of your pastor directly contributed to *your* child's decision to abandon their faith? Pastors have no recourse against their flock when the sheep do exactly that to the pastor's children.

Family should be an "untouchable" area, an area that, for most people, there can be no outside manipulation or influence without express consent from the pastor. Job related/business ethics would prohibit an employer of a company from firing, manipulating, or chastising any employee for the happenings in their home and family. I understand that the analogy is incongruent with a "ministry job," and yet we often treat our pastor as a "Hireling."

Remember that your pastor should also bear many qualities possessed by a friend. Have you ever visited a friend's home? Even with close friends, stepping into their bedroom is often an uncomfortable place because you know it is a place where all walls come down, an intimate place—a person is revealed and most vulnerable in their bedroom. The family boundaries of your pastor should have that same aura—involvement in the home life of a pastor, his or her interactions with their children, are intimate; they should be respected and honored. If you're invited into your minister's home, the first thing you do isn't walk into their bedroom and start exploring the contents of his or her underwear drawer. Likewise, respect the sanctity and sovereignty of the family.

Let your pastor parent as he or she sees fit. Don't chastise or berate the pastor's children unless you are in a position to do so—don't attempt to parent someone else's child: your pastor's or anyone else's.

Christopher Schmitz – Why Your Pastor Left

My wife and I will never forget an encounter when we were ministering in one particular church, the same church in which a parishioner stole my wife's purse. My son, our oldest child, was almost four. After a Wednesday evening service, he was playing with several other children his own age; these children were all wound up having fun playing like young boys do, hiding around corners and stepping around them to scare their friends. One of the parents of three teens in the youth group, a very severe man with no sense of humor stepped around the corner and spooked my son. The child stuck his tongue out at the man and ran off giggling.

The father immediately came over to me; I was standing only a few feet away talking to another parishioner. He told me how he thought it utterly disrespectful of my child to stick his tongue out at "one of his elders." I did inform him that my boy was only three years old, but promised to have a serious discussion with the toddler about reverence and respect. Parenting is never as much fun as when other people with very little interaction in your life tell you exactly why you are failing as a parent.

I appreciated [sarcasm] how the parent was concerned enough to follow up with me the next morning. He came to my office right away in the morning to deliver a book on how to "properly raise children." At the time, I was in my mid-twenties and the publishing date was a decade older than I was. The source material wasn't exactly relevant—I don't think the chapter on the dangers of the new "color TV" was going to help me much.

Sometimes people just need to lighten up; they certainly need to understand influence, respect, and boundaries. Even if the parenting book had

Christopher Schmitz – Why Your Pastor Left

any amount of real-life bearing, I would have been loath to read it after my parenting had been called into question (and for the record, many people have commented on how well-behaved our children are.)

There is a famous quote. "Those who live in glass houses should not throw stones." One thing that the ministry demands is transparency, but at what cost and how transparent must we be? Are we required to answer any deeply personal question any person demands of us? I am frequently transparent and very genuine when I preach. Pastors should retain a modicum of privacy; it is a necessity to maintain authority and order. There should be some areas of a pastor's life that he can choose to keep off limits.

Gary Smalley, in his seminars on relationship-building and communication, talks about the "closed spirit." A closed spirit is like a shy clam that has closed to protect itself; you can never force a calm to open up without violating it—causing damage to thing itself, harming your relationship. Churches cannot force a pastor to be more transparent than he or she is willing without wounding them and hurting their ministry. Forcing a pastor and his or her family to live inside a glass house, while the congregation is allowed to pick and choose what they choose to reveal, creates a double standard that will cause resentment and breed an attitude of judgmentalism. Further, that fishbowl scenario strips the pastor of their ability to deliver the "hard messages."

Here's an example of the danger of living in a "glass parsonage." Pastor feels led to preach about gambling; the sermon convicts sister Ethel in her spirit. Ethel is a board member's wife and she spends every Saturday in the casino in her neighboring community. Forgetting that sermons are directed by

236

God, Ethel feels upset and offended that Pastor would preach a message "specific to her." She already saw how Pastor's teen boy got into a heated argument with another student at school—shouldn't he be preaching on hatred instead? Angry, sister Ethel is tempted to spread dissention, feeling justified in her need to bring the pastor "down a notch" so that he's not a hypocrite. During the week, her "anonymous prayer request" trickles down the prayer-chain: Pastor and his family need help getting close to God—we need him to find that balance and *bring the Word properly in the future.*

I know many people, even pastors, who advocate that a pastor *must* live this transparently so they can be a living demonstration of Christlikeness. That's a faulty idea. Our example of perfection is Christ; human pastors cannot be expected to fully live in that perfection at all times and be subject to judgment when they commit human failures.

Unfair comparisons inherent in "glass parsonages" dilute the authority that your pastor wields. In 1 Corinthians 10:29, Paul asks, "Why should my freedom be judged by another's conscience?" This is Paul, an Apostle. Paul understands that we have personal freedom, and even as a leader of the church he is within his rights to exercise that freedom. Expecting your minister to live under the judgment and expectations of other men holds the pastor in greater bondage than any other person in the congregation. Pastors should instead model the epitome of freedom in Christ! If you are a pastor and an advocate for a glass house, for the sake of your family at least consider tinted windows.

The oft-overwhelming transparency of the glass parsonage can lead to burn-out in the ministry family. Unlike their pastor-parent, "they didn't sign up

Christopher Schmitz – Why Your Pastor Left

for this." For many PKs, the abundance of people watching their every step and misstep can make them feel like the star of the Truman Show. And like the character Truman Burbank, who discovers his entire life has been a televised setup and he had been raised on an enclosed movie set, the final moments of stage-time in his show saw him angry, escaping through the rear exit, and disavowing the entire production.

PKs tend to have an unusually high rate of church disaffection and even defection. I've known many PKs and I can vouch for that statement with personal experience. Chances are, if you know half a dozen pastors and have met their kids, you can probably vouch for it too. Richard Willowby writes about this disaffection in his article "Prodigal PKs." "If teenage PKs feel they must sing in every youth group concert or live flawlessly because they exist in the spotlight ... they may want to escape the glare of expectations." He adds, "The evening and weekend nature of church life can make ministers seem like absentee parents who don't have time or energy to be involved with their children or provide oversight." [71]

Dennis Rainey, author and president of FamilyLife also writes about this in "Caring For Your Family."

> The key is to view our children as our privileged responsibility and assignment from God. This is the quality one young man, himself now a pastor, saw in his relationship with his father, who was a pastor: "My dad could teach spiritual principles from the most ordinary circumstances. When Dad walked out the door, I was invited. When he

---

[71] Willowby, Richard. "Prodigal PKs." Pastor's Family, Oct/Nov 1996.

Christopher Schmitz – Why Your Pastor Left

played golf with his preacher friends, I rode in the golf cart... he did not have to alter his schedule, just his focus... The other day my dad commented, 'I regret not being more consistent in my family devotions when you were growing up.' I reminded him that our family altar was often a boat, a field, or a golf cart."

Another child of a pastor has painful memories. At her father's funeral she watched and listened as mourner after mourner described all the wonderful deeds done by this shepherd for his sheep. When at last the crowd departed, she asked, "Who was that man of whom they spoke?"

All the deceased pastor's children agreed that others had known the heart of their father better than they did. In sadness the daughter of this wonderful servant of God wrote of her father, "To Dad every request from a [church] member constituted a command performance. Family plans were canceled without question. Protests were pointless. Even the youngest child could recite Dad's response: 'Don't you understand? God called me to serve these people. My work is to do the Lord's work. How can I refuse? They need me.' And he would be gone."[72]

Rainey goes on to recommend some steps for pastor-parents. Cultivate a focused relationship with each child. Explain to your kids what you do and why. Save some pastoral care for your own sheep. He says, "For about a decade

---

[72] Rainey, Dennis. "Caring For Your Family, How Not to Lose the Battle at Home." Enrichment, Winter 2011: 70-74. 73

Christopher Schmitz – Why Your Pastor Left

I declined opportunities to lead Bible studies for businessmen because I did not want to always be rushing off to help others know God while failing to introduce my own children to Him… After your wife, your children are your most important disciples."[73]

Church people find it so easy to cross over those boundaries and either place those expectations upon the family, or monopolize the pastor's time. No pastor walks into ministry thinking it is a "Forty-Hour per week, punch-clock job." We understand that the dynamics are different than any other job in our culture; those dynamics do not change the need for the pastor to take personal time for themselves and additional quality time for his or her family. An overabundance of time spent on church business at the expense of the pastor's life comes at the expense of the church as well as the pastor. It's kind of like having a choice between eight bags of quality, fresh groceries or fourteen bags of outdated, spoiled and moldy groceries. More is not always better.

The mandate in 1 Timothy 3:4,5 reads, "He must manage his own family well and see that his children obey him, and he must do so in a manner worthy of full respect. (If anyone does not know how to manage his own family, how can he take care of God's church?)" NIV. While the word "manage" is the most accurate translation of the word proistēmi, the Greek text for verse 3 is more accurately reflected by the King James Version. "One that ruleth well his own house, having his children in subjection with all gravity." The Greek text leaves the specifics of managing open to interpretation only by the notion that Greg Hickle suggested earlier in this book: if it is not sin, then it is permissible.

---

[73] Ibid. 73

Christopher Schmitz – Why Your Pastor Left

The word "subjection" is hupotagē and means "in subordination to." Hupotagē *can* mean obedience, but more accurately represents respect—it doesn't rule out the possibility that a person in subordination might choose a different path; the text requires that the candidate for eldership remain honorable and worthy of their child's respect regardless of their child's decisions.

This passage in 1 Timothy is a prerequisite to assuming a position as an "elder" in the church, a group to which the office of Pastor belongs. Eldership has more to do with requirements of the office and Godly calling than it does with age. By Paul's own account, the pastor Timothy, who the epistles of 1 and 2 Timothy were written to, was young, even by standards in that day (lifespan of the Greeks and Romans was not too drastically different than they are currently.) As the head pastor in the church at Ephesus, he was between his mid-twenties and thirties. My studies incline me to believe more on the early twenties model—scripture is filled with gifted, trained, and called *young* people called to do great things. Study on the story of Jesus telling Peter to catch a fish and take two coins from its mouth reveal that the majority of Jesus' disciples were considered "underage" according to the Jews because, by age, only Jesus and Peter were subject to the Jewish Temple Tax, even if the fact of an individual Bar Mitzvah made them a technical adult; there were two standards.

That one must keep his family affairs in order is a biblical command for your pastor. That said, ministers *must* have adequate time for "maintenance" of their family. That is not an area where a lay-person can offer a rebuke. Reproving a minister for insufficient family time only further burdens him or her with yet another expectation. If you see tension building in your pastor's

241

family, find loving ways to let the pressure off. If you have authority, or can make suggestions to another who has authority, ask about giving your pastor opportunities to spend time with his or her family—make the setting closed, enable the family to reconnect with itself—outside of church relationships and church business.

Find unique ways to bless the pastor and his children. To do that, you must first *know* the family. Don't expect that they are just like *your* family or like the last minister's family. Each family unit is different—which is what's so great about them. They can reach new people and bless you in ways that others couldn't.

Nearly every year, without fail, I've been approached by other people who feel it absolutely necessary that I attend a seven to ten day-long church "family camp." One group of church people exerted great pressure on me, verging on making it a direct order. As much as that camp blessed those other people, it fell sandwiched between two other camp weeks that consumed 100% of my time and took me away from my family entirely. While our family would have been together at the camp, I wanted to be with *just* my family and not have to worry about outside schedules.

Mark Elliott describes many pastors in his book. "He may look like he has it all together on the outside. The truth is he may be lonely, hurting, insecure, depressed, struggling, and ready to quit. You could make a big difference in his life and family! Watch his kids so that he can take his wife on a date. Give him a gift certificate to a nice restaurant in town. Give him and his wife a weekend away at your cabin, timeshare, or a nice resort… Why not spoil

242

your pastor so much that he would give you the best years of his ministry and never want to leave your church? What could happen if Christians ministered to their pastor and his family without expecting anything in return?"[74]

If your church is anything like the ones I've been involved with, you've probably had a few "charity cases" in your body. It's great to see it, when the congregation bends over backwards to make a newcomer, usually one that doesn't meet the same standards of social class as the rest, feel welcome. Congregations bless them and use that person as a central focus point to demonstrate Christ-like love. I enjoy being a part of that, yet I wonder what keeps congregations from blessing their leaders, especially pastors, in a likewise manner?

Prevention of this ministry killer is a must. It is more than a ministry killer, it is a child killer, and it's having a dramatic impact on the future generations of men and women who've been groomed to become ministers and church or community leaders. We must learn how to properly deal with the boundaries and navigate the false expectations that surround the parsonage and pastoral family.

---

[74] (Elliott 2009) 211

Christopher Schmitz – Why Your Pastor Left

Chapter 14

(The Remedy)

You may have read this book hoping for some closure on how to deal with your grief over the loss of your pastor. I know that up until now, this book has mostly been about preventing a pastoral loss, or explaining the circumstances that might have factored into his departure. I do want to give advice on how to cope with the grief that often results from these circumstances. I also want to warn you against letting bitterness consume you. You may see the validity in some of the situations I wrote about in previous chapters and that might make you angry, you might also become angry because it's a natural stage of the grieving process. Do not turn that anger inward and let it become bitterness. I write about an experience I had with bitterness because I know how anger so easily turns into bitterness, and how anger is a natural stage in the grieving process.

Growing up, I went to High School in a town where football was everything. The coach I played under is the winningest coach in the state football records. He was known for his stern demeanor that demanded respect and for his violent outbursts at poor reffing decisions—he was a man who was passionate about the game. I had the chance to play with an incredibly gifted bunch of guys. In my junior year we went to the state championship game and lost—our only loss of the year in what amounts to the Superbowl of High School football games. In the following year, we won that State Championship game and held an undefeated record. It was kind of like a Disney movie,

244

actually. The team we lost to the previous year had been undefeated and hadn't lost a game up until the rematch against us at the State Championship game, only this time, we walked away with the trophy.

Despite the honor of being on that team, my heart was filled with anger and bitterness that almost consumed me during my final year of high school and my first couple years of college. That game was the biggest game of my athletic experience and a major moment for anyone growing up in a "football town." Yet, for me, I couldn't help but be resentful of that game. I know, it sounds like a setup for the sequel to Varsity Blues, but bear with me.

The head coach I played under was a deeply respected member of our community. There was an assistant coach, however, whom I didn't get along with as much as I should have. My sister had some issues with him in the past; perhaps that had something to do with why he and I chaffed. There were other, complicated issues in our past as well—there always are in smaller communities like the one I grew up in—interpersonal problems in smaller communities easily become magnified. Our personalities likely clashed most because he and I had a heated disagreement in one of his classes a year or so prior to that game. In retrospect, I can see how I had been an arrogant teen boy (as most teen boys are) and had disrespected him with my attitude—which is inexcusable—but there hadn't been any team problems except that trespass upon his pride. The Assistant Coach was also one of the persons responsible for the local FCA (Fellowship of Christian Athletes,) and was an outspoken church advocate. One of the reasons for our clash of personalities was due the incongruity that I saw between what he "preached" and how that played out on the campus... not that

245

the judgments of a high school teenager are anything, but "the truth is in the eye of the beholder" as they say.

Shortly before the Prep Bowl game, we'd had a colorful disagreement. Publicly, in front of an entire class, some issue had flared up. I don't remember much about it except that the whole class paused to watch what resulted in a teenager and a teacher yelling at each other. I do remember that I was saved by the bell—the period ended and the class dismissal interrupted the dispute (which had *not* been about class material.)

During this final game, the Championship, the Head Coach grabbed me by the sleeve and gave me the play about to send me to the huddle to replace one of the starters. The Assistant Coach grabbed me by the shoulder-pads and shoved me behind the cluster of "bench-warmer" freshmen that had no chance of playing in a game of this magnitude without the upperclassmen blowing out the opposition.

I'll never forget the look he gave me when he pushed me back past the underclassmen. He gave another player the play-call and sent him to the huddle. On two occasions, during time-outs, the players in the positions I backed up specifically requested that I relieve them, but the Assistant Coach reassured them that they were fine. I never left the sideline that game; I didn't get to play in the biggest game of my career—the game I'd spent six years preparing for. I felt robbed. I was angry, but I held my anger in check, trying to show as much respect as possible.

I turned that anger inward, not wanting to be the villain. I dropped any classes from that point on that the Assistant Coach taught. My parents were

Christopher Schmitz – Why Your Pastor Left

some of the few who knew my frustration and I had standing parental permission to receive detention from this particular teacher if I flew off the handle and said or did something stupid that got me into trouble. I never did blowup, though. I buried my anger—the issue was dead; my sports involvement was done. I'd been cheated—story over, right?

Turned inward, my anger just boiled inside. I didn't recognize until years later, but I liked that feeling—the power and control that buried hatred gives a person. Bitterness is a powerful thing, it makes a person feel vindicated, validated; it gives them an unwarranted sense of righteous indignation that they can used to justify whatever actions they like. It's like a drug; you just draw on that memory and let the anger and power consume you a little bit, it gives you an edge.

Because of that anger I'd held onto, I purposefully decided to forego any interest in collegiate athletics, even though I'd received calls from college coaches wanting to discuss possibilities of athletic scholarships. I didn't want to play; I loved the power and anger of my bitterness more than the game, and I saw continuing to play as refusal to play the victim role. That would sacrifice a big portion of this power I felt inside of me. It was something that never should have been. It affected me in college; especially studying ministry, I should have realized that I was in need of serious correction, spiritually.

On a trip with a number of other students, I remember hanging out in some condo in a tourist-trap town in Colorado. One of the students was an upperclassman and a far more mature believer than I was and he helped me forever change that night. As one of the clear leaders in our rag-tag band of

Christopher Schmitz – Why Your Pastor Left

college students, he dictated the flow of the conversation. Somehow the corporate banter turned to teachers, or football, or some topic that set me off. I ranted the preceding story, playing the angry victim.

He looked right at me and said, "You've got a real problem with bitterness." Then he changed the subject like it'd never happened. I don't remember his name; I never thanked him. I was too busy being angry at that moment. He'd just publicly called me out for a personal problem, and then changed the subject—both not letting me dwell on it and feel empowered in my anger, and not letting me react or respond to his comment. I could only think about it. That was exactly what I needed—the self-realization of the problem and the right circumstances that made me heed his diagnosis coupled with some time to mull over the warning.

Realization set in. This was no longer the coach's problem: it was mine. There comes a point in the consummation process of bitterness where you refuse to release your anger and hold onto it—taking ownership of that sin. Whatever that past hurt was, it's in the past; your maintenance of the memory is the only thing keeping it alive. The sin becomes yours and *you* are responsible for it, rather than your abuser. This is exactly what I had done; while it was a big deal to me, something I thought of frequently, I'd guess that this coach never thought about it. The onus of the problem was solely with me. His conscience was likely clear, with God. Now, aware of the problem, it was only with me that there was any sin.

A year or so later, I'd transferred colleges, but been faithfully studying scripture and learning how to deal with bitterness and anger. One Sunday, a

Christopher Schmitz – Why Your Pastor Left

visiting minister at the church I attended preached on the topic of bitterness. He shared a similar story to what I'd dealt with—it wasn't football, but some other matter entirely. He'd gone through some personal conflict where he felt deeply wronged by anther believer; the situation festered and then the culprit moved away and so the unresolved nature of the conflict embittered him. This was the day when I finally felt as if that bitter spirit broke within me and I had victory. I learned to let go of it.

Bitterness is hatred turned inward; you can't hold onto Hatred and God simultaneously ("God is Love" 1 John 4:8.) God must be the source of your power because that source is your master and you cannot serve two masters.

He taught some practical ways to resolve your spirit and break bitterness. First, is to obviously pray and ask God to uproot that bitterness from your life and then actively work to release it. That's a continual battle. I'd been working on that part for over a year by the time I heard this wise minister speak on the topic. He also realized that his enemy didn't know that they'd caused any pain.

Once he'd understood all of these things, the second thing he did was take ownership of the problem and recognized that it was now *he* that was the sinner in this situation, holding a grudge against his brother. He felt God call him to repentance and to write a letter to this person and explain how and why he felt the way he did and then to ask for forgiveness for his bitterness. He wrote many drafts of that letter and kept them all in a box. Finally, when he felt that he'd written the letter with a perfectly clear conscience, he felt released from that hatred. He was going to mail that letter when he felt God instruct him to

249

take the box full of letters and burn it. While he was prepared to do it, he didn't need to mail the letter. God had brought about resolution.

So why am I writing about all of this in a book dealing with coping after the loss of person's pastor? The same ways to deal with bitterness may help you work through other stages of grief, in addition to anger. It should also warn you against going down the same road I did if you've been wronged corporately or personally by a specific person, group, or faction in your church. Let God deal with those others in His own way, let God be God, you need only serve Him and rely on Him. Even if the situation that led to your pastor's departure or dismissal was entirely human in its making, God can still work. He can still operate and make miracles as long as there is at least one person believing that He will show up in power. God can still transform and redeem your church with an even greater work. Abraham prayed if there be at least ten righteous men inside of Sodom, his cousin's home, God was willing to spare it. He was sending his angels to that city, and whenever the presence of God arrives something will be changed. God was sending destruction or renewal. Lot lost two of his daughters to the rapists of the city; staying in the midst of those who have caused pain can be difficult, but the departure of the Godly may result in the destruction of those remaining.

So how do we use these techniques to bring personal healing and resolution in the wake of losing our pastor? Remember, be open to prayer changing *you* as much as the situation or object of your appeals. Prayer is always a first resort. Invite God to operate and give you the proper context and vision. For the deeply wounded, I don't hesitate to recommend counseling and

Christopher Schmitz – Why Your Pastor Left

can't claim to be any sort of expert; *do not* use my advice in the place of solid, qualified counseling techniques.

As Christians, we are all walking through a process of sanctification. We should continually be giving our lives over to God. We must "daily take up our cross" and follow Christ (Luke 9:23). That means dying daily to the things that *we* want and renewing our minds (Romans 12:2) to become more like Christ and strive to accomplish God's will rather than our own. Maybe, in order to cope and work through your specific events, you should write down your feelings, write letters to those who may have hurt you. Maybe a journal would be a good way to get your thoughts articulated so you can work through them. Consider an independent party as a private counselor; if you are the sort who talks through your problems for catharsis, make sure you're not just venting anger to a person close to the situation or someone that isn't legally bound to confidentiality—don't let your hurt become compounded by letting it spread to others and/or cause division as you seek healing.

Sometimes, we can only surrender our hurts to God and let Him sort them out. That may necessitate a departure, a sacrifice of things. In college, I sacrificed athletics. I was spotted playing some inter-mural football by members of my college team—a team that held nigh-unbreakable records for losing; they needed all the talent they could muster. At one point the entire team was in my yard begging me to join for my senior year. That would have been a huge feather in my hat—a big ego boost had I joined. I didn't feel, at that point, that I was ready yet to return to the game—knowing that I would never compete. I sacrificed that in order to ensure I had overcome that thorn in my flesh. I was

251

unsure of myself then and wanted to ensure that I had, indeed, overcome that problem in my past. I didn't want to walk into a situation where I may be tempted to fall into those same pitfalls. Now, I can say that I don't have grudges or hold bitterness against those who have wronged me in ministry or caused me undue hardships—even hurt me financially. I wish things had happened differently, and I will guard myself against future hurts from those persons, but I don't hold bitterness against them.

Surrendering those things might mean walking away from a church or group if that is the only way healing can be achieved. I know some people who have been so deeply wounded by their church peers that they had to find a new place of worship. This is regrettable, but understandable in some cases. Just make sure to check your heart; make sure that this is indeed the will of God and not a decision made from anger or a refusal to compromise or love your Christian brethren because of their past decisions. Make sure you aren't harboring unforgiveness in this process.

Before you make any of those decisions, do what I did when confronted with my bitter spirit. Take some time and think about it. Evaluate yourself—only *you* can know your motives. Be honest and examine your own heart. It's okay to be hurt; it's okay to be angry. Just don't let those things consume you and guide your future.

Be sure to maintain your boundaries. Establish them if you need to. Let love guide your life, but let it be tempered with firmness. Don't allow yourself to be burned in the same manner. Give the benefit of the doubt whenever possible, yet if someone has wounded you in a specific way or has a habit of

252

reacting in certain manners—*expect that it will happen again*. Take steps to bring about healing, but also restoration of your brothers and sisters wherever possible. Pray constantly for strength and guidance and seek a divine call!

Everyone has a call. God has a will and plan that He will unfold. Partner with the vision, be instrumental in that process, find your purpose and calling in your church. As a lay-person, if you leave, let it be because God is calling you to something or somewhere else. If you stay, assume a role and a purpose as God directs (He calls everyone to *something*!) When you are in the will of God and walking in His purpose and His call, you can be effective and only then will you walk in the authority and power to which he calls agents of change.

Love and prayer must temper everything. Open your heart for change. If you've lost your pastor, know that someone else *will* come to replace them. Prepare your heart for that day and seek closure in the past circumstance so that it does not repeat itself.

Prayerfully consider your next candidate. When he or she comes, be involved in whatever way you can with the selection process. Stay involved after they arrive—be part of the minority that works diligently within the church. Grow with your new pastor; become an integral part of your churches' ministry. A relationship with your new pastor is not a betrayal of the former. Growing in a new relationship will help heal any past hurt. Don't judge your new minister's successes or failures on the basis of past ministries! Allow him or her to cast vision and mold ministries as God calls. If God is truly given free reign, change isn't restricted to the face in the pulpit!

Christopher Schmitz – Why Your Pastor Left

Remember that change can be a good thing, after all. Sometimes God calls pastors away so that He can mold something new, as He desires. Your church has, perhaps been in the process of becoming a beautiful, clay bowl on the potter's wheel. Now, though, that form changes, the top is closed over and pulled high into a cone and cut off. The Potter punches another hole through the side and all seems lost. Then, He takes that cone and makes a spout, attaches it and forms the top into a lid, creating a teapot. During the process of the wheel, it's easy to question the Potter's sanity. But resisting will only slow us or withhold us from our destiny in fulfilling His purpose that He envisioned in us when He first put that clay on the wheel.

Some of the ways we resist that wheel, those Ministry Killers were:

• Disillusionment

Ask your pastor about his or her call. Encourage them at every turn! Partner with your pastor for success and join them for the hard times as well as the good ones. Never, ever, abandon your pastor and leave them as a lonely shepherd on the hillside.

• Abuse and Power Struggles

Don't fight your pastor! He or she has authority because they are ultimately responsible for the welfare of God's church. Let the pastor cast vision and lead; that's why God called them! Pray.

• Ministry Incongruity/Unclear Expectations

Make the church boundaries clear. Communicate exactly what is expected and be willing to have those expectations compromised in order to pursue *God's* vision for a ministry. Expect things to be

Christopher Schmitz – Why Your Pastor Left

different now than in the past and value the fresh point of view others bring. Empower and release others into ministry.

• Financial Concerns

Honor God with your pocketbook and not just your words. There is a direct correlation between how God blesses you and your generosity (in this case, giving honor to His called and sent ones). Know whether your pastor is a shepherd or a hireling.

• Jealousy

Affirm each other in ministry. Understand your specific calling, boundaries, and strengths/weaknesses. Kill your pride in the interest of the Kingdom.

• Respect Issues in the Ministry

Tread lightly near another person's boundaries; don't stray over them. Accept correction and understand what rights your pastor has over his or her self. When you remove another's rights over their own finances, decisions, schedule, etc. you are endorsing slavery. Don't be a Nabal.

• Divine Calling/Ministry development & growth

Pray for your pastor's success and that he or she is constantly in touch with the will of God. If it's your opinion that your pastor needs to leave, pray that God deals with that situation and thought—either that the Pastor sees it's time to go or that *you* see what God is up to.

• Hurting the Pastor's Wife

People have no idea how much a pastor's wife can suffer. It is a doubly hurtful thing to watch your spouse sacrifice; when you are his help-

255

mate, all of the pastor's concerns and trials become her pain as well, in addition to her own stressors. Show her love! There is no better way to love a pastor than to passionately love his wife.

• The Fishbowl

Be careful that in your zealousness to see ministry happen as you expect it that you don't ruin a family. Don't force your idea of a perfect pastoral family onto your minister's kids. That will only make the next generation of humanists and deliberate atheist sinners that much more zealous; it's not love when you ruin a pastor's kids on God.

In every follow-up to each chapter on "Ministry Killers" I offer the preventative advice of encouragement. This is no mistake. Churches need to recognize that vocational ministry is perhaps the hardest job in the world. Pastors find the job difficult enough to do without discouragement. In several books, one frustrated and honest pastor has been quoted as penning:

> "If I wanted to drive a manager up the wall, I would make him responsible for the success of an organization and give him no authority. I would provide him with unclear goals, not commonly agreed upon by the organization. I would ask him to provide a service of an ill-defined nature, apply a body of knowledge having few absolutes, and staff his organization with only volunteers who donated just a few hours a week at the most. I would expect him to work 10 to 12 hours per day and have his work evaluated by a committee of 300 to 500 amateurs. I would call him a minister and make him accountable to God."[75]

Christopher Schmitz – Why Your Pastor Left

Change is a natural part of our progression, part of our growth. I'll never forget those pamphlets that they give you as a kid around the time puberty strikes. You remember those pamphlets from school. They all start the same, "You may begin to discover that as you grow your body begins changing." Change is instrumental to growth! I find it ironic that churches that so vehemently resist change, to the extreme that they sometimes excise a pastor who yearns for it, those churches are radically implementing the very thing they are resisting. It's all so very Obi-Wan Kenobi in its resolution.

Sometimes God uses change. Sometimes He uses faithful consistency to bring about His plans. Often, those two partner for a deep and powerful move of God that cohesively blends those two elements together.

I can offer no other sincere advice except to love God above all others and seek first only His kingdom. You can never fully please man, but your sincerity can touch the heart of God. Love Him above all others and the rest will follow.

---

[75] (London 1993) 54

Christopher Schmitz – Why Your Pastor Left

Christopher Schmitz – Why Your Pastor Left

Appendix A

(Quick Reference of Statistics and Resources)

From Wayde Goodall in "Handling Stress and Avoiding Burnout."

Characteristics of Burned-out Ministers[76]

Feelings of apathy, anger, resentment	Vulnerable to illness
Feeling let down	Avoidance of office and daily work
Feelings of cynicism	Changing churches (job change)
Blaming parishioners for personal problems	Increased marital and family conflict
Rigid resistance to change	Inappropriate humor at others' expense
Avoidance of involvement with others	Derogatory, impersonal references to members
Aloofness from others (withdrawal into self)	Loss of concern and sympathy
Boredom, frustration, loss of enthusiasm	Avoidance of social times with parishioners

Factors that contribute to Burnout[77]

• Lack of awareness of one's personal need for recreation and leisure

---

[76] Goodall, Wayde. "Handling Stress and Avoiding Burnout." In The Pentecostal Pastor: A Mandate for the 21st Century, edited by Thomas, Goodall, Wayde, and Bicket, Zenas Trask, 160-169. Springfield: Gospel Publishing House, 2000. 166
[77] Ibid. 167

Christopher Schmitz – Why Your Pastor Left

- Unrealistic expectations about the nature of ministry

- Limited opportunities for promotion, inadequate remuneration

- Excessive commitment to work (workaholism)

- Excessive need to be liked and accepted by others

- Over-involvement in rescuing or helping others

- Accepting too much responsibility for parishioners' successes or failure

- Equating parishioners' rejections of help with personal rejection

- Inadequate professional training in intervention skills

- Parishioners who criticize one's ministry

- Constantly focusing on parishioner's weaknesses and problems

- Lack of opportunity to talk about personal attitudes, feelings, and trials

- Long working hours

- Inability to delegate (not enough help)

- Frequent focus on the problems and negative aspects of ministry

- Not being able to say no

- Unrealistic blaming of self for lack of church growth

- Feeling that one has to be at every church event

- Feeling overwhelmed because of the great need

- Not finding balance between ministry (work), family, rest, and play

- Not maintaining a consistent prayer and devotional life

- Being a loner in the ministry

- Unresolved family and personal problems

Number	Statistics Related to Depression	Source
80%	Pastors dealing with depression	Life Enrichment 1998
84%	Pastors spouse dealing with depression	Dobson 1998
40%+	Pastors would self-diagnose they are suffering from burnout	Dobson 1998
25%	Pastors do not have a trusted friend in ministry	Focus on the Family
75%	Pastors reported a significant stress related crisis at least once in their ministry	Fuller Inst. Church Growth 1991
50%	Pastors who feel unable to meet the demands required by the job	Fuller Inst. Church Growth 1991
90%	Pastors who felt inadequately trained to cope with ministry demands	Fuller Inst. Church Growth 1991
70%	Pastors who say they have lower self-esteem now compared to when they started in ministry	Fuller Inst. Church Growth 1991
40%	Pastors reported serious conflict with a parishioner at least once a month	Fuller Inst. Church Growth 1991
70%	Pastors who do not have someone they consider a close friend	Fuller Inst. Church Growth 1991
12%	Ministers reporting they were depressed "often or always in their ministry"	Blackmon & Hart
70%	Clergy who experience major distress	Malony & Hunt

33%	Clergy have considered leaving the ministry	Malony & Hunt
$64million	Annual stress related claims within one denomination	Southern Baptist Conv.
88%	Pastor's wives who experience depression	Cecil Paul
23%	Pastor's wives who experience depression 1-2 times annually	Cecil Paul
17%	Pastor's wives who deal with self-destructive thoughts	Cecil Paul
81%	Insufficient time with pastor spouse	Leadership 1992
71%	Percentage of ministry families stressed by use of finances	Leadership 1992
70%	Percentage of ministry families stressed by income level	Leadership 1992
20%	Ministers suffering from long-term stress	Thoughts & Trends 1992

Christopher Schmitz – Why Your Pastor Left

Number	Statistics Related to Church Growth/Decline	Source
1,500≈	Pastors leave their assignments each month, due to moral failure, spiritual burnout or contention within their local congregations.	Dobson 1998
10%	Dismissed pastors who left pastoral ministry entirely	Christianity Today 1997
4k-7,000	Number of churches closing each year	Census Bureau
1000	New churches opening per year (20 yr avg)	FASICLD
450	Average number of new churches each year between 1990-2000	FASICLD
50%	Churches adding no new members in previous 2 years	FASICLD
2,700,000	Church members becoming inactive per year	FASICLD
27	Churches per 10,000 people in 1990 America	FASICLD
11	Churches per 10,000 people in 2000 America	FASICLD
5,000,000 (-9.5%)	Combined membership decline of all Protestant denominations in the USA from 1990-2000	FASICLD

Christopher Schmitz – Why Your Pastor Left

24,000,000 (+11%)	Population increase in USA	FASICLD
-20.5%	Total lost footprint given the above	*calculated from above
-21%	Church volunteerism since 1998	Barna 2009
-17%	Sunday School involvement since 1998	Barna 2009
75%	At any given time in America, percentage of ministers who want to quit.	Church Resource Ministries – 1998
2,000+	Pastors leaving ministry each month	Marble Retreat Ctr 2001
+400%	Number of clergy leaving the ministry during the first five years of ministry, compared with the 1970s	Presbyterian Church survey 2005
1,600	Ministers terminated/forced to resign monthly	Sunscape
99	Median number of adults who attend a mainline church on any given weekend	Barna 2009
78%	Christians who have not shared their faith in the last six months	Lifeway 2014
55 years	Median age of pastor	Barna 2009
20%	Churches with 2 or more paid staff members	Focus on the Family
33%	Clergy have considered leaving the ministry	Malony & Hunt

Christopher Schmitz – Why Your Pastor Left

FASICLD Poll: Those Attending Church "Frequently"

*"frequently" is defined as attendance at least two times per month:

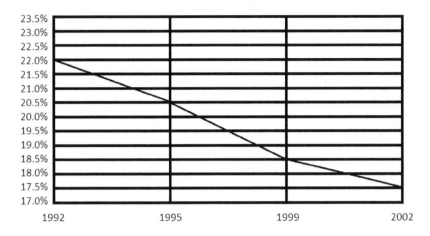

Number	Statistics Related to Ministers' Finances	Source
40%	Don't have an opportunity for family vacation or continuing education.	Barna 2002
70%	Pastors whose compensation contributed to marriage conflicts	Leadership 1992
22%	Pastors who feel forced to supplement their church income	Leadership 1992
$31,234	Average pastoral salary and housing package if serving a congregation of less than 1,000 attendees	Census Bureau
40%+	Single Staff Pastors who feel underpaid	Thoughts & Trends 1992

Christopher Schmitz – Why Your Pastor Left

33%	Senior Pastors who feel underpaid	Thoughts & Trends 1992
50%	Pastoral Salary increases versus minimum wage	Thoughts & Trends 1992
90%	Pastors who work more than 46 hours a week	Fuller Institute 1991
60%	Clergy whose wives hold full time jobs or are involved in careers	Malony & Hunt
71%	Percentage of ministry families stressed by use of finances	Leadership 1992
70%	Percentage of ministry families stressed by income level	Leadership 1992

Number	Statistics Related to the Pastoral Family Unit	Source
84%	Pastors spouse dealing with depression	Life Enrichment 1998
47%	Believe their Pastor-Spouse is suffering from burnout	Dobson 1998
80%	Clergy who feel their families have been negatively impacted by the church	Fuller Inst. Church Growth 1991
33%	Believe ministry to be an outright hazard to their families	Fuller Inst. Church Growth 1991
25%	Pastors who don't know where to go for help with personal or family conflict or concerns	Barna 2002
40%	Don't have an opportunity for outside renewal like a family vacation or continuing education.	Barna 2002
94%	Ministers who feel pressured to have an "ideal family"	Leadership 1992
77%	Ministers' spouses who feel pressured to be "an ideal role model for the Christian family"	Leadership 1992
88%	Pastor's wives who experience depression	Cecil Paul
23%	Pastor's wives who experience depression 1-2 times annually	Cecil Paul

Christopher Schmitz – Why Your Pastor Left

17%	Pastor's wives who deal with self-destructive thoughts	Cecil Paul
81%	Insufficient time with spouse	Leadership 1992
63%	Percentage of ministry families stressed by congregational differences	Leadership 1992
71%	Percentage of ministry families stressed by use of finances	Leadership 1992
70%	Percentage of ministry families stressed by income level	Leadership 1992
28%	Pastors who said "ministry was a hazard to family life"	Thoughts & Trends 1992
53%	Pastoral family having difficulties raising children	Leadership 1992
56%	Ministry family suffering sexual problems	Leadership 1992
35%	Ministry family experiencing differences in ministry career	Leadership 1992
25%	Ministry family experiencing differences in spouses career	Leadership 1992

Number	Statistics Related to Pulpit Eviction	Source
91%	Pastors know 3+ peers who have been forced out of pastoral positions	Christianity Today 1997
34%	Polled ministers serving congregations who either fired the previous minister or actively forced his or her resignation	Christianity Today 1997
23%	Number of current pastors who have been forced out at some point in their ministry.	Christianity Today 1997
10%	Dismissed pastors who left pastoral ministry entirely	Christianity Today 1997
43%	Conflicting church vision/direction was a precipitating cause of their termination	Christianity Today 1997
38%	Personality conflict with board member(s) was the cause of their termination	Christianity Today 1997
13%	Of pastors forced out, these were directly fired	Christianity Today 1997
58%	Of pastors forced out, these were forced to resign	Christianity Today 1997
29%	Of pastors forced out, these resigned because of the perceived pressure	Christianity Today 1997
66%	Terminated pastors cited "conflicts with powerful members" as a partial cause for eviction	Southern Baptist Conv.
78%	Percent of churches evicting ministers	Southern Baptist Conv.

Christopher Schmitz – Why Your Pastor Left

	which previously terminated pastors or staff members	
2,000+	Pastors leaving ministry each month	Marble Retreat Ctr 2001
+400%	Number of clergy leaving the ministry during the first five years of ministry, compared with the 1970s	Presbyterian Church survey 2005
1,600	Ministers terminated/forced to resign monthly	Sunscape

Christopher Schmitz – Why Your Pastor Left

Bibliography

Barna, George. "Gracefully Passing the Baton." *The Last Christian Generation?*

December 7, 2009.

http://fourpercent.blogspot.com/2009/12/gracefully-passing-baton-

by-george.html (accessed August 2014).

—. *Revolution.* Tyndale: Carol Stream, 2006.

Bordelon Alder, Donna. "How to Encourage Your Pastor's Wife." *Thriving*

Pastor, 2005.

Carroll, Jackson W. and Becky R. McMillan. *God's Potters: Pastoral Leadership*

and the Shaping of Congregations. Grand Rapids: Eerdmans, 2006.

Earley, David and Wheeler, David. *Evangelism Is: How to Share Jesus With*

Passion and Confidence. Nashville: B&H Academic, 2010.

Elliott, Mark. *Confessions of an Insignificant Pastor.* Lima: Faithwalk, 2009.

Fischer, David. *The 21st Century Pastor.* Nashville: Zondervan, 1996.

Foster, David. "Anne Rice Announces She's Leaving Christianity. I Knew That

Would Happen. Did You? ." *DavidFoster.TV.* august 2, 2010.

http://www.davidfoster.tv/anne-rice-announces-she's-leaving-

Christopher Schmitz – Why Your Pastor Left

christianity-i-knew-that-would-happen-did-you/ (accessed August

2014).

Goodall, Wayde. "Handling Stress and Avoiding Burnout." In *The Pentecostal

Pastor: A Mandate for the 21st Century*, edited by Thomas, Goodall,

Wayde, and Bicket, Zenas Trask, 160-169. Springfield: Gospel

Publishing House, 2000.

John C. LaRue, Jr. "Forced Exits: a Too-Common Ministry Hazard." *Your Church*,

1996.

Kent Crockett and Mike Johnston. *Pastor Abusers: When Sheep Attack Their

Shepherd.* Whole Armor Press, 2012.

Kessler, J. "Being holy, being human: Dealing with the expectations of

ministry." *The Leadership library*, 1988.

Krejcir, Dr. Richard J. "Statistics and Reasons for Church Decline." *Church

Leadership.* n.d.

http://www.churchleadership.org/apps/articles/default.asp?articleid=

42346 (accessed 2014 August).

—. "Statistics on Pastors." *Into Thy Word.* n.d.

http://www.intothyword.org/apps/articles/default.a (accessed August

2014).

—. "Why Churches Fail: Part I." *Francis A. Schaeffer Institute of Church Leadership Development.* 2007. http://www.churchleadership.org/apps/articles/default.asp?articleid= 42339 (accessed August 2014).

LaGrand Bouma, Mary. "Minister's Wives: The Walking Wounded." *Leadership,* winter 1980.

Lawrence, Brother. *The Practice of the Presence of God.* 24th Printing. Grand Rapids: Revell, 2009.

Lifeway Research. "Study: Churchgoers Believe in Sharing Faith, Most Never Do." *Lifeway Research.* January 2, 2014. http://www.lifewayresearch.com/2014/01/02/study-churchgoers-believe-in-sharing-faith-most-never-do/ (accessed August 2014).

Lindner, Eileen, ed. *The 2007 Yearbook of American and Canadian Churches.* Nashville: Abingdon Press, 2007.

London, H. & Wiseman, N. *Pastors at Risk.* Colorado Springs: Chariot Victor Publishing, 1993.

MacArthur, Dr. John. *Rediscovering Expository Preaching.* Nashville: Thomas Nelson, 1992.

Manning, Brennan. *The Ragamuffin Gospel: Good News for the Bedraggled, Beat-Up, and Burnt Out.* Colorado Springs: Multnomah, 2005.

Christopher Schmitz – Why Your Pastor Left

Maxwell, John. "When to Quit." Vols. 10, no.1. El Cajon: Injoy Life Club, n.d.

McManus, Ron. "Changing Pastorates." In *The Pentecostal Pastor: A Mandate for the 21st Century*, edited by Thomas, Goodall, Wayde, and Bicket, Zenas Trask, 514-521. Springfield: Gospel Publishing House, 2000.

Murrow, David. *Why Men Hate Going to Church*. Nashville: Thomas Nelson, 2005.

Powell, Christina M.H. "Interpreting Research Results Related to Ministry." *Enrichment Journal* 15, no. 3 (Summer 2010): 118-121.

Rainer, Thom. "13 Issues for Churches in 2013." *Church Leaders*. n.d. http://www.churchleaders.com (accessed August 2014).

Rainey, Dennis. "Caring For Your Family, How Not to Lose the Battle at Home." *Enrichment*, Winter 2011: 70-74.

—. *Ministering to Twenty-First Century Families*. Nashville: Thomas Nelson, 2001.

Rice, Anne, interview by Michele Norris. *Today I Quit Being A Christian* NPR. August 2, 2010.

Rienas, Gabriele. "Q & A For Ministry Wives." *Enrichment*, Winter 2011: 128-129.

Christopher Schmitz – Why Your Pastor Left

Sage Publications. "Work, leisure attitudes of Baby Boomers, Generation Xers and Millennials compared." *Science Daily.* March 10, 2010. http://www.sciencedaily.com/releases/2010/03/100310083450.htm (accessed August 2014).

Secrist, Dan. "Growing From a Pioneer Church to a Multistaff Church." In *The Pentecostal Pastor: A Mandate for the 21st Century*, edited by Thomas, Goodall, Wayde, and Bicket, Zenas Trask, 482-491. Springfield: Gospel Publishing House, 2000.

Strauch, Alexander. *Biblical Eldership: An Urgent Call to Restore Biblical Church Leadership.* Colorado Springs: Lewis and Roth, 2003.

The Barna Group, Ltd. "Report Examines the State of Mainline Protestant Churches." *Barna Group.* December 7, 2009. https://www.barna.org/barna-update/leadership/323-report-examines-the-state-of-mainline-protestant-churches.

Thomas, Viv. *Second Choice: Embracing Life As It Is.* Crown Hill: Paternoster Press, 2000.

Thumma, Scott, Travis, Dave & Bird, Warren . *Megachurches Today 2005 Summary of Research Findings.* Survey, Hartford: Hartford Seminary, 2005.

Vander Laan, Ray. "He Went to the Synagogue." *Follow The Rabbi.* n.d.

    http://followtherabbi.com/guide/detail/he-went-to-synagogue

    (accessed August 2014).

Vitello, Paul. "Taking a Break From the Lord's Work." *New York Times*, Augus 2,

    2010: A1.

Walls, Randy. "A Place at the Table." *Enrichment*, Summer 2010: 8.

Wheeler, Dr. Raiford S. *A View from the Parsonage.* Maitland: Xulon, 2012.

Whitehead, William. "Praise the Lord, Fire the Pastor!" *Spiked Online.*

    November 13, 2007. http://www.spiked-

    onlinc.com/ncwsite/article/4073 (accessed 2014 August).

Willowby, Richard. "Prodigal PKs." *Pastor's Family*, Oct/Nov 1996.

Zoba, Wendy Murray. "What Pastor's Wives Wish Their Churches Knew Part 1."

    Christianity Today, April 7, 1997.

—. "What Pastor's Wives Wish Their Churches Knew Part 2." *Christianity Today*,

    April 7 1997.

Appendix C:

(An Essay on Arminian/Calvinism and Determinism)

Against the Divine Machine:

The Nature of Determinism, Which is the Logical Conclusion at

the Far Edge of the Calvinistic Pendulum

Introduction

Humorist and cartoonist Bill Watterson named half of the iconic duo

Calvin and Hobbes after theologian John Calvin. Ironically, or perhaps with

purpose, Calvin once asks his friend if he believed his destiny was already fixed

by cosmic forces. Hobbes is a nonbeliever while Calvin is sure. "Really? How

come?" Hobbes asks. "Life's a lot more fun when you're not responsible for

your actions," Calvin replies.[78] While meant in jest, it is this Deterministic creed

which many live their lives by, even if only subconsciously.

Determinism is the belief that human actions are the result of

antecedent causes which have been formulated naturalistically or theistically.

The natural viewpoint sees every action as resulting from, and causing another,

action *ad infinitum*. This makes humans a part of "the machinery of the

universe."[79] Theistic Determinism sees all of these predetermined actions as a

direct result of God's control. While it may be a nice platitude meant to reassure

---

[78] Watterson, Bill. The Authoritative Calvin and Hobbes. Kansas City: Andrews and McMeel, 1990. 152
[79] Elwell, Walter, ed. Evangelical Dictionary of Theology. 2nd Edition. Grand Rapids: Baker Academic, 2001. 467

Christopher Schmitz – Why Your Pastor Left

the troubled soul, how much control over daily minutia do we mean to infer God actively has when we say, "Don't worry; God is in total control." How does that impact the nature of God, specifically His love and justice?

Many scholars, even those theologians normally opposed to each other, make the same point that God's loving character or his loving nature (as revealed to us in scripture) would be inaccurate if there were no such thing as free will[80]; as typical to such a debate, such a war is won in the definition of the terms and thus "Free Will" becomes hotly debated. Even most hardcore determinists claim there is such a thing as free will and the exercise thereof, however they redefine freedom or will in order to fit their theology into an acceptable mold. The devil is in the details.

Problematic Deterministic Theodicy

The primary apologetic Calvinists are determined to reinforce is to find a way to reconcile this nature of God with predestination or election, especially when the concept of double-predestination is scrutinized (whereby the "nonelect" are condemned to Hell after judgment: a sentence which they had no control to avoid).[81] It seems that a God of such Deterministic machinations is neither just nor loving. A loving, omnipotent God cannot predetermine the damnation of certain souls while his love remains intact; does He truly love everybody if the option of Hell remains on the table and such Election or

---

[80] John Walvoord, William Crocket, Zachary Hayes, Clark Pinnock. Four Views on Hell. Edited by William Crocket. Grand Rapids: Zondervan, 1992. 140
[81] Erickson, Millard J. Christian Theology. 2nd Ed. Grand Rapids: Baker Books, 1998. 930

Christopher Schmitz – Why Your Pastor Left

nonelection remains unconditional? A God of love is not omnipotent if he cannot simply save the souls of the ones he loves.

Justice cannot truly exist under the umbrella of Determinism. Sometimes God may seem to appear unjust, but only ever at the benefit of those He loves; God does not give what is undeserved except when he gives a reprieve, this is fundamental to Grace.

Debate over this specific issue has raged for generations, and for good reasons. Either point taken to the extreme results in an unbalanced theodicy and potentially discredits the rationality behind Theology. Taken to the far edge, Calvinism becomes staunchly predestination and stifles all free will—humans have no capacity to make their own decisions and God is a great machine; this results from the second point of Calvinists' TULIP: Unconditional Election. We will examine this concept further.

On the other end of the spectrum, Arminianism risks infringing upon the sovereignty and power of God. The same was mentioned in regards to Determinism, though more in the hyperbolic context of love and the nonelect. Arminianism, taken to the edge, elevates human authority above the rule and dominion of God; presented as a theodicy the extremity of this viewpoint is the Open Theism view[82].

This paper deals primarily with the side of Determinism. Admittedly, it leans towards an Arminian bent. Particularly this is because of my belief that I am a sinner and my acceptance and acknowledgement that I cannot do otherwise

---

[82] Caner, Ed Hindson and Ergun, ed. The Popular Encyclopedia of Apologetics. Eugene: Harvest House, 2008. 241

Christopher Schmitz – Why Your Pastor Left

without the help of a savior. This may sound like the exact opposite argument Calvinists expect, perhaps even like a point in their favor. I expect Justice, however, and I know and understand that no penance can recompense God for violating His laws. But if God chose for me to commit my sins, and will then punish me for them, then He is not just. If God cannot stand sin and foreordains all mankind to sin, thus expelling us yet desiring us to come to Him, then He is not logical. Chiefly Justice, but also other of God's traits are of primary concern to this study.

Any study of God's Justice or Love must include a logical theodicy, or a whole theology that explains the existence of sin or moral evil. At Determinism's worst, a skewed theodicy results whereby God willingly forces men to commit atrocities that violate the moral law the theodicy is meant to explain.

While many Calvinists might argue that such a belief is not the intent of TULIP theology, it is the natural outcropping of this theology. In fact, the position that God causes humans to sin was taught by Theodore Beza, John Calvin's immediate successor.[83]

Calvinist theologian and philosopher Gordon Haddon Clark makes his thoughts expressly clear in his writings. "I wish very frankly and pointedly to assert that if a man gets drunk and shoots his family, it was the will of God that he should do it."[84] It is this position of Clark, and similar positions, which this paper explores. Clark presses his point, "Let it be unequivocally said that this

---

[83] (Erickson 1998) 926
[84] Clark, Gordon H. Religion, Reason, and Revelation. Philadelphia: Presbyterian & Reformed, 1961. 221

Christopher Schmitz – Why Your Pastor Left

view certainly makes God the cause of sin. God is the sole ultimate cause of everything. There is absolutely nothing independent of him. He alone is the eternal being. He alone is omnipotent."[85] Clark's position is hotly contended by many passages of scripture.

Natural Determinism

Clark's type of theology is certainly dangerous to the health of the general public. While not endorsing the view that theology mesh with contemporary existential understanding, it would certainly make the topic less hotly debated.

John Calvin insisted that the doctrine of predestination does not lead to carelessness regarding morality, or the cavalier attitude that one can continue to sin care-free since his or her election is assured. Calvin insists that knowledge of our election leads us to pursue holy living.[86] One wonders how much time Calvin spent with other humans given that viewpoint; like utopian communism, such an idea looks good on paper but seems contrary to human nature. Psychologist Kathleen Vohs and Jonathan Schooler enacted experiments to examine whether participants who believed that human behavior is predetermined would be more encouraged to cheat. Exposure to a message implying a deterministic worldview increased cheating on a task in which participants could passively allow a flawed computer program to reveal answers to mathematical problems which they'd been instructed to solve themselves. Increased cheating was mediated by decreased belief in free will. In another

---

[85] (Clark 1961) 237-238
[86] Calvin, John. "book 3, chapter 23, section 19." In Institutes. n.d.

Christopher Schmitz – Why Your Pastor Left

experiment, participants who read statements endorsing free will did not cheat while their counterparts did. These findings suggest that the debate over free will has societal, as well as scientific and theoretical, implications.[87]

The worst of these implications is the total abandonment of any form of theology and the universality of atheism. The rejection of free will emasculates any concept of moral obligation. Author-philosopher and Faraday Institute Associate Nicholas Beale asserts that denying free will "is the closest thing I can imagine to a scientific refutation of Christianity."[88]

Beale differs from modern scientific thought in that his philosophical presuppositions leave room in the framework for the possibility of a god. Beale's quote is a common assertion among the atheistic community. Much of those, touting science as the ultimate answer, have worked the Deterministic angle as a proof against God. Beale claims a personal belief in evolution and even makes a philosophical argument for its logical necessity to increase the attribute of Love and goodness of God[89] although it seems to disagree with his position regarding causation of "natural evils" such as earthquakes. Thus, we see what science has to offer Determinists.

Stephen Hawking notes the impossibility of scientific Determinism explaining nonquantifiable, factual data. "Gödel's theorem, Heisenberg's uncertainty principle, and the practical impossibility of following the evolution

---

[87] Kathleen Vohs, and Jonathan Schooler. "The Value of Believing in Free Will: Encouraging a Belief in Determinism Increases Cheating." Psychological Science (Wiley-Blackwell) 19, no. 1 (Jan 2008): 49-54. 49

[88] Beale, Nicholas. "Free Will, Free Process, and Love." Think Autumn (2009): 115-124. 117

[89] (Beale 2009) 118

Christopher Schmitz – Why Your Pastor Left

of even a deterministic system that becomes chaotic, form a core set of limitations to scientific knowledge that only came to be appreciated during the twentieth century."[90] Hawking is admitting that any phenomena that cannot be measured or empirically observed and cannot therefore be reduced to quantitative analysis (things such as "meaning," "beauty," or "justice") cannot be explained by science. Heisenberg's uncertainty principle alone wrecks any argument for Determinism.

Science, then, has left us bereft of answers. The scientific community can agree that they place their faith in the Darwinian model and the evolutionary process. They cannot agree, however, as to the best way to disprove God: to invalidate their agnosticism with proven cause for atheism. While determinism seems an option on face value, it alone cannot explain justice and other philosophical concepts outside the realm of science. Scientific based Determinism cannot touch God and so philosophy is appealed to. Beale notes, "The idea that [Determinism] is, philosophically, a defeater for religious belief is mistaken."[91] And so, science appeals to philosophy to sound the death knell of God, and philosophy demands the same of science. Science cannot answer these questions because these concepts are immeasurable and unobservable.

Philosophy tries to grasp onto the theological precepts, however, philosophy does not operate with an accurate concept of evil. Beale, and other philosophers, often define "evil" from within an existential framework. Evil is something which causes feelings other than pleasure. "It is clear that, if you love

---

[90] Hawking, Stephen. The Universe in a Nutshell. New York: Bantam, 2001. 139
[91] (Beale 2009) 124

Christopher Schmitz – Why Your Pastor Left

someone, you do not knowingly allow them to suffer serious pain or evil without sufficiently good reasons. People do suffer serious pain and evil, and at least some (most Christians would say, all) of them are people whom God loves."[92] Beale's view of evil, that it would include natural disasters and such occurrences, seems to compromise God's loving nature. How does one reconcile those positions? The answer is the opposite of Determinism, or Open Theism, whereby God surrenders his omniscience and sovereignty except to act in specific situations to ensure His will is enacted. Arguing for some form of Determinism we arrive at its antithesis and neither conclusion integrates well with the Biblical source data.

Theological Determinism

Since philosophy and science both fail to adequately come to terms with the God of the Bible, the only logical place to turn is to the pages of Scripture itself. The Determinism concept, in various forms and doctrines, is something that theologians have grapple with for ages; even in the 1800s it was pointedly asserted that the Determinism paradigm was unsolvable and yet is also a topic that we cannot just sweep under the rug. Francis Garden wrote about Gordon H. Clark's God/murder situation a hundred years prior. "How can we say of the very same thing that it has been decreed by the will of God, and that it is contrary to that will? ...an absolute shutting up of the question is unsatisfactory, and in reducing ourselves to silence we may bring on an oblivion of much important truth."[93] Either something is God's will or it is not. Clark

---

[92] (Beale 2009) 115
[93] Garden, Francis. "Divine Predestination: An Attempt Approximatley to Solve the Main Difficulty Connected With It." Contemporary Review, June 1872: 423-

Christopher Schmitz – Why Your Pastor Left

takes the notions set forth in Puritan Calvinist Jonathan Edwards' Freedom of the Will, whereby God decrees what he foreknows and mankind acts on this (thus redefining "Free Will,"[94]) and eradicates the attempted separation of the individual's freedom to act from God's compulsory, decretive will.

In Garden's version of the murder story, a man is murdered and he asks the hypothetical question of how we counsel his widow. If we believe in predestination, then surely the murder must be the will of God. "A large portion of the events which happen in this world is made up of men's crimes, sins, wrong-doings of every imaginable degree. Has God predestined them? And if not, where are we to draw the line?"[95]

Is there a theology that treads the middle path? Free will Theism, a form of *Self*-Determinism, is any type of theological model that affirms that, contrary to Process Theism, (which is a facet of Open Theism,) "God can unilaterally intervene in earthly affairs and does so at times" while still denying a fundamental precept of Theological Determinism, "that God can both grant individuals freedom and control its use."[96]

<u>Scriptural Analysis</u>

In decoding the theological impetus behind Determinism, one must look at the biblical concept of election. In the New Testament, Paul the Apostle joins love with the principle of election on at least four occasions.[97] As

---

429. 425

[94] Edwards, Jonathan. Freedom of the Will: Which is Supposed to be Essential to Moral Agency, Virtue, and Vice, Reward and Punishment, Praise and Blame. London: Hamilton, Adams, and Co, 1860. 1-10
[95] (Garden 1872) 424
[96] Basinger, David. The Case for Free will Theism A Philosophical Assessment. Downers Grove: InterVarsity, 1996. 12

Christopher Schmitz – Why Your Pastor Left

mentioned earlier, love is a fundamental aspect which must be reconcilable within one's theodicy.

Very specifically, it is worth looking at Paul's background as he penned the manuscripts surrounding election. Timo Eskola does an excellent job forming a solid exegesis of Paul's writings. He begins with the Jewish context for Paul's theologizing. Eskola focuses especially on the demonstrably pre-New Testament material such as select apocalypses, wisdom books, and the Qumran documents.

Using Sirach as his key witness, Eskola argues that the sapiential tradition reflects a significant departure from the Deuteronomic approach to Israel's salvation. The varied responses to persecution among Jews compelled the wisdom teachers to adopt a new eschatological dualism, according to which personal salvation was not ultimately determined just on the basis of covenantal election, but also on the basis of fidelity to the law.[98] There exists, then, a significant departure in electoral belief structure from one Testament to the next, that departure can be traced back to the inter-testamental period.

A similar picture emerges from a study of key apocalyptic books (*I Enoch, Jubilees, 4 Ezra*) and of the Qumran material. In all these sources, the soteriology is also synergistic: one's covenantal status is not, in itself, sufficient for deliverance. One must validate that status through observance of the law. Proof was required of commitment to that elected status. Important to this

---

[97] Horton, Stanley, ed. Systematic Theology. Revised. Springfield: Logion Press, 1995. 356

[98] Eskola, Timo. Theodicy and Predestination in Pauline Sotenology. Tübingen: Paul Mohr Verlag, 1998. 41-44

Christopher Schmitz – Why Your Pastor Left

soteriology within Eskola's argument is that predestination in these writings is not deterministic. Even at Qumran, the destiny of human beings is not fixed by divine decree but left open to the choices people make either to follow or to reject the way of law-keeping.[99] Given the background material it is reasonable to suggest that the original audience of the Pauline writings would understand the concept of "election" under similar terms.

Eskola's theodicy is complete, allowing fully for both God's wrath and his salvation. Paul radicalizes the Jewish understanding in that all people are bound by sin and subject therefore to God's wrath. No longer is there a basis, at least at the outset, for positive human response to God. Paul's solution is not the predestination of individuals, such as in the Augustinian and Calvinist tradition, but a universal Christological predestination. "All human beings have first been predestined to damnation. All men have been 'elected' to find salvation in Christ"[100]

Eskola concludes that predestination involves universal election in Christ, but this universal election does not necessarily bring salvation to all. Election involves the provision in Christ of atonement for all, but "does not yet deliver salvation to individuals."[101] This is perhaps the most frank and literal reading of the scripture one will find when they study the topic both systematically and exegetically.

Conclusion

---

[99] (Eskola 1998) 273
[100] (Eskola 1998) 185
[101] (Eskola 1998) 185, 186

Christopher Schmitz – Why Your Pastor Left

The idea of God's omniscience, free will, and predestination in most current thought and theology is linear. In Theistic Determinism, God created originally and set everything in motion, this makes all subsequent events contingent and thus predestined. The problem with this is that we are limiting an infinite God. "Determinism is the view that there is at any instant exactly one physically possible future,"[102] according to Peter van Inwagen, the noted philosopher and metaphysicist. Limiting the dimension of God by our human perspective, we act just like the residents of Abbott's Flatland, not able to see beyond our own dimension and understand that some objects transcend our own reality; who better fits that description but God.

Imagine a world map with a pin on a specific location; the map fails to take into account the fact that the earth is not a mere two dimensional layout (which anyone not believing the world is flat can agree with.) A point on a map is insufficient for a miner wishing to harvest minerals from a mountain marked by the map, there is also a depth or elevation necessary with the dimensional coordinates; any person who has installed a satellite receiver on the roof knows that they cannot receive the proper signal with just the number of circular degrees, but must also measure and pinpoint the dish's azimuth in order to locate their signal source. An exponentially increasing number of possibilities might exist in a true free will scenario, though only one reality exists, as far as our base assumptions on the nature of the universe (which some philosophers

---

[102] van Inwagen, Peter. "An Essay on Free Will." In The Incompatibility of Free Will and Determinism. Oxford: Clarendon Press, 1975. 10

Christopher Schmitz – Why Your Pastor Left

may argue is a weighty assumption) and therefore we base our theodicy and theology on destiny and election on this very notion.

Perhaps it would be more fitting with the character and nature of God, especially his infinite nature, to re-envision the base model of divine knowledge as a visual family tree where every branch is a point in time related to an individual and to their available options at that point in time (even taking into account contingency and natural leanings of that man). This would obviously create quite an immense, tangled and intertwined tree branching off with such a large and ever expanding number of variables that it boggles the mind... the human mind that is. This a limitation of the human mind, however, and must be reconciled with a limitless God who can easily encompass far more than our mind can ever achieve—we cannot compare our perception of reality versus the Infinite One. While this thinking might be less understandable, it is perhaps easier to reconcile with the concept of sovereignty, omniscience, and the Calvinist accusation of a limited God given an Arminian perspective. Perhaps that is what is called for in developing a new theodicy for a contemporary rational age: that we finite beings surrender the need to understand everything about an infinite God, or even begin to open ourselves to the possibility of things beyond our finite dimension. Perhaps then we can find some genuine common ground with each other.

Election must remain within the realm of soteriology and not venture beyond its doctrinal borders without doing much harm to the doctrine of free will. In any discussion of election, we must begin with Jesus and restrain taking

Christopher Schmitz – Why Your Pastor Left

liberties with any theology we have merely inferred from the text.

Bibliography

Basinger, David. The Case for Free will Theism A Philosophical Assessment. Downers Grove: InterVarsity, 1996.

Beale, Nicholas. "Free Will, Free Process, and Love." Think Autumn (2009): 115-124.

Calvin, John. "book 3, chapter 23, section 19." In Institutes. n.d.

Caner, Ed Hindson and Ergun, ed. The Popular Encyclopedia of Apologetics. Eugene: Harvest House, 2008.

Clark, Gordon H. Religion, Reason, and Revelation. Philadelphia: Presbyterian & Reformed, 1961.

Edwards, Jonathan. Freedom of the Will: Which is Supposed to be Essential to Moral Agency, Virtue, and Vice, Reward and Punishment, Praise and Blame. London: Hamilton, Adams, and Co, 1860.

Elwell, Walter, ed. Evangelical Dictionary of Theology. 2nd Edition. Grand Rapids: Baker Academic, 2001.

Erickson, Millard J. Christian Theology. 2nd Ed. Grand Rapids: Baker Books, 1998.

Eskola, Timo. Theodicy and Predestination in Pauline Soteriology. Tübingen: Paul Mohr Verlag, 1998.

Christopher Schmitz – Why Your Pastor Left

Garden, Francis. "Divine Predestination: An Attempt Approximatley to Solve the Main Difficulty Connected With It." Contemporary Review, June 1872: 423-429.

Hawking, Stephen. The Universe in a Nutshell. New York: Bantam, 2001.

Horton, Stanley, ed. Systematic Theology. Revised. Springfield: Logion Press, 1995.

John Walvoord, William Crocket, Zachary Hayes, Clark Pinnock. Four Views on Hell. Edited by William Crocket. Grand Rapids: Zondervan, 1992.

Kathleen Vohs, and Jonathan Schooler. "The Value of Believing in Free Will: Encouraging a Belief in Determinism Increases Cheating." Psychological Science (Wiley-Blackwell) 19, no. 1 (Jan 2008): 49-54.

van Inwagen, Peter. "An Essay on Free Will." In The Incompatibility of Free Will and Determinism. Oxford: Clarendon Press, 1975.

Watterson, Bill. The Authoritative Calvin and Hobbes. Kansas City: Andrews and McMeel, 1990.

CPSIA information can be obtained
at www.ICGtesting.com
Printed in the USA
LVHW080951210223
740042LV00010B/139

9 781530 838554